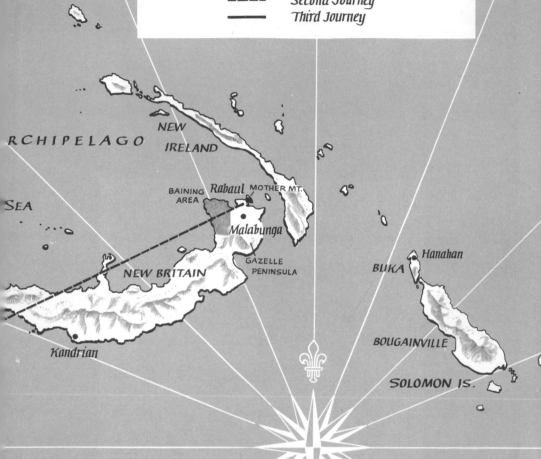

STONE AGE ISLANDS

········· First Journey
▬ ▬ ▬ ▬ Second Journey
▬▬▬▬ Third Journey

RCHIPELAGO

NEW IRELAND

SEA

BAINING AREA

Rabaul   MOTHER MT.

Malabunga

GAZELLE PENINSULA

NEW BRITAIN

Kandrian

BUKA   Hanahan

BOUGAINVILLE

SOLOMON IS.

NLEY RANGE

AZON BAY

SOLOMON

SEA

palacios

THE STONE
AGE ISLAND

THE STONE AGE ISLAND

NEW GUINEA TODAY

MASLYN WILLIAMS

DOUBLEDAY & COMPANY, INC.
GARDEN CITY, NEW YORK
1964

To

M & JW

and

LWP

ACKNOWLEDGMENT

For the most part this book records my personal feelings about the strange and complex country in which I have worked during the past eight years: but inevitably much of what is written in the following pages derives directly or indirectly from other people who live and work there.

Most of them are friends or acquaintances who are native to the Territory of Papua and New Guinea, or who belong there by an adoption which is of the mind as well as of the body. Where I have attributed significant actions or opinions to them by name I have sought, whenever possible, their permission to do so. Other people, in positions of authority or special knowledge, have gone to much trouble to give me specialized information or to check the manuscript, thus giving the book such semblance of authority and accuracy as it may have.

However, I wish to make it clear that it is not a scholar's volume, nor have I set out to provide information that is available in official reports or in books written with a more serious intent than to entertain. This book is merely an account of some of my travels in New Guinea, together with stories of such strangeness, told to me in many wild and lonely places, that I have thought them worth retelling.

If the reader be moved to reflect that primitive people are curiously like ourselves, I shall not be surprised, for that is what I have found. I have also found that something more than material advancement must be provided for them if they are to live fuller lives than they do now.

Photographs for the book have kindly been provided by Mr. John Leake, Assistant District Officer James Sinclair, and Patrol Officer Neil Grant, all of whom have been good companions on many of my travels, and by the News and Information Bureau of the Department of the Interior, Canberra.

PREFACE

I have known the author of this book for nearly twenty years. For the past seven years I have watched his progressive involvement in the drama of Papua and New Guinea—a drama of primitive peoples being thrust, by the swiftly mounting pressures of history, out of their hidden valleys into the life of the twentieth century.

He had a double charge: To document the life and customs of stone age peoples, and to use the medium of film for a crash program of instruction in the arts, crafts, and usances of civilization.

He has flown, driven, and walked over thousands of miles of one of the most rugged countries in the world. He began as an observer with a camera, and has ended as an intimate participant in a swift, occasionally bloody, but always fascinating and constructive drama of human progress.

Like every participant, he has been changed by the action of the play. He has suffered physically, and spiritually, but he has emerged tougher and taller from the human experience.

This book is a record of his observations, experiences, and conclusions. It was I who urged him to write it. I am very proud to introduce it to all those who, whether they know it or not, whether they like it or not, will be caught up in the consequences of thrusting stone age man out of the twilight of history into the sudden glare of modern civilization.

MORRIS L. WEST

CONTENTS

PART 1

FOREWORD

The letter began "The Minister directs" and it said that he would see me at ten o'clock. I was given to understand by officials of his department that he would be able to spare me ten minutes, or perhaps fifteen. It was clear that I was not expected to speak during this time unless invited to give technical information on the production of documentary films. I was a little resentful because I like to speak, but I know that the Australian Minister for Territories is a busy man and not just a politician.

As I walked between the frosted beds of late roses, and the rows of golden poplars turning brown, and up the long lawn to Parliament House, I realized that I had forgotten how lovely Canberra can be in the last days of autumn; for I had lived in this district, and was in love here as a young man. But, looking back through the long perspective of time I remembered best the more dramatic seasonal climacterics in these wide upland valleys of the Monaro—the bitter winters, and summers when everything burned.

There was that Christmas Eve when we slaved all day to get the lucerne stacked, so that we could have Christmas in peace, without the worry of crops getting wet as they lay in the paddocks; for the summer storms were bad that year.

We harnessed the carts a little after four o'clock in the morning, and when we stopped for a rest and a quick meal of cold mutton at midday, the temperature was over ninety and still rising. It cleared the hundred during the day, and when we stopped work at eight o'clock that night, with the top on the stack, I was burned black, and giddy with the heat and fumes of lucerne, and felt as though I had been flogged across the back with thick rods.

I remember, too, a day in early spring, colder and wilder than the worst of winter, when her father sent my girl and me to look at

the lambing ewes in a far paddock near the foothills of the lower
Alps. The thin rain blew slantwise into our faces, and froze into a
skin of crinkly ice on our eyebrows and round our wrists, and our
ponies kept throwing their heads back and showering us with drop-
lets of frost and the spume from their nostrils.

We separated, and I found a young ewe down, near-frozen stiff,
and the lamb just coming. It was too late to move her into the
shelter of a log, and I stayed half an hour, keeping the wind and
the rain off her, and trying to make it easy. And I was thankful
that I wasn't a doctor, and having to deal with women in this state.

I was riding a dark brown mare named Lucy. She had a mouth
like iron, and when we turned for home she pulled on the bridle
with every step, so that my hands ached trying to hold her in; for I
had picked up a couple of motherless lambs and had them in front
of me across the saddle, and was taking it gently. She was a fine
mare and a good galloper, but needed a lot of work.

There was a young man who lived in the town who used to hire
her at weekends to go riding. He was a rising diplomat who later
represented Australia in the General Assembly of the United Nations, in New York. His name was Paul Hasluck. And now I was
walking up the lawn toward Parliament House, to see him.

"The Minister directs . . ."

He received me courteously.

He also made it clear that he had no high opinion of the kind
of work that I was doing. I looked discouraged, but secretly agreed
with him. He explained, as politely as possible, that he had sent
for me against his better judgment, having been importuned into
it by his departmental advisers. He believed that the greatest weakness in my kind of work was its dishonesty. My respect for him
mounted steadily.

He had been persuaded, he said, by his advisers, to commission
a number of informational films that would illustrate the work being
done under his direction in the Australian-administered Territory of
Papua and New Guinea. He did not want, he added, looking me
firmly in the eye, dramatic representations of patrol officers striding
across the landscape sowing crops of adverbs and adjectives all over
the place.

I was not very interested. I am fond of comfort and civilization.
I would have preferred to have returned to work in Europe, or

even America. However, his immediate requirement was a simple one. He required a professional film-maker to go to New Guinea and, after careful investigation, to propose for his consideration a limited program of useful film-making, together with an estimate of the cost in terms of time and money. This preliminary survey, he suggested, might take six weeks. It did not seem a great slice out of a man's life.

That was eight years ago.

Since then I have been sixteen times to the Territory of Papua and New Guinea and have made more than thirty films there. I have come to regard the Honorable Paul Hasluck with some admiration and considerable respect, although I fear that history may overtake many of his plans for the future of New Guinea.

I have also come to feel personally involved in the future of the two million people whose image I have tried to capture and present in my films, and now in this book.

Sydney 1963

The island of New Guinea has a prehistoric look even on a flat map, like the fossil of some misshapen Mesozoic reptile. Its gaping head bites into the entrails of the Moluccas, its breast rests on the topmost tip of Australia, while its tail dips into the Coral Sea. It is bigger than any other non-continental island in the world except Greenland and, with the hundreds of smaller islands that are geographically and politically attached, covers an area roughly 1700 miles from east to west and 730 miles from north to south. It hangs just below the equator and has a land space greater than that of France and Great Britain combined.

Like ancient Gaul it is divided into three parts, first by a line that cuts north and south through its middle so that the reptile's head is in Asia and its tail among the islands of the Pacific. On the western side of this line is West Irian, included for some centuries in the fabulous Dutch Empire of the Indies but now part of the Republic of Indonesia. This book is not concerned with West Irian but deals only with the country and the islands that lie on the eastern side of the line.

This eastern half of New Guinea is again divided into two parts, this time by a massive mountain chain that runs along it lengthwise, like the spine of a dragon. On the north side of the mountains is the United Nations Trust Territory of New Guinea, taken from Germany and put under Australia's protection and tutelage by the League of Nations after World War I. South of the mountains is Papua, an Australian colony. The two areas are governed as one and are known together as the Territory of Papua and New Guinea. The center of administration is at Port Moresby, capital of Papua.

Walking along the waterfront with sea and sky stretching together into a silver infinity, the little town behind me seems suspended in time and space beyond the edges of the earth. The rest of the world, almost out of reach and mostly out of mind, speaks to the people only through the radio news broadcast from Australia. It comes strained through static and atmospheric noises, so that frequently the listeners become impatient and turn it off in the middle of a sentence.

There is, then, little contact with the world outside. One cannot reach out and touch any other part of it. The nearest major point of physical communication is Sydney, six hours away to the south by aircraft, and joined by a single service each day, except Monday.

Rising up behind the little capital, almost at the backsteps of the town itself, is this great and strange island of New Guinea, one of the few remaining places of any size that has not yet been gathered into our present age. To the rest of the world it is either unknown or a vague curiosity, so that almost everyone who comes to visit comes only to search out its deficiencies and its strangeness: to make suggestions for improvement or to show how things might be done better, or by what means New Guinea tribesmen might most quickly enter into the modern world. Nobody comes for the food or the wine or the conversation.

One man comes to measure the amount of sweet potato that a mountain family eats in a week, and computes its dietary deficiency. Another studies the pattern of disease, or the sexual habits of clans living in isolated places. One man looks for nickel or for oil, so that New Guinea may be self-supporting, while another assesses the amount of money to be made by selling cosmetics to young men of the Gulf country who spend all day making up for a village dance. Some come to study the life cycle of strange insects and plant parasites, and others are interested in one or another of the tribal languages and dialects. Pundits come to analyze the mistakes being made in Government and administration, and journalists, sensibly comfort-loving, stay a while and then hurry back to civilization to publish the answers to New Guinea's manifold problems.

This coming and going of experts from outside makes the people of New Guinea self-consciously aware that they are backward, and this breeds feelings of inferiority and embarrassment. The goodwill and wisdom of the experts is not questioned, and the suggestions stir ambitions for improvement and progress. Seeing themselves through the eyes of these erudite visitors, the people of New Guinea begin to realize the extent of their spiritual isolation from the rest of the world.

But there are not yet many among the two million native people of this territory whose ears have caught and held whispers of the history of the world outside, or who have learned to read and to reason in terms of today's civilization. There are many more, by thousands upon tens of thousands, to whom the outside world is less than a myth and its ways utterly inconsequential; whole tribes live in the far western highlands, and in the upper reaches of the Fly and Sepik Rivers, to whom this untidy little frontier town itself would seem like a city of miracles, an astonishment, something to be seen before it could be believed.

I saw a few such men yesterday, in the street, escorted by a Government officer. They were mountain people, recognizable by their square build and dark skins, and by the way they stayed close to each other and looked around fearfully all the time, their fingers feeling instinctively for the axes which they normally carry in their bark belts. For where these people live a stranger is an enemy and death is the immediate and expected end of trespass.

They had been disarmed for the visit and, in spite of their escort, felt naked and afraid. There were eight men of middle age, and a youth wearing the uniform of a Government interpreter. The lad would most likely be the son or nephew of the most influential of the older men, who themselves would be important clan leaders brought out from their tribal lands for the first time to see the wonders of the white man's world, and to be given, by this means, at least a partial understanding of the future being planned for them by the Government.

This has become a necessary step in the process of quickly civilizing primitive tribes who live in places so cut off and isolated that they have no way of knowing what lies outside; and in this era of urgency, when some compulsion of the age demands that all shall be civilized equally, there is no time to teach stone age people first to read and write, or to reason out and choose for themselves a new way of life that might suit them best.

I spoke to the Government man with them, for I knew him, and he told me where they came from and said that they had seen so

many new things that they were bewildered and stayed awake all
night whispering.

He recited a litany of things and places they had seen. The hospital, with women sleeping in beds and no pigs tied up beside them.
Light shut up in bottles and hung in houses so that inside it was
never night. The sea left them speechless, and so did the motion
pictures, where spirit men stand as high as trees and appear and
disappear at will, and speak with great voices that can be heard
a mile away. They visited the prison, a place where criminals are
fattened and protected behind fences so that their victims cannot
be revenged; and they saw the big village where only policemen
live. The policemen's brass band played for them and they nudged
each other and smiled for the first time since leaving home. The
bakery, the telephone exchange, and much else they found inexplicable, and they were greatly surprised by the apparent poverty
of the people, for none wore the certain signs of wealth; no necklaces of giri giri shell or dogs' teeth, no mother-of-pearl plates, no
pig tusks or bird of paradise or cassowary plumes.

He said that this rather dampened any mild enthusiasms they
might have had for civilization, and added that they were rather
anxious to get home in case tribal fighting should break out in their
absence. But first they had to attend a meeting of the Legislative
Council because, next year, they would be voting to elect their own
representative, and the Government thought it a good thing that
they should take the opportunity to see the council in action so that
they could tell their people all about it.

He grinned, and said that as none of them understood a single
word of any dialect or language spoken beyond their own tribal
boundaries it was unlikely that they would gain much from the
experience, but on the other hand the sheer mystery of it all would
impress them, especially listening to the debates through earphones
linked to the translation system. This would be considered magic
of a very high order indeed. I left him trying to induce them to go
aboard a launch for a short cruise in the harbor, but they were
afraid of so much water, and reluctant to leave the land.

Port Moresby township starts on the waterfront and spreads back
over the foot of a high hill in a tight compact of storehouses, shops,
and offices which cover two blocks. It started eighty years ago with
a tin shed, as a convenient center from which to exploit the meager

but exotic resources of the New Guinea islands. The shed was used for storing copra. Its owner was a Scottish storekeeper who became very rich trading among the islands of the Pacific.

It now has two main streets. One runs along the waterfront and has wharves on one side, and warehouses, cargo sheds, and the Harbour Master's office on the other. A short offshoot from the street leads past two stores and a freight depot, to the Customs House and post office. The other street is a microcosm of material civilization. It has several insurance offices and banks, two hotels, a movie, and the police station. It takes ten minutes to walk around the entire town although it is the capital of a country of two million people. The Government offices are two miles away and they also verge on the waterfront. The population, both native and white, lives in outlying suburbs and villages, so that the town itself is impersonal and lacks style of any kind. But it is beautiful.

It seems always to be washed with a filtered light, so that its shapes and colors have soft edges. Its hills sit all around it covered with the thin green of eucalyptus through which show rough patches of iron-red earth and scars of yellow shale. Huge, flat-bottomed galleons of colored cloud ride across the open sky, puffed endlessly along by trade winds sweeping in from the sea. Heavy-scented frangipani grows among stones, mauve and orange bougainvillea clambers undisciplined over walls everywhere, and the great rain trees in the streets drop blotches of crimson blossom on the footpaths.

A bus leaves from the corner of the main street, and goes out along the waterfront to the Government offices, and to the villages beyond. I paid my fare and sat beside a man from the village of Poreporena who looked at the great clouds moving across the sky and said that the wind would soon be right for the start of the canoe-racing season, and that many villagers were taking white people as passengers on their canoes and charging them five shillings (fifty-six cents) each. I said that I thought this too cheap for an afternoon's sport, and he replied that he did not hold with the commercialization of village activity. There is a strong feeling of inner privacy among the Papuan people, and although they treat friendly white people with courtesy they do not invite any kind of intimacy.

There was a clean coastal vessel at the small-ships wharves, discharging copra and taking on general stores, and I asked him what it was, for I had not seen it before. "It is," he said, "the new ship bought by the Native Co-operative Societies and it is called *Hiri* to please our ancestors." He took half a cigarette from the pocket of his shirt and asked me for a light, but I do not smoke, so he excused himself and went to the driver and borrowed his lighter, then stayed talking with him. I twisted my neck to take another look at the new ship and thought how good it is that tradition should be remembered in the naming of her, for *hiri* was the word given to the voyage made each year by these Motu people in other days when they went trading along the coast, setting out in their great seagoing canoes at the beginning of the season of the southeast wind and coming back again, many months later, when it turned to the northwest.

Beyond the wharves, out on the open harbor, a flying boat gathered its strength together and set off with a roar, lumbering like an overweight duck struggling to become airborne. And having freed itself it soared easily upward trailing silver drips, then turned, flashing for a moment in the sun, and headed off along the coast on its daily run. To me these things are familiar, yet in my grandfather's day this harbor was not known to Western men, and the map of New Guinea was still incomplete.

The history of the discovery of these islands has yet to be written, and whoever undertakes it will engage upon the labor of a lifetime and much love. There are no legends, widely held, with roots in pre-European times. No relics in stone or old wood-carving or architecture that would indicate some beginnings. Even the written records of our own times go back no farther than the first decade of the sixteenth century and are scattered and untabulated, and need to be translated from a number of languages long out of fashion. Such scant records and evidences as exist cause much dispute and even mutual rudeness among scholars and students.

This curious lack of documented history is ascribed by some scholars to the fact that in 1495, His Holiness Pope Alexander VI drew a line around the globe dividing the world in two. And according to this story, he apportioned the rights of exploration and colonizing on the one side to Spain and on the other to Portugal. He did this in order to avoid conflict between the two great Catholic kings, but the result might well have been that when a captain discovered new islands, he either kept the matter secret or else marked each new discovery falsely on the chart to the advantage of his own king. This story is held to be true by many honest historians but is heatedly denied by others equally erudite.

But there are a few facts upon which most are agreed, and a number of names may be safely associated with the early days of exploration and discovery, at least in the northern part of New Guinea. For instance, in 1511 Afonso d'Albuquerque, Governor-General of the Indies, sent ships to find new spice islands, and one of these ships foundered, the crew being rescued by a local sultan who made a practice of raiding New Guinea for slaves. It seems likely that when these shipwrecked men were returned to their home port they made mention of the great island to the south, from which slaves might be had for the taking.

Then the Spanish Governor of the Moluccas, Don Jorge de Menezes, became lost in these parts in 1526, getting his islands mixed either by accident or design. And two years later another Spaniard, Alvaro de Saareda Ceron, in the employ of Cortez, explored part of the northern shore of New Guinea and gave it the name of Isla del Oro, though there is no record of his having found gold there, and the name soon fell into disuse.

Another sailor, Inigo Ortiz de Retes, remarking that this coast reminded him of Africa, gave it the name New Guinea. This was in 1545. Afterwards came other seamen, Dutch, English, and French, and although there were famous navigators among them the map remained incomplete through three hundred and fifty known years of exploration, until 1873, when Captain John Moresby filled in the final outline of the southern shore by discovering the harbor that bears his family name today.

He was a young man, son of a high admiral of England and commander of Queen Victoria's survey ship *Basilisk*, working out from Australia. He was also, it seems, persistent and a stickler for detail, for whereas each previous explorer had bypassed the harbor entrance, thinking it no more than a minor river mouth hemmed in with dangerous reefs, Moresby was curious and persevered, and finally got inside. He found himself in sheltered waters of such area that they could, he thought, accommodate the world's biggest fleets with safety.

Having dropped anchor and made things shipshape, he noted in his diary, "I am determined that the outer and inner harbours shall

bear the name of my father, the venerable Admiral of the Fleet,
Sir Fairfax Moresby." So it is today. Port Moresby is the name given
to the outer harbor as well as to the town, and Fairfax Harbour is
the sheltered, inner anchorage.

All day long, following his first arrival, the harbor was lively and
excited with the passage of canoes coming and going between the
Basilisk and the villages. Most of them were nimble, single-hulled
canoes with outrigger, used as a rule for visiting within the harbor,
or fishing, but because of the excitement of the day a great many
trading canoes were used for viewing the strangers: huge, double-
hulled, seagoing craft with multiple masts, and sails shaped like the
pincer claw of a crab, with two curving jaws coming to a point so
gracefully that they were almost breathtaking against the sunset.

Captain Moresby watched for a while, then went back into his
cabin. Picking up his pen once more he wrote, "The natives flocked
aboard in hundreds, eager and curious, chattering like monkeys as
they pointed out to each other the marvels that took their fancy."
He was a perceptive and systematic note-taker and kept conscientious diaries which were for the most part disciplined and conservative in comment. But like many who have since fallen under the
spell of Papua, his ingrained loyalties faltered now and then before
the onslaught of its persistent loveliness, so that he felt impelled to
finish a later page with a doubt and a sigh, writing, "What have
these people to gain from civilisation? Pondering the fate of other
aboriginal races brought into contact with the white man I was
ready to wish that their happy home had never been seen by us."
Then feeling a little ashamed of this display of sentimentality, and
remembering that he was not only an Officer of the Queen but a
good English Churchman, he added sententiously, "But Providence
must surely be trusted to work out its own ends." Later he, too,
became an admiral like his father.

But it seemed to Captain Moresby that Providence might accept
some little assistance in this matter, so he sought out the English
missionary, Dr. Lawes, who already had evangelists working along
the Papuan coast, and suggested to him that he should establish
the headquarters of his mission among the villagers inside the harbor. Then he recommended to his own superiors in England that
the newly discovered Port Moresby would provide a most suitable

and safe place for a naval base, and that the center of any projected civil administration for Papua might also be set up there. These propositions were accepted.[1] Thus did Providence and a young sea captain together provide the framework of piety and paternalism within which the people of these villages have grown up during the past four or five generations.

A number of their descendants were clambering about among the branches of the Mango trees outside the mainblock of Government offices when I got off the bus. They were chattering, as Moresby would have said, like monkeys as they busily stripped the trees of unripe fruit to save it from birds and flying foxes. The policeman on guard duty helped them, pointing out clusters that hung out of sight above their heads. A file of slim village girls aged between ten and twelve, wearing neat school tunics, walked by on bare feet with mincing dignity, pretending not to notice the boys. Mothers in grass skirts, some with tattooed faces and carrying food or household goods on their heads, followed behind. Two religious women in denim-blue habits, wearing sandals and girded with rosary beads, strode swiftly along the footpath toward town.

Four generations of missionaries, traders, and Government officials have laid a thin skin of civilization over most of New Guinea, especially on the coast; and out here among the Government offices, within sight of the villages which Moresby found, visitors may see many gentle Papuan clerks who wear shirts and shoes and speak careful, respectful English, bearing files from one office to another. They quietly murmur, "Yes, *taubada*"[2] and "No, *taubada*" to the officials with whom they work, but beneath the neat gentleness and courtesy there is often a resentment—a feeling that they have been kept too far from civilization, removed not only from its threats but from its promises.

Captain Moresby did what was right according to his conscience to help Providence defend the Papuans from any unchecked onslaught of civilization, but there are some who feel that he and those who came after may have been too solicitous—that what began as protection has become a bondage, however amiable and benevo-

[1] Five of the biggest of the harbor villages have, over the years, become contiguous and are now collectively known as Hanuabada which means, in the local language, Big Village.

[2] *Taubada* is Motuan for "chieftain"—tau (man), bada (big).

lent; that of all the people of New Guinea, the Papuans who live in the villages near Port Moresby are the most cultivated but the least content.

It was a member of their village council, a man who lives in Hanuabada and works in the Government offices, who said to me one day, not long ago, "You have given us many good things. You have taught us much and we should be grateful. But you have not taught us how to achieve these things without you. And if you go away somebody else will come to look after us because we are not ready to look after ourselves. It is, I think, time that we stopped being grateful to you and saying, 'Thank you,' all the time."

Two

The Chief Native Lands Commissioner, Ivan Champion, is the most traveled man in New Guinea. He has an advantage over most other men in that he was born here and has lived here all his life. Forty years ago, with Assistant Resident Magistrate Charles Karius, he walked across New Guinea from south to north at its widest part. They were the first to do this. Their two attempts to achieve the feat occupied eleven months, and for most of the time they lived off the land, bargaining for assistance and for food with headhunters and cannibals. They had no means of communication with the rest of the world and were, for months, given up for lost. Karius is dead these twenty years or more, and nobody has attempted to repeat their achievement.[1]

I came to the door of his office which was open, but hearing voices stood for a moment wondering whether to interrupt or to go away and come back later. The voices were subdued and the language seemed to be Suau or Mailu, which meant that the people in the room were villagers from the southeast coast. I wanted to stay because he had promised to help me work out an itinerary for my current assignment, but after a while, there being no lull in the conversation, it seemed clear that the Commissioner was busy with visitors who had come a long way to discuss a land dispute or some other important matter. So I turned to go away. But at that moment the voices ceased abruptly and there was a click, followed by the unmistakable sound of a tape recorder running backwards, so I went in.

[1] In 1959–60 Dutch and French scientific and film-making teams crossed what is now West Irian. These expeditions carried radio and were supplied by airdrops. Even so these crossings were regarded, rightly, as feats of remarkable endurance, though not all members of the teams were able to complete the journeys.

Ivan Champion's office is small and uncarpeted. There is a table and swivel chair, and along one wall a chest full of shallow drawers, of the kind used by draftsmen and surveyors. Most of the transitory furnishings seem more appropriate to a ship chandler's store than to the office of a senior Government official. They include a roll of canvas sails wrapped around a spar and propped diagonally across one wall. Then there is a pair of oars from a dinghy, a ship's compass in a box, a sextant, a chain-measure of steel tape, and under the table an iron box of the kind used by field officers on patrol. He sat crouched over the table, writing in a minute and meticulous hand. The tape recorder stood beside him on the table. As I came in he looked up.

It has been a long time since he walked across the island, and his close-cut hair is now white, but there are few other outward evidences of more than middle age. The light blue eyes remain guileless and still seem more used to searching horizons than to peering into office files; and although Authority tries to pin him down to a desk, giving him assistants to do much of the field work, a telephone, and a lad to bring cups of tea, he stays faithfully in love with far places and finds frequent reason to leave his office to visit some distant village, preferably one that is close to the water's edge and has a good anchorage.

He is able to do this surprisingly often, especially since the Department of Agriculture has so successfully encouraged villagers to plant coffee and cocoa and other permanent crops for which there is no provision in the traditional systems of land usage and ownership. Under the old systems a piece of land seldom belongs outright to any one man or family, but is owned communally and its usage shared, so that one family may have the right to grow food crops on it, another to gather firewood, a third to hunt on it or to collect the fruit of certain trees, or edible insects. If water runs through this piece of land another family might have the right to fish in it. Consequently, when such areas of land are planted with permanent commercial crops, disputes are bound to arise between families, so that the Government has now decreed that title to tribal, clan, and family lands must be examined, ratified, and registered by a lands commissioner. A thousand years ago William the Norman, conqueror of England, had something of the same problem; and presumably had people like Ivan Champion to deal with it.

He looked at the heap of files stacked on top of his chest of drawers, affecting an expression of despair, and said, "I'm afraid that it rather piles up and I'm not really able to spend as much time in the office as I would like." I made no comment and he seemed to suspect that I was not convinced, and grinned like a boy, then put his hand on the tape recorder and added, "But this thing helps a lot." He used it, he said, when working in the villages for taking down conversations, because it was not always easy to catch the exact meaning or inference when discussing involved domestic relationships among villagers, especially if there was some undercurrent of feeling that caused them to argue and interrupt each other, and talk more than one at a time. And often they spoke a language or local dialect that one did not know and had to get at through an interpreter.

Also to be taken into account is the fact that the average villager has an instinctive suspicion of writing, and is inclined to dry up when he sees his words being written down in a notebook. It is fear of magic more than any distrust of authority but, as the Commissioner pointed out, they do not realize that the tape recorder is taking down what they say, and so are not inhibited by it. It is simply another piece of the white man's cumbersome luggage. Afterwards one is able to listen carefully to the discussions and arguments and to sort out the relevancies, and so produce a much more accurate assessment of the truth of the matter than one could by simply scribbling down disconnected phrases and trying to remember details some weeks later.

So he goes to the villages with his recorder and sits down among the men to talk about the things their fathers and grandfathers did, how they came to own a certain piece of land or to have special rights over it, by inheritance, marriage, exchange, or simply by some tradition of usage rooted back in unremembered times. As a rule they talk freely with him because there is scarcely a village in Papua where he is not known, few indeed that he has not often visited and in which he does not recognize a man as having been with him on a patrol in the old days, or on a voyage to the outer islands, or one whose son has come to work with him in Port Moresby. He grew up with Papuans and has many of their ways and manners, never shouting or getting angry or hurrying about, speaking slowly and just loudly enough to be heard above the murmur of surrounding sounds, the whisper of the sea or the wind, and the background of children calling to each other.

He understands the tempo of Papuan life and does not rush the men when he is talking to them, or try to force answers, or keep them from the things they normally do at certain times and seasons. When they must go fishing he stops talking and takes two or three young boys to help him measure out the village lands and make neat maps that are later filed away in his office in Port Moresby. He does much additional work on these expeditions, charting inlets and harbors that might be improved by the addition of jetties or other facilities that could encourage new commercial or social activity among the villagers; and this work he likes best.

He took me once to such a place among the islands of the Mailu Group, out from Amazon Bay on the southeast coast of Papua: and in the late evening when the sea was a sheet of violet glass in the last light, and the coconut palms along the shore stood black and stiff like stage scenery cut sharply out of cardboard, he put sextant, compass, and lead line into a dinghy and we rowed away from our work boat into the middle of a wide estuary. We sat there taking sights on landmarks and fixing them on the chart, and making soundings with the lead line, while a few late-homing pigeons fled swiftly past in the gathering dark, seaward, to their roost on an off-shore atoll. High in the last diminishing circle of gray daylight a solitary sea eagle swung slowly to and fro, searching the sea for a late supper. Sirius was already bright in the sky.

We had worked quietly, without strain or angularity, easy and as fluid in our movements as the water slapping at the sides of the dinghy: then, when the sun had quite gone and everything but ourselves and the tide had stopped moving, he took the lead line for a last cast and let it go with a soft splash that seemed, in the utter silence, like the first sound ever made, or the last. We looked at each other and sighed, then took the oars and paddled back to our boat.

That night the island people danced the Govi dance, in which one man is decorated to represent a bird of paradise. He wore a cape of shredded palm leaf over his shoulders, and tufts of other leaves stuck into arm and leg bands, and a turban of feathers on his head. He performed his dance on a square platform raised some four or five feet above the ground, and simply hopped around its periphery like a mating bird hopping anxiously along a branch, while a group of decorated men and women beat drums and chanted and danced in the center of the platform. The villagers sat on the ground surrounding the platform, staring up at the dancers.

There were big fires all around, which cast black shadows and threw patches of red and yellow light on brown skins shiny with coconut oil; and suddenly above the sound of the drumming and singing, there was the squeal of a pig being killed so that the visitors could be given something to eat. There were other dances later, and much gossip, for a great many people had come from other islands and from villages along the coast, and most of them being related in one way or another, there was much to talk about. When the moon came up it threw a soft light over their canoes, drawn up on the beach, and a little breath of wind stirred in the sails loosely furled around high masts. One day, I know, I will go there again and stay.

Ivan Champion taught me much about New Guinea in those days, and wherever we went told me the history of the seaways in which we sailed, pointing out a passage through which this or that explorer had passed or might have passed; and whenever he could, he checked his own soundings of reefs and inlets and anchorages with those of Matthew Flinders, who made the first reliable charts in these island waterways not long after Australia itself was first settled. Now I had come to get his help again, and with map and notebook we worked out my next journey, dividing New Guinea into three parts, each quite different in aspect, history, and in the level of advancement reached by its people.

First I would go westward along the Papuan coast to visit villages of the Motu and the Mekeo people, whose ways are little changed from the old days. Then I would cross the great dividing range by air, to the northern part of New Guinea where great changes of all kinds are creating social and political ferment. And finally into the central highlands, where the twentieth century and the stone age have lately come face to face. In this way I would gain at least a general idea of the infinite variety of culture, custom, and achievement to be seen among the people of Papua and New Guinea, and to assess and see the aims and labors of those who live and work with them to ends that are honest, if sometimes theoretical, and not always understood by those most concerned. And before I left him we had arranged, for some time later, a short voyage to the outer islands.

Unfortunately, because of limited time and money available for this assignment, I was not able to include a visit to the Sepik River area on this occasion, though I have been there before and since; so having left the Chief Native Lands Commissioner listening to his tape recorder, I sought out those who might best be able to tell of the most recent advancements and happenings in the remote, malodorous, and fever-ridden swamplands of northwest New Guinea, where a quarter of a million people live in riverine villages spread along five hundred miles of main waterway and the twists and turns of its uncounted tributaries, many of them never yet explored.

The annual Education Conference was sitting in Port Moresby, which meant that there would be many missionaries in town from all parts of the country, so that I might easily find one of the priests or brothers belonging to the Australian Franciscans or Americans of the Divine Word Mission, who between them do most of the educational work in the Sepik River District. These Americans also run an aerial medical and supply service. But instead of missionaries I found Tas Hammersley, a pioneer Government schoolteacher from the Sepik area, and Patrol Officer Graham, who has recently discovered a number of previously unknown clans at the lower end of the river. They were in the hotel lounge, drinking cold beer.

Hammersley, I knew, had not long ago established the first Government school on the river; not only established it, but he had built it himself, having walked through the bush to a site well placed in relation to several villages, and there set to work with ax and saw and a carpenter's outfit to put up a boarding school by himself. He was his own architect, carpenter, and laborer, but as the building took shape and the purpose of his work became understood, men and boys came to help him. Some carried the timber from where it had been felled, others gathered saplings and grass for the roof, while others dug land to make food gardens for the students who were to come. Then women planted taro, yams, and sago around about so that soon after Hammersley opened the school and began to teach the boys the alphabet and numbers, they were already, in part, self-supporting, though their parents afterwards continued to visit, bringing fruit and other food.

Patrol Officer Graham, like Hammersley, is a young man, perhaps younger than the schoolteacher, in his early twenties. He looks like a champion football player, solid, square, and implacable; but like almost all patrol officers he is, in fact, gentle, modest, and sentimental about the people among whom he works. He is going home to Sydney for three months' vacation. After that he will spend six months at the School of Pacific Administration, also in Sydney. In the course of this six months he will study a number of subjects including anthropology, agricultural economics, political history, office management, and civil administration. Life in Sydney will be a pleasant change for him, but already he says that when the course is finished he will be glad to get back to his friends in the lower reaches of the Sepik.

He said that he had much to do in Port Moresby before catching his plane the next day. He had, for instance, to call on the Welfare Section of the Administration to try to speed the delivery of a sewing machine promised months ago for the native women's clubs. Then he must go to the Public Health Department with a rather vulgar message from the doctor at Ambunti about the urgent need for an additional medical assistant, and a new part for the refrigerator which was, at present, out of order. He glanced at his beer and smiled, and said that I had best sit down and have one myself because he had some photographs that might interest me, and if I would wait a moment he would go to his room and get them.

The pictures were interesting, especially those of the Shu'amu people, one of the clans which he had recently discovered. He thought they might be the remnants of a semi-nomad mountain tribe reduced to a few survivors by continuous warfare and who, having heard rumors of the Government, had moved down toward the river to put themselves within its protective reach. There were several other such fragmentary groups finding their way from the interior, looking for peace and a respite from a life of continuous fear and fighting.

These Shu'amu seem a pleasant and gentle people though very primitive, the men wearing practically nothing other than gourds over their private parts and quill feathers stuck into holes pierced through their nostrils. A few of the older men wore little necklets

of cowrie shell, obviously old and much-handled, having been used
as currency in trading ventures that originated on the coast many
years ago. Like the last inferior goods in a peddler's pack, they have
found a final owner among the most isolated and impecunious people in the land.

There were no more than thirty of these Shu'amu men, women,
and children, and no old folk. These had no doubt been the most
easily killed off by raiders or had been abandoned one after the
other in a succession of peremptory flights. But there were a few
children, and one woman suckling a baby. There were also a few
pigs in one picture, a sow with her litter. So the clan will probably
survive.

Patrol Officer Graham sorted through the pictures and put one in
front of me. "That's Gani," he said. The man had an intelligent
though not friendly face. His earlobes were bound with thin spirals
of cane and he wore a short stick of bamboo through his nose. "He's
supposed to have eaten his wife, but I don't believe it. The Crown
Prosecutor got the story from a man of the Augot clan who has a
grudge against Gani over some missing pigs." Patrol Officer Graham
seemed a little offended that the Crown Law Department should
seem to harass his friend Gani, fight leader of one of the remote
May River clans who live in the backwaters of the Sepik.

He and Gani have a relationship that is fairly common between
Government officers and local leaders in areas that are not yet fully
under Government control. Through several wives, and their relations in a network of interclan marriages up and down the river,
Gani has family contacts and right of access to most of the villages
within reach of the May River Patrol Post. He also speaks Pidgin
English, as well as most of the local dialects, and these several
factors make him extremely useful to the patrol officer as a guide
and interpreter during his journeys on the river.

In reverse, Gani's prestige in the villages is enhanced immeasur-
ably by the fact that he has the ear of the patrol officer, shares in
the food and tobacco rations issued to the patrol personnel, is privy
to the magic of firearms, radio, and the outboard motors that drive
the Government canoes, and enjoys the luxury of living in a tent
and under a mosquito net, so that when people see him coming
they say, "Here is Gani, who speaks with the Government."

Gani is no angel. He was involved in the Yellow River killings, and his ability to speak Pidgin English was acquired in prison. Yet I incline to believe that he would not eat his wife. Somebody else's wife perhaps, given the appropriate opportunity, but not his own wife. He might well have killed her in a fit of pique, but he wouldn't eat her. He is a fairly conservative type, cautious, and unlikely to risk being himself the victim of a pay-back murder organized by the dead woman's clan. He is the kind of primitive leader who will probably become a sturdy back-bench politician when self-government is thrust upon the two million people of the Territory, as seems likely before very long.

The Yellow River massacre was a textbook case, in which the people of Gani's village invited the inhabitants of another village to a reconciliation picnic, then murdered them all and ate them. The victims, men, women, and children, numbered some thirty or more. When the Government patrol sent to investigate stories of the orgy entered the murderers' village, they found the skulls of the victims hanging in the houses of those who had eaten them, each skull being neatly cleaned of meat and autographed by the man who had been responsible for the death of its owner.

The men of Gani's village were removed to a corrective institution, leaving behind only the women, children, and very old men. So it became necessary for the Government to establish a patrol post in the area to protect these defenseless dependents from other cannibal clans, until the men came home again. Patrol Officer Graham has been happy among these people, exploring other tributaries of the river even more remote, and discovering new clans never before seen. Some of these, too, he has been able to send to prison for cannibalism, so giving them the opportunity to see the outside world and to learn something of civilized ways. He drained his beer and stood up, gathering the photographs together. "Now, if you'll excuse me, I'll go and see about that sewing machine."

When I first came to New Guinea the Legislative Council met in what was little more than a wooden shed at the water's edge, in a grove of coconut trees. The winds of change that roared around the world, provoking a cyclonic violence elsewhere, in Africa, Indonesia, and other parts of Asia, seemed to sound less loudly in the ears of those who met in this shed than did the soft clicking of the wind in the palm trees above their heads, or the flip-flap of wavelets along

the beach at low tide—sounds so soft and seductive that sometimes
they lulled to sleep those members who had eaten too much lunch.
At that time the majority of the council members were public officials. There were a few selected representatives of missionary
societies and business interests to give the council some semblance
of democracy. And three natives of New Guinea, chosen by the
Government.

Now, the council meets in an air-conditioned chamber that stands
on a hill overlooking the town, and is reached by a road that curls
upward from the main shopping block like a wide stairway. The
majority of its members are elected by the people, and native representatives have the decisive voting strength. The change came
within a matter of two or three years, without any loud demand on
the part of the New Guinea people themselves. Some of the new
native representatives have been to school, are sophisticated, and
represent groups which have been living a semi-Western way of
life for fifty years or more. Others are themselves illiterate in the
Western sense, and speak self-consciously for tribes who are still
practically primitive. Nobody seems to be quite sure how or why
this change came about so quickly, though it is clear that pressures
exerted from within the United Nations have had something to do
with it. Otherwise it is simply as though history, having dealt with
major issues elsewhere in an area of disintegrating colonialism,
now turned to New Guinea and said, "You're next."[2]

It is unlikely that members of the House of Assembly will go to
sleep in the new chamber, for in the past two years each session
has seen dramatic paragraphs of history written into the statute
books. One after another new regulations and ordinances have been
framed, removing any vestige of racial discrimination from the law,
and making the least practice of such discrimination illegal. Other
and more positive legislation has been enacted to provide all New
Guinea people with equal rights and opportunities, so that suddenly
young men and women, who a few years ago had no future outside
their villages, are theoretically able to occupy any position in the

[2] The Legislative Council has recently been reconstituted as a House
of Assembly, and elections held in March 1964 have given native members a majority in the new House. It will still be necessary for legislation
to be ratified by the Australian Government before it can become effective.

country. They require only the opportunity of experience and the chance to gain educational status.

When I entered the chamber Miss Wedega was speaking and there seemed to be a ripple of quiet laughter and comment among members as she spoke. This surprised me because Alice Wedega, though very pleasant and good-humored, is not as a rule actively humorous. She is, in fact, a serious-minded lady, modestly conscious of being the only native-born woman in the council and given to speaking without rhetoric or extravagance, mostly on matters that are of practical concern to the women of New Guinea. She comes from southeast Papua, and when not engaged on council matters or traveling abroad to represent her country at international gatherings, is busy with the organizing of women's clubs and agricultural committees, and the affairs of the Girl Guides Association in which she holds the rank of Commissioner.

I took a seat next to a man I knew and asked him what had caused the amusement. He handed me a copy of the local newspaper, pointing to a paragraph in the gossip column which ascribed to Miss Wedega the statement that her grandfather had eaten better men than some of those now sitting in the Legislative Council. Nobody would believe her capable of saying any such thing, but it seemed to some members too good a joke to let pass.

A woman of outstanding charm and sincerity, mission-trained since girlhood in social graces and emotional discipline, as well as in letters and simple addition, Alice Wedega is something of a rarity among her own people—a middle-aged, unmarried woman, who lives a detribalized life and devotes herself almost entirely to good works sponsored by the Government or her church. She inherits, through this mission church to which she belongs and whose imprint upon her character is indelible, the tradition of generations of gently bred English women who, living in cathedral towns or pretty villages, have conducted Sunday schools and women's guilds, taken charge of Girl Guides, visited the sick with bottles of broth, and who have died bravely and chastely, vaguely pitied by lesser women and loved by everybody. It is an outstanding achievement by the mission that has trained her, and very few other Papuan women can match her blend of instinctive and cultivated dignity.

When the laughter died she continued her speech. She was much concerned with the ill effects of the repeal of the liquor laws, saying that now that the native people are permitted to drink, some men hold liquor parties in the villages, while many others who live near towns spend too much of their time and money in hotels, and are disastrously neglecting their families. The Government should, she thought, do something to protect women and children from the evils of its own legislation.

The council members listened quietly, respecting her honesty but a little embarrassed by the naïveté of the plea. They let her continue without interrupting, and when she sat down there was a pause. Then a Government member said, diffidently, "We fully appreciate Miss Wedega's point of view, but she must understand that the right to self-determination and self-government includes the right to be exposed to temptation." The President rose for an adjournment and the members left their places. I followed them into the corridors to talk to some whose districts I might soon visit.

Members of the Legislative Council in session look thoughtful but not anxious. They are keenly busy with the mechanics of political change but there is no sense of panic, nor does there seem any immediate reason why there should be. There are no signs on the surface of impending disaster or startling change. There seem to be no smoldering hates nor any evidence of anxious or passionate nationalism. There are, of course, resentments here and there, and even localized outbreaks of minor violence in which people have been killed. But the Government maintains an almost God-like calm and seems majestic in the certainty that all is well. It frowns upon but is patient with the few who say loudly that they think otherwise. There are two such in the council itself who cry, "Danger!"

One of them, Ian Downs, is President of the Highland Farmers and Settlers' Association. He nodded to me but was busy in discussion with a small group of other members. Ian Downs, an Australian, was a District Commissioner before he left the Government service to become a planter, and is a power not only among the settlers but among half a million highland tribesmen whose goodwill and respect he earned when working among them for many years as senior representative of the Government in their area. Now he suspects the Government of wanting to relinquish its responsibilities in New Guinea, believing that it plans to withdraw and leave the United Nations to deal with the problems of administering this backward and uneconomic territory, and of bringing its people to a secure independence. He says that such a policy would betray both the New Guinea people and the white settlers who, given a little time, can and will work out a way of running the country together to their mutual satisfaction.

The other voice is that of John Guise who, like Alice Wedega, is an Anglicized Papuan with strong missionary affiliations. But though equally courteous, he is more outspoken and says publicly that Australia's past help and her present gestures of good intention are unreal and empty so long as she continues to govern New Guinea as a totally dependent colony. Some Australians are indignant with him for saying this sort of thing. They write, telling him that he is "an ungrateful native" and "a tool of the Communists." But there are many among the most senior of the Government officers in New Guinea itself who see in John Guise, politician and lay preacher, the man most likely to emerge as a national leader. Of the two million New Guinea people, he is the one most at home in all the worlds that lie between the Sepik River savages and the sophisticates of our present civilization, for he has mixed with both kinds and has spoken in the meeting rooms of the United Nations as well as on open hillsides in the high valleys of the great divide.

Not long ago he stood before a crowd of Highland tribesmen who still paint their faces when they assemble, and wear great sprays of feathers on their heads and carry axes. They sat along a hillside, their grass-fiber aprons tucked between their legs, listening to the Papuan with the brown skin who spoke to them as though he were a white man. He said, "I have crossed the great salt water and I have talked with men from other lands whose skins are the same color as ours, and these men are the chosen leaders of their people. They have said to me that they, too, were once governed by white men but that they grew tired of this and rose up and threw the white men out. And they ask me, "When will your people get rid of the white men, and be happy like we are?"

When John Guise said this there was silence until he spoke again, and said, "Soon I will go again to talk with these men and once more they will say, "When will you throw the white men out?" He paused and asked, "What shall I tell them?" Slowly he looked over the crowd, seeking out the clan leaders with his eyes. Then pointing his finger at one of them he demanded, "Tell me, what shall I answer?" There was no answer and he let his arm drop. "I will tell you what I will say. I will say that we do not like being a colonial people but we are not yet ready to throw out the white men to let others in, nor do we wish to see in our country the things that have happened in Africa."

John Guise is not "an ungrateful native" or "a tool of the Communists." He is a Papuan patriot and a fledgling politician with a flair for rhetoric. He is inevitable and necessary in this period of his country's history. It remains to be seen whether he or any other educated, mission-trained, and Government-sponsored political leader will gain the support of the big traditional leaders, many of whom are illiterate but still wield more influence than the Government and the missionaries combined. As we sat talking one such man came toward us and hesitated shyly, having no English and not wishing to break in upon our conversation uninvited. But John Guise looked up and smiled, and so did I, and we both stood to speak to Kondom Agaundo, elected member for the Highlands and spokesman in the Legislative Council for half a million people.

John Guise and Kondom Agaundo come together from opposite ends of two thousand years. Between them as they stand, native-born inhabitants of the same country, there is a cultural and educational gulf at the bottom of which lies the stone age from which Kondom has lately emerged, and upon whose rim stand people like John Guise and Alice Wedega, the first full-ripened fruits of Western culture transplanted into Papuan soil. And thinking of Miss Wedega I thought of Kondom's wife, his number one wife, whom I had met when I went into his valley in the heart of central New Guinea to see him elected by his half-million countrymen to this seat in the Legislative Council.

Kondom's number one wife (he has eight) is a Catholic. She wears a necklace of dogs' teeth and a girdle of spun grass fibers. She has the face of an aged matriarch and the simple humility of an uneducated saint. Her hair is short and wiry, and she wears a loop of fencing wire pendant from her ears. Her breasts are small and like empty purses of wrinkled brown leather. Her father was a big man of the Chimbu people. Kondom's family gave twenty pigs, fifty plumes of the bird of paradise, forty gold-lipped pearl shells, and much other wealth to her clan when she and Kondom were betrothed.

Her eldest son is a schoolteacher at the Catholic Mission. He speaks English as well as Pidgin, the New Guinea lingua franca. He also wears a white shirt and shorts. Her youngest daughter, Ahna, is one of the most beautifully built women I have ever seen. At sixteen she is nearly six feet in height and perfectly proportioned. Apart from a tribal tattoo on her face her skin is without blemish. She wears nothing but a narrow apron of grass fibers. She smokes twist tobacco rolled in newspaper. She is completely illiterate, but plays a swift and efficient game of baseball introduced by American missionaries. To look at her is to be reminded of the Shulamite of Solomon's song, "I am black but very beautiful Oh daughters of Jerusalem."

I have not yet been able to record the number of Kondom's children, not that it is important. I have seen his eight wives and have watched them at their daily tasks, working in the garden, drying coffee beans, cooking the family meals, living almost exactly as their mothers lived and their mothers' mothers for unknown generations back. The world in which their husband, Kondom, moves when he is not at home is a complete and utter mystery to them, as unknown as heaven is to us, an abstract that does not even tempt serious thought.

Each of them tends a garden that came with her as dowry when Kondom took her to wife. Her principal occupation is to tend that garden and from it to supply daily the food necessary to keep herself and her children alive, to feed Kondom and to provide him with a surplus sufficient to enable him to give feasts of a magnitude that accords with his status and dignity.

Kondom lives in a small weatherboard cottage of Australian country town design, at the foot of a high mountain that is called Waiye. His wives share a cluster of small, native-style grass huts that surround an earthen enclosure or courtyard where they cook and execute other daily domestic chores. The central fixture in this courtyard is a forty-gallon gasoline drum partly buried in the earth. Each day this is filled with the food that constitutes the daily main meal: a gutted young pig, two or three scraggly chickens, the carcasses of any small bush animals (rats, mice, or small marsupials) that might have been caught by the children; layers of wild or garden-cultivated greens, taro roots, and other tubers. These are laid on top of hot stones and covered with the thick, fleshy leaves of

banana palm or taro that are tied down over the lip of the drum to
keep the cooking sealed.

Meanwhile Kondom receives visitors, mostly fellow members of
the Native Local Government Council of which he is the elected
President, who come to discuss affairs of tribal significance with him
in the Council House that stands just across the road from Kondom's
own house, on a small grassy plateau at the foot of Mount Waiye.
A signboard outside the Council House announces that this is the
meeting place of the Waiye Native Local Government Council, and
the council clerk, an educated young man from Rabaul, will tell you
that in the old days, less than twenty years ago, the fight leaders
of the clans met on top of the mountain to settle disputes with
spears and clubs while today they meet in the Council House at the
foot of the mountain with weapons no more lethal than the President's gavel. The clerk, whose family has attended school for two
generations back, tends to be slightly patronizing about this transformation.

Among Kondom's regular visitors is the Assistant District Officer
in charge of the Government Station at Kundiawa, eight miles
away. Even more frequent are the visits of the Government Officer
responsible for guiding the operations of the Waiye Native Council.
When these or other officials call on Kondom he knows without
telling that it is "something belong Government" that brings them.
He will be asked to discuss the organization of some new public
works with the other members of the council, or to arrange a display of tribal dancing for a visiting politician from Australia or
the United Nations, or to use his influence to promote some new
campaign or experiment planned by the Departments of Agriculture
and Health.

Kondom receives each visitation with dignity and responds with
goodwill and efficiency to every practical suggestion. For instance
in the past few years he has built a model Council House, a neatly
carpentered medical aid center and a school, together with teachers' residences, and European-style houses for the council clerk
and the council carpenter, although every one of his neighbors in
the valley lives in a primitive grass hut.

He himself is illiterate and speaks even bush Pidgin with difficulty. In the Legislative Council he is regarded by some of the least
patient Australian members as a bore, and by some of the more
sophisticated Papuan and New Guinean members as an embarrass-

ment. Yet Kondom knows in his simple countryman's way that he is a historical figure, even though he may not understand completely the detailed significance of this transitional importance.

At his first official engagement as a member of the Papua-New Guinea delegation to a South-Pacific Conference, Kondom was clearly the boy-from-the-bush having his first look not only at the outside world, but also at a new kind of civilization. Other delegates, Fijians, Samoans, New Caledonians, and other Pacific islanders, as well as fellow members of his own delegation, speaking fluent English or French and sometimes both, noted the silent, withdrawn, and ill-at-ease bushman without realizing that in his own valley alone he could claim the personal and tribal loyalty of 165,000 Chimbu highlanders.

Smart young typists and secretaries smirked and giggled at his self-consciousness, at his inability to sign his name to documents, to respond to questions and inquiries in English or French, or to follow many of the technical discussions on social, political, and economic developments in the South Pacific. They nudged each other when he fell asleep with his mouth open in the afternoon sessions during speeches that he could not follow. They beamed in anticipation when, on the fourth day, he stood up to speak on local government. He cleared his throat noisily and a girl laughed outright, then blushed with embarrassment. Kondom waited a moment, then began to speak in mutilated Pidgin that was translated as he went along.

"My name is Kondom. I come from the bush. I have no English, I cannot read or write. My tongue is thick, my head is a stone. In my own country I am a big man, yet I stand before you as a child. I have been a leader in battle with bow and arrow and spear, but today I am a baby feeding at his mother's breast. Soon I will die, and in a little while my son will come here in my place and sit among you and speak to you in English, and write his name, and be a leader among you. And you will not laugh at him." When Kondom sat down there was silence, and the young typist was wiping her eyes.

The warning bells rang to call the members back into the chamber. John Guise excused himself and hurried away. I said goodbye to Kondom and arranged to visit him at Waiye within a few weeks. Members passed through the lobbies on their way back to the chamber. Vin Tobaining, a wealthy cocoa planter, and school-teacher Efram Jubilee, both smooth, big-bellied men of the well-to-do Tolai tribe from the northern islands, stopped to shake hands softly and to murmur quiet politenesses before moving on. Ian Downs, still talking with colleagues as he walked, stopped briefly to ask if I would be going to the Highlands and if so would I call on him for any help I needed. I said that I would like to film a meeting of the Highland Farmers and Settlers' Association, if that were possible. He said, "Of course, write to me about it."

The bells stopped and the doors of the chamber closed. The men inside resumed the polite, ritualistic procedures of democratic discussion, some alive with ideas for New Guinea's future and their own, some frightened for it, others cynical, feeling that the history of New Guinea is being shaped elsewhere and that these debates in the new air-conditioned chamber are part of a game of make-believe.

I went out into the hot, white light and walked down into the town. Tomorrow I would leave Port Moresby and try to find in the villages of the coast and the northern islands, and in the mountains, some true picture of New Guinea and would plan for the Minister a film that would show the work being done, under his direction, to bring its various people to a stage where they might decide their own future.

Like him, I could only do my best.

Three

I was at the airport early, for flying in New Guinea is safest in the mornings before the clouds rise out of the valleys and fill the passes through the mountains; and three aircraft that I have flown in during the past year have since been lost, so as I get older I tend to be careful about flying. Not that I am going far today, only to Yule Island, along the coast to the northwest, a trip that takes all day by the missionary's launch *St. Francis,* but little more than half an hour by plane.

The four-engined aircraft from Sydney is already on the tarmac, having come in on schedule at dawn, and the hangar is full of people meeting or being met. Those meeting the plane look as though they belong here, the men in shorts or casual slacks and open shirts, the women in flimsy frocks. The people in city clothes have just arrived from Australia, many of them returning from vacation for "just one more two-year term" before going back home for good. Nobody believes them and usually they stay longer, perhaps for two or three more terms, either because their work is absorbing, or they can save money, or the small-town social life of the tropics suits their nature.

Mother Geneviève is first through the Customs and into the arms of her Little Sisters, Handmaids of Our Lord, all soft-cooing sounds and smiles and tiny flutterings of brown hands, so very happy to welcome their Mother back from her native France where she has been bustling about, appearing on television, giving interviews, trying to raise funds to keep her Order going because, as she says, the Holy Ghost cannot be expected to do all of the work. A remarkable woman, tall, well-boned, and with a strong, wide face. Her brother was a general in the Foreign Legion.

Her Little Sisters are Papuan and New Guinea girls, dedicated to the service of the Christian God. When they are trained and disciplined in spiritual and human skills they go out, truly as hand-maids, to help the missionaries working in the field, some as school-teachers and nurses, most as cooks and housekeepers. Many of them speak beautiful English, some with overtones of a French accent. All have that miraculous serenity which is the hallmark of mystical union. It is a strange thing. I compare them immediately, whenever I see them, with village girls of the same age and tribal background, whose faces, however fine of structure, are usually empty, sullen, and vague, like the faces of tired and aged animals, before they are out of their teens. Nothing so much underlines the limitations of primitive life as the transformation that takes place when people from isolated and backward tribes come into close contact with in-telligent and sympathetic people from the outside world.

This effect is always evident among school children at mission stations, but it is also seen frequently at remote patrol posts where there are men waiting trial for murder and other crimes. Here, for the first time, they are freed from the tensions of savagery and pro-tected by a system of law and order that does not recognize revenge as a social compulsion. Nervous suspicion gives way to trust and ease of association, and each individual seems to develop a separate and untrammeled relationship to the new environment. It is, of course, a transitory stage of metamorphosis, but for the civilized on-looker it is an exciting thing to see an anthropological curiosity be-come, in a matter of weeks, a recognizable player in the charade of mankind's social evolution.

A group of laborers sits on the tarmac in the wing shadow of a DC-3. There are forty of them or more. By their tribal markings and the shape of their heads they come from the New Guinea side, from beyond Mount Hagen. Each has a bundle wrapped in a woven palm mat which contains his clothing, a blanket and mosquito net, and cup, plate, cooking pot, and spoon. Most of them also have a small wooden case in which they keep their more precious and per-sonal belongings. A small package of letters, photographs, news-paper clippings, and job references (the magic of pieces of paper that communicate), a pack of dirty playing cards, armshells and other decorations for dancing, a special piece of clothing for best, usually a Hawaiian shirt or a football jersey, maybe a watch or a clock. One or two of them have guitars. One has a cricket bat. Another even has a shotgun.

They have been working down the coast on a coconut plantation, on contract for two years. During this time they have been paid a minimum of twenty-five shillings ($2.80) a month, plus food, clothing, accommodation, and medical care. Their working conditions have been checked from time to time by a Government labor inspector. Thirty thousand young men from the villages sign these contracts each year and go away to work in another part of the country. After two years the employer must return them to their villages.

If they have been sensible they have saved some money to put toward the price of a bride. If they have been foolish they have lost it all playing Lucky, a simple card game. Most of them seem to enjoy the adventure and gain from the experience, though much depends upon the plantation manager for whom they work. Some of them are very good employers, most are average like the rest of us, but a few are uncouth and barbarous and the laborers hate them and run away and cause trouble for the Government and everybody else.

A Papuan employee of the airline, considerably superior in his own estimation to these bush *kanakas* from New Guinea, comes and orders them into the aircraft. Slowly they get up and move out of the shadow into the stark light of the sun. Inside the aircraft it is already like an oven.

A Cessna takes off and heads toward a gap in the Owen Stanley Range. The baggage boys working for the airline stand and watch it until a hot and exasperated official shouts at them to get back to work. This shouting and sweating and getting hot is very bad for white men who work at the in-between jobs in the tropics, jobs that are full of responsibility but carry very little prestige or reward. Jobs like airline booking clerks and baggage supervisors. Their whole motivation and devotion is to efficiency as it is understood in Sydney, where most of them come from, or New York or Djakarta or Rio de Janeiro and other such places on the international roundabout. But the Papuan baggage boy was born in a village where there is no clock and where, if anybody contemplates a journey, even to the next village, it is discussed for several days. They are expert fishermen and canoemakers, but they do not understand the urgency of moving pieces of baggage from one point to another fifty yards away. They stand and wait about until instructed to do something, and when told to move a heavy bag onto a truck they quietly pick up a much smaller bag and shift it a few feet and then move away instinctively to stand in the shade.

Before the Sydney plane has been ten minutes on the tarmac, the officials, and occasionally an impatient passenger who hasn't seen it all before, being a newcomer, will be pushing and pulling and lifting heavy baggage and freight, while the Papuan, unemotionally and without evidence of deliberate guile, will go on quietly and slowly picking up the lightest and most trivial parcels and pointlessly moving them from place to place in order to seem conscientiously occupied.

The Government anthropologist is on the plane, from a conference in Canberra where they are planning a social survey of native urban settlements; and Toua Kapina, President of the Hanuabada Local Government Council, back from a short course of instruction at the School of Pacific Administration.

I saw Wilfred Moi in the hangar, slight and soft-smiling, the center of a group of Papuans and Australians, and realized that he must have come through on the Sydney plane from Fiji where he has been doing some additional medical training. I hoped that he was going on to Rabaul, back to take charge again of the rural health center that he started at Tapapipi among the Tolai people three years ago. It would round off what to me had been a quite moving story.

Moi is in the same category as Alice Wedega, a Papuan educated in the tradition of the gentle, well-spoken, and modest English person of the nineteenth century, a species practically extinct in its homeland, but still possible to find in Papua, and presumably other mission lands, where Anglican clerics and their ladies have lived out their lives in a kind of quarantine, cut off from the cauterizing influences of the past thirty years in Europe, and so have retained the lucent outlook of their youthful English schooldays.

His father was a village schoolteacher in the mission, and Wilfred (named for a nicely mannered English saint) received as good an education as was possible in Papua before the war. He learned to respect the Establishment and to aspire to attach himself one day to its outer fringes though, being a Papuan, he neither expected nor hoped to occupy any important position within its solidly Anglo-Australian framework. He married a village girl and they have three children. He learned to be a Medical Aid Post Orderly and when, after the war, the tempo of native social advancement quickened and Government departments looked around for likely young men to push ahead, Wilfred Moi, a favorite son of the Anglican mission and its widely respected Bishop, found himself one of half a dozen young men chosen to attend for training at the British Medical Centre in Fiji.

There was no question of making these young men fully qualified doctors. None of them had the basic education required of doctors in most parts of the world. Some of them qualified as health inspectors, a few as assistant medical practitioners. Wilfred was among these few who came back to practice as doctors among their own people. It was a step forward for the Papuan and New Guinea people as well as for Wilfred Moi and his companions.

On casual acquaintance one would not regard him as a pioneering type. He is shy, physically slender, inward-looking. It was a surprise when he was sent to Rabaul and asked to start the first rural health center in New Guinea among the burly, truculent, race-proud Tolai people of New Britain.

Today there are several of these rural health centers. They are established at points from which they can serve a group of villages. They have a doctor's office and dispensary, an infant welfare clinic, and in some cases a maternity ward. There is an assistant medical practitioner like Moi in charge of each center, two nurses, a health inspector responsible for village hygiene and building regulations, and usually a malaria control officer or aid post orderly. This is an all-native staff, and the cost of maintaining them is shared by the Native Local Government Council in the area, and the Government. They provide a basic out-patient and domestic health service which supplements the centralized hospital and specialized medical services provided by the Government and missionary organizations. It was the first of these health centers at Tapapipi, about twenty miles from Rabaul, that Wilfred Moi, with the local courtesy title of doctor, was sent to open.

The forty thousand Tolai people of New Britain in the Trust Territory of New Guinea are the most compact, literate, and vocal group in the whole of the Territory, ahead of all the others in every

material aspect of advancement. The administration seems to favor
them with considerable attention because they are responsive to
new ideas of "progress" and are usually prepared to co-operate in
schemes of advancement put forward by Government planners. But
they are not a tractable group: they do not consider themselves
particularly obliged to the administration for its special attention to
their advancement. They do not respond with unquestioning loyalty
and affection. On the contrary, some Tolai clans tend to be stubborn and at times violent. They have even been known to throw
stones at the district commissioner. Recently they staged a street
fight against "foreign" plantation laborers from the Sepik District.
To send the gentle Papuan Dr. Moi into this environment seemed
to be testing him unduly.

I had a note from him soon after he had finished his first two-year
term at Tapapipi and was off to Fiji for further training. I had
written to ask him what he felt about his work with the Tolai, and
in his reply he said, "I did not like it when the Government told me
that I must go and work among these people. They are New Guinea
people. I am a Papuan. It is not easy for two people with such
different backgrounds to understand each other exactly. Every man
is part of the things that have made him. His father's house, the
village, his mother's face, uncles and aunts and the children he
played with. In his heart are the songs the people sang at night in
the houses, the words, the sounds. He has his own pathway to the
sea, his own God to speak to. Every man in a strange place is by
himself.

"I can never forget when I came first to Tapapipi. My house was
not finished. All about was mud and grass trampled into the dirt.
There was no garden. No one was there to welcome me. I could cry.
It will stay in my memory forever. By myself I finished my house
so that my wife could come with the children. Only one old man
from the village came to help me and because I could not speak
his language we could not talk together. But, in my heart I spoke
to him with thanks. He made a garden for me with taro and sweet
potato and beans.

"I waited every day, but nobody came to my house. The people
who were sick went to Rabaul to the hospital or stayed in the villages until they got well. Only sometimes at night young men would
come and wake me up to tell they had a pain in the head or the stom-

ach. I knew they were making jokes with me, but I treated them with every attention and seriously. When they went away they laughed and called out to the people that they had been to visit the Papuan.

"Each day I walked to the other villages to talk to the people and to tell them I am here to help you, but they did not respond. Even the Village Councillors were against me, although they had asked the Government to send a doctor to work in their villages. Only Council President Nason Tokiala was for me. He called the Councillors together and spoke angry words to them, but they turned away and would not listen. They were angry because the Government had not sent them a Tolai doctor.

"One day a man came to me and asked me to visit his house. I came and he told me all his troubles even about his quarrels with his friends. I was very happy. I told him to come to my house and bring his friends. Then a woman came from a village far away. She had walked for many days with her sick child. I put her in my house and cared for her and the child. It got better. I felt at last a man who is alive. My work had started. When the nurses and my other helpers came it was better. The people became used to us. After some months the Councillors came to me and asked if they could build a maternity hospital at the centre. I replied, 'I am here to help you in all medical work. If you have the money to build your hospital I will work in it.' So they built the hospital.

"After two years the Government told me that I should leave Tapapipi and go back to Fiji to study some more. I was proud, but a little sad to leave my work. When it was time for me to go all of the people came to see me. There was a great crowd. Council President Nason made a speech. He said the people wished me to come back to them when I have finished my study. I told them, 'I was sent to help you, if you want me to come back I will be glad.' Everybody came to shake my hand. We have won our battle, the Tolai people and me."

The passengers from Sydney were moving out of the hangar with their baggage, to get into cars waiting to take them to town. Hank van Santen, chief pilot for Patair, passed me on his way to the briefing room. "We're taking you up to Yule Island this morning?" I nodded and Hank smiled. "A big shot from England going with you, I believe." He passed on, and I walked out onto the tarmac to wait for my fellow passengers.

The "big shot" of whom Hank had spoken became my friend on this day and in view of what happened to us it would be ill-mannered of me to use his name. It is sufficient, therefore, to say that he was a person of authority from England, an expert of considerable status who had come to New Guinea at the invitation of the Government.

He was large and stately, and had he not been so badly advised as to be wearing short trousers, would have looked regal. Even so, the immaculate shining whiteness of his clothing, from knee-length stockings to sola topee, set off with the neatly striped and distinctive tie of a famous British institution, caused him to stand out among the other people at the airport like a potentate among lesser men.

He arrived on the tarmac accompanied by the Directors of Agriculture and Finance. A Papuan assistant carried his monogrammed briefcase. The Cessna that was to take us to Yule Island stood ready. I was introduced, then the pilot, who seemed momentarily taken aback by the size of his load until the Director of Finance smiled and said that he was not coming on the trip.

We all stood back and made respectful signs suggesting that the distinguished visitor should enter the aircraft first and occupy the comfortable back seat, but the pilot seemed suddenly anxious and whispered to the Director of Agriculture, who shyly whispered to the visitor, who nodded agreeably and stood back. It seemed that he was too large to sit anywhere but in the co-pilot's seat. I got in quickly, followed by the Director of Agriculture. The visitor was reverently squeezed into the front seat with his briefcase, and we took off.

It had been explained to me the night before by the Government public relations officer. We were to fly to Yule Island and be met there by the officer in charge of the area. After a short exchange of official courtesies and a cup of morning tea, the Government officer would take us by launch across to the mainland to carry out the purpose of the expert's visit. This, briefly, was to inspect and assess the possibilities of a community rice-growing scheme about which there had been some disagreement in the Department of Agriculture and some growing doubt in the Department of Finance. My own function was to supply conversation of a lighter kind if necessary.

Having crossed from Yule Island to the mainland, we would make a short journey by road, of about an hour, to the District Agricultural Station where we would have lunch. Then another short road trip through the prospective rice-growing area during which we would pass through an interesting village before arriving at the substation from which the rice-growing experiment was being conducted. Here we would find the Cessna waiting to return us to Yule Island, where we would have dinner with the French Bishop of the Society of the Missionaries of the Sacred Heart, whose headquarters are on the island. It seemed a fairly simple and pleasant program. The visitor looked forward to it with serenity and confidence. He had, clearly, not traveled in New Guinea before.

The short flight to Yule Island was uneventful. It was a clear morning. On one side of the aircraft the great mountains of the Owen Stanley Range spread away from us fold after fold into the interior. To the northwest, rising above the rest of the peaks, Mount Yule hid the tip of its ten thousand feet in cloud.[1] Looking out on the other side of the aircraft, the ocean lay flat to a hazed-in horizon, pale blue fading to nebulous silver mist. Below us the narrow coastal plain planted with coconut palms in ordered rows, then the ribbon of beach, and patches of green and orange reef broken with surf.

The engine droned. The Director of Agriculture frowned as he read through reports that had been lying on his desk for days, waiting time to be read. The pilot pointed out the landmarks to the visitor, who acknowledged each snippet of information with appropriate expressions of interest and surprise. I sat and contemplated with quiet anticipation a reunion with the Bishop and his priests, and having a French omelette again.

The aircraft swooped over the island, then circled once to let everybody know that we were about to land, with passengers, freight, or mail. We could see the *St. Francis* discharging stores at

[1] Yule Island and Mount Yule are both named after Lieutenant Charles B. Yule, Commander of H.M.S. *Bramble*, a British survey ship that took part in the survey of the Papuan coast during the second part of the nineteenth century, and during which Captain Moresby discovered the harbor that is named after his father.

the mission wharf, and at the other end of the curving bay the Government launch standing by the jetty, presumably to take us soon across to the mainland. A jeep was snaking through the coconut palms in Chiria village, throwing up a tail of gray dust. This would be somebody from the mission, or from Mr. Slaughter's Trade Store, coming to see if there was anything for them on the aircraft. The Cessna bumped along the grassy strip and tick-tacked to a stop. George Canavan, the Government officer, stood a few paces ahead of his highly polished Land-Rover, waiting for us to alight, his round face full of amiability and quiet assurance.

I like George very much. He is intelligent, educated, zealous, and round. He organizes efficiently and does not panic when things go wrong, as they must frequently do in a country where the natural tempo and order of things is contrary and perverse, and resistant to organized change. He waited with easy patience while the visitor lowered himself out of the cockpit and to the ground, then saluted smartly, though without ostentation, and advanced smiling.

The Director of Agriculture introduced them and when they had shaken hands George indicated a group of Papuan police drawn up in line close by, rigid, tense, and barefooted, staring fixedly ahead. "I wonder," said George, "if you would mind inspecting them, they rather enjoy it and it gives them a chance to get a good look at you without peeping." The visitor looked surprised but answered that if it were proper for a civilian to inspect them he would be delighted. So they walked over and passed with solemn dignity along the line of seven men, stopping at each man as George announced his name and the visitor murmured alternately, "Good morning" and "How do you do?" When they had done this the visitor seemed quite pleased and stood back smiling, while George saluted the corporal of the guard and dismissed them in fluent Motu.[2] He then indicated the Land-Rover, the passenger door being held open by George's personal driver. As we embarked he winked amiably at me behind the visitor's back. We drove off to morning tea.

---

[2] Although the official language of Papua and New Guinea is English, each of the two territories has a vulgar lingua franca used to overcome the problem of the multiplicity of tribal languages. In Papua the lingua franca is Police Motu, a simplification of one of the main tribal languages. In New Guinea the lingua franca is Melanesian Pidgin, commonly called Pidgin English.

"Everything," said George a little later, "is organized. I will take you up the river to a landing-stage where a vehicle from the agricultural station will be waiting. This will take half an hour or so. We then drive for another twenty minutes on a fairly good track to the station, where you can look around a bit before lunch." He turned to the distinguished visitor, "There is quite a bit of rice being grown there in experimental plots that might be of interest to you." The visitor inclined his head graciously. He had so far been out of his bed at the hotel in Moresby for some five hours and had not as yet seen a single grain of rice, but he knew how to be patient. "We then," George said, "go by tractor up to the rice-farm where we have the mechanical farming equipment that is loaned out to the villages to that they can plough, sow, and harvest their crops efficiently."

The visitor again approved with an inclination of his head, but a slight rise of the eyebrow seemed to query the tractor. The Director of Agriculture was quick to observe this and said to George, "Why the tractor, is the road out?" George pursed his lips and looked dubious, "Well, there's been a bit of rain lately and you can never tell if there is going to be a road or not. It's better to be sure than sorry, you know." He turned again to the visitor and explained, "It's not so much the rain down here on the coast, but it's up in the mountains." He waved his hand toward the Owen Stanleys. "A couple of inches up there overnight and we have a flood down here next morning." For a second the visitor looked doubtful, and again he inclined his head in acquiescence, but as we walked along to the jetty I began to feel sorry for him.

In the launch, crossing from the island to the mainland, George explained to us the syntactical and grammatical peculiarities of Mekeo, Fuyuge, Roro, and half a dozen other languages spoken in his subdistrict. How, for instance, many of these people have no words in their own language for such concepts as love, peace, joy, and pleasure, but many different words having fine shades of meaning in matters of death, fighting, disputes, and so on.[3] When George talks on such subjects he is admirable, and I never cease to wonder

[3] Some tribes have local expressions of affection, as for instance that of the Fuyuge people, who say *"Naur'ua ga nu gotsia,"* which means "My insides jump after you." On the other hand they have no words for "Thank you."

how he comes by his apparently encyclopedic knowledge. We were all most interested in his discourse when the launch bumped gently to a stop.

The visitor looked up quickly, and seeing that we were in the mouth of a wide river, half a mile or more from either shore, seemed surprised that we should have come to a sudden stop. George said, "Tch . . . tch . . ." and spoke sternly to the steersman in a language that I could not place. He then turned to us and said briefly, "Goilala, an ugly language, very difficult grammar." He turned back to the steersman and spoke at greater length and with considerable firmness. The Director of Agriculture looked apologetically at the visitor and said, "It's the mud bank, these coastal rivers are full of them, it's the rain you know, bringing down the silt." The visitor looked politely surprised. We all jumped when George suddenly broke off his flow of Goilala and shouted with impatience, "Well get over the side and push us off, you bloody idiot." He turned penitently to the visitor and explained, "Sometimes they will only understand English."

The steersman and his two assistants carefully tucked up their lap-laps and lowered themselves over the side. We were surprised to find that the water came only to their waists. We disposed ourselves geometrically so that the weight would be evenly distributed. George stopped the engine and the only sound was the lapping of the river against the sides of the boat, and the muttering of the three men pushing. It was approaching midday and the sun was high. The visitor took off his sola topee and wiped his head. There was a small spot of black engine oil on his white shorts. His eye caught it and a small frown flickered across his forehead. I noticed that his knees were already turning pink.

An outrigger sailing canoe came skimming past, carrying a Yule Island family with vegetables and fruit gathered from their garden on the mainland. George hailed them and they steered alongside. The family obligingly dropped into the water and helped push. In ten minutes we had the engine started again and moved on upriver at a steady three knots against the stream.

The water in the St. Joseph River, named by the French missionaries when they first came in 1884, is gray-green and has the viscosity of engine oil. It flows slowly between monotonous banks of stunted mangroves that seem to stand up to their thighs in water, holding sickly gray-green branches aloft like bent, arthritic arms. There are tracks of crocodiles on occasional mud banks that slope into the river. A flicker of white and a raucous, melancholy cry, emptied of everything but despair, comes from behind the green curtain of trees where a lonely yellow-crested cockatoo looks for company. Six hornbills emerge from the right bank and cross to the left, oblivious and undeviating. Their batlike, black, ungainly wings swish and creak in slow but perfect synchronization, making them look like a batch of mechanical toys. The sky is transparent, with no trace of color.

The ancient marine engine that drives us against the stream chatters and stammers and chokes as it gulps down gas and oil and coughs up smoke. The hot smell revolts the stomach. George is now comparing the local government movement in Tanganyika with that in New Guinea. He thinks that we might have something to learn from the former. The visitor listens courteously and the Director of Agriculture is silent. I look over the side watching for fish. The flies are bad. There is not the remotest sign of habitation.

It was a pity that the engine broke down when we were, as George said, "Only five minutes away from the jetty." And he was quite justified in speaking very harshly to the crew when it was found that we had no anchor and consequently drifted back down the river for half a mile until another mud bank stopped an unscheduled return to Yule Island. George felt quite resentful about the anchor. He explained that he had made a special call on the radio to Port Moresby to have the new ringbolt fitted and returned, and the marine branch had done a very efficient job in getting it back in time for this trip, knowing that we had a distinguished visitor to take out on a tour of inspection. The visitor felt that he should be grateful to George for having made the special effort, and inclined his head in acknowledgment. Secretly, he told me later, he had begun to suspect that there was in New Guinea a particular and mischievous Puckish deity whose function it was to punctuate traveling with a series of seemingly trivial inconveniences that in the sum created a kind of quiet chaos. The more he thought of this the more he began to admire George's calm, and his resolute refusal to be either surprised or embarrassed by each successive inconvenience.

It was approaching two o'clock when we reached the jetty and

climbed ashore. "We will now," said George, "soon be there." The
Director of Agriculture, feeling that something should be said, remarked that he was certainly ready for his lunch. "It shouldn't be
more than a half hour," said George. But the vehicle that was to
meet us was not in sight and I wondered how we were going to
complete the journey to the agricultural station if it didn't come.

A road that started at the jetty disappeared back through the
mangroves, making a gray, diminishing slit in the all-enveloping
green. There was a tiny clearing where road and river met, and on
the edge of the clearing a single tin shed. A heap of untrimmed
logs lay alongside, waiting to be taken downriver to some building
job. We sat on the logs and waited. After a while I excused myself
and walked a little way along the road and found fresh wheel tracks
where a vehicle had recently come, then backed and turned and
gone away again. I went back and sat with the others on the logs,
but thought it best to say nothing for a little while at least.

A mosquito landed on George's arm and he examined it with
interest, drawing our attention to a minute red parasite on its neck.
"It is," said George, "a flea." Being previously unaware that mosquitoes have fleas we found this momentarily interesting, but as
George went on to describe the life cycle of the malarial parasite
and the variety of effects of its lodgment in the human intestine,
our attention lapsed and the visitor gave the first evidence of cracking. "There is," he asked with feigned assurance, "a vehicle of some
kind coming for us?" George stopped talking immediately and
looked up and around as though surprised that there was no car
standing there, but all he saw was a shy schoolboy with a bicycle.
Nobody had noticed his arrival.

"*Oi mai*," said George to the lad, "*Oi diba namonamo?*"⁴ "I cannot
speak Motuan," replied the lad gravely. "Where do you come from?"
said George. "I am from Mainohana," said the boy, naming the
Catholic Boarding School that serves the district. "Have you seen
our motorcar?" said George. "No," said the boy, "But there was a
trailer here, and when you did not come it went away because the
driver wanted his lunch. He will come back when you send for
him." "Hm . . ." said George, and for a moment I thought that his
patience might desert him. But he merely raised his eyebrows and

⁴ "Come here, can you understand me well?" (Police Motu).

turning to us said, "It was arranged that a car should meet us here but as you can see you can't trust these fellows an inch, they've no sense of responsibility." He gave a brave smile and added with mock indignation, "Gone to lunch, good heavens, what next?" He turned to the boy again. "Now you, boy, get on your bicycle and go and find the driver and tell him to hurry up, we have a number one *taubada* here from England and he wants his lunch too." The boy said "Yes, Father," absent-mindedly and walked away up the road, wheeling the bicycle. George shouted after him, "Get on the bicycle and hurry." The boy looked around. "I cannot, it is too big." He disappeared around a bend in the road.

The visitor said, "If you will excuse me I think I will walk a little way along the road to stretch my legs." No one answered. He got up and walked away. After having gone twenty yards he stopped and looked down at his feet, then turned and came back. There was a tide line of gray mud halfway up his beautifully shined shoes, and a few spots on his white stockings. He sat down on a log some distance from us and we felt it better not to interrupt his thought. Thirty minutes later a bigger boy appeared on the bicycle, and soon afterwards we could hear the chug-chug of a tractor. Fifteen Papuans appeared silently out of the mangroves on the other side of the road.

Among them were a middle-aged man and a young woman, both bleeding copiously from huge open slits in their backs and on their legs. Standing close to them were a younger man, and a slightly older woman who was bleeding from a cut across her forehead, but nevertheless looking smug and well-pleased. Their appearance put new heart into George, who now turned to the visitor and explained. "Those members of the Mekeo people who have not embraced Christianity or adopted its social customs still practice traditional polygamy." He spoke defiantly in the manner of a professional guide. "When a man takes a second wife it is customary for the first wife to show symbolic resentment by striking at the new wife with a bush knife. The husband then aims blows at the first wife to teach her better manners, and then the brother of the first wife is duty-bound, for the honor of his family, to aim blows at the husband."

The visitor listened courteously, seeming to find the information interesting, though thinking, obviously, that the blows had been delivered with somewhat more enthusiasm than required by simple symbolism. But he was clearly more interested in what was going on now that the tractor had arrived, towing behind it a four-wheeled flattop onto which the fifteen Papuans, including the wounded, were busily piling themselves and their belongings.

George excused himself and went to speak to the driver of the tractor, pausing to deter the cyclist who was lifting his vehicle onto the flattop. He came back to say that heavy rains during the night had caused the river to flood badly and damage a bridge a few miles farther along, and that a car was waiting for us on the other side. He seemed relieved that blame for this latest delay could be laid at the door of Providence.

We set off, with the visitor, the Director of Agriculture and myself sitting on two wooden cases slightly elevated above the Papuans, who sat at our feet creating, as it were, a tableau of paternalism. In this ensemble we made steady progress for two miles and came to the bridge, on the other side of which stood a solitary house, a shed (which I knew to be a trade store), and a jeep.

Whatever one feels about the English one must admire the silent dignity with which they do idiotic things. It is not proper for a right-minded, intelligent, and middle-aged gentleman of dignified build to have to propel himself hand-over-hand on a steel cable stretched as taut as a fiddle string across a rushing torrent, with nothing to sustain him but another such cable stretched above his head. We all admired our visitor, and for one briefly wicked moment I even hoped that George, going ahead of him uttering polite and anxious encouragement, might lose his footing and fall in. Some gesture of the kind seemed called for to please our visitor and to recompense him for the trials that he was suffering so nobly. But George has spent many years exploring in the wild highlands of New Guinea and truly enjoys walking tightrope across rivers on strands of rattan.

It was four o'clock when we all got to the other side, and I thought a trifle sadly of the Cessna pilot waiting for us at the rice-farm and the French omelette going flat at the mission. But it seemed clear, after so many delays, that we would not complete the journey in one day, and that we should be content to go no farther than the agricultural station and spend the night there, and go on to the rice-farm in the morning. "This," said George, "will give us a chance to get to bed early and have a good night's rest." He smiled with sympathetic encouragement at our visitor, who was at that moment looking around hopefully for somewhere to wash the rust and grease from his hands.

An elderly, gray-haired, gentle, but weather-worn lady in faded clothes came out of the house and stood smiling kindly at us. She was, I remembered, a widow continuing alone the life that she and her late husband had made for themselves here on the bank of the river among the Mekeo people, buying copra and rice, selling tinned meat and flour and cheap kitchenware to the women, and hair oil, scent, face powder and colored cloth for lap-laps to the men. She went into the house and came back with towel and soap and a dish of water which George took from her and gave to our visitor.

The Director of Agriculture came with us into the store where a Papuan assistant sold us tins of meat and fish, butter and biscuits. When we came out George was standing between the tractor and the jeep watching the driver, assisted by his friends, sucking benzine from one to the other through a rubber hose. When the operation was completed we got into the jeep, relief tinged with doubt that so aged and ill-used a vehicle could continue to perform the mechanics of locomotion.

It had no shred of upholstery, indeed, no superfluous part of any kind, nothing but a metal framework on four wheels. The visitor sat in front with the driver—a Mekeo dandy with crimson lap-lap, a Superman T-shirt, and a hibiscus bloom in his beehive of black hair. The Director of Agriculture, George, and myself sat in the back with the food we had purchased. Fifteen Papuans hung on. We set off.

The visitor sat upright and looked straight ahead, expressionless, never flinching over the bumps. He ignored the full breast, shiny with pig fat, resting on his shoulder, its owner clinging with one hand to the back of his seat while with the other she fended off head-high stems of kunai grass that threatened to sweep her from her perch. He did his best also, but could not ignore the stems which, having been pressed into the mud under our front wheels were flung back in our faces as we passed. I watched closely and saw him mutter, and my heart went out to him, striped with mud like a zebra, face scarlet from the sun, briefcase held upright on his burning knees; forever England.

It was a little after six o'clock when, after two stops to let the engine cool, we reached the agricultural station. There was nobody at home. The refrigerator was padlocked. The boy said, "Master, imi go walkabout." George stood looking down at the floor, thinking. After a while he lifted his head and said, "I'm afraid, sir, that we are not having a very successful day." The visitor silently unstrapped his briefcase and produced a bottle of whisky.

The moon was full and very beautiful. Sitting on the steps of the house, looking across a field of rice ripe for harvesting, I watched it rise like a living thing from behind the jagged backdrop of the Owen Stanley Range, huge and yellow, the color of butter. The trials of the day seemed of no account.

Inside the house, built of rough-hewn timber with walls of plaited kunai grass, George sat reading a book, freed at last from responsibility. The visitor and the Director of Agriculture talked quietly about New Guinea and the difficulties of its development. The houseboy had made a stew with our tinned beef and some sweet potatoes from the garden. Hunger is the most effective sauce. Our appetites were satisfied. Some of our Papuan passengers were sitting with the houseboy in the kitchen. I could hear the murmur of their voices, and could see them in my mind passing the lime gourd back and forth as they chewed betel nut together and discussed our visitor. Flying foxes quarreled in the mango trees at the back of the house.

Suddenly there was an uproar of dogs barking wildly, a hysteria of yelps and whines and rattling chains that brought George out onto the top step to search the night. Two hundred yards away, coming toward us in silhouette, black against the light of the moon, between the rows of tall red cannas that marked the road, came a young man with a gun over his shoulder and a dog running at his heels. George turned to speak to the men inside, addressing himself to the Director of Agriculture. "It's him, your lad, coming home." And to himself, resentfully, "And about time, too."

The visitor did not seem unduly surprised when the Director said, "This is Mr. Addlington, a cadet agricultural officer relieving at this station while the regular man is on leave"; even though young Mr. Addlington wore nothing but a pair of threadbare shorts, sandals, and a yellow beard. Perhaps he was too tired. On the other hand Mr. Addlington seemed all at sea and fluttered a little like a frightened bird, emitting strained and anxious fragments of inquiry, "Have you had anything to eat . . . when did you come . . . I'm sorry I wasn't here but I had given you up when you didn't come . . . can I get you a drink . . . Marco . . . Marco . . ." he shouted desperately in the direction of the kitchen.

His dog, excited by the sudden andante, came running into the house uttering wild canine cries, until Mr. Addlington, unable to stand the emotional strain, seized his gun and fired it, sending the animal yelping out of the house. There was a moment of immobility and silence as we all remained still, listening to the long diminuendo of the dog's frightened cry disappearing into the far reaches of the night. Mr. Addlington ejected the spent cartridge and peered professionally through the barrel of the gun. He put it in the corner of the room, then came and stood among us and said, "Would anyone care for a beer and some Camembert cheese?" adding apologetically, "I'm afraid it's only tinned." Suddenly everything seemed quite normal. Though later Marco came and said that the dog was dead and could he, please, cook it for his guests.

Four

We made an inspection of the rice-farm on the following
day, visited a village school, watched Mekeo farmers threshing rice
with Government machinery, got bogged twice, and met three nuns
on bicycles who said that they were going to Yule Island on retreat
and would be there this evening. We did not ask them the route
they proposed to take but one of them, sensing our interest, explained that they would cycle as far as the river and then load their
bicycles into a canoe and paddle themselves downstream to the
mouth of the St. Joseph, there to be picked up by the mission
launch. It seemed quite simple. They estimated that five hours
would see them to their journey's end. I thought back over the two
days we had spent covering the same distance with every modern
aid to locomotion at our disposal.

They cycled away through the wide street of Inawaia village,
bobbing their heads respectfully as they passed the great wooden
cross set up in the center of the village, carved and painted with
tribal designs, on the spot where their first priest had made peace
with this village. That evening at Yule Island I met them again,
crossing the open space in front of the church, going to Benediction.
They smiled, and showed no signs of fatigue or achievement. I
passed on reflectively to visit the Bishop.

"*Monsieur* William, 'ow are you! *Vous êtes bien gentil de me
visiter.*" The Bishop advanced with shining eyes and wide smile,
holding out his hand in welcome. I knelt quickly to kiss his ring
and as quickly he touched my head to bless me. Then he lifted
me up, put both hands on my shoulders, and looked into my face,
peering through thick-lensed spectacles, his mouth for a moment
still and concerned behind the untidy gray-forked beard.

"You are tired, sit down and I will get you some wine, Australian, it is very good, and cheap." He strode back across the big untidy room to a rough cupboard of packing cases fitted one above the other, and pulled out a bottle of wine and two glasses. "It is all right, this wine from Sydney. We buy a keg and bottle it ourselves."

He stood pouring, then nodded toward a heap of untrimmed photographs lying on the table. "Some new pictures, I have just printed them, not bad," he shrugged. "They will make all right for Christmas cards." I made a mental note to see Brother Jacques, the mission printer, and to order my annual supply before leaving the island. We raised our glasses briefly to each other and sipped the wine.

He came and stood beside me as I sorted through the photographs. I asked him, "You are just back, my Lord?"

"Yes, only yesterday—it was a good progression, many baptisms and confirmations, thousands of Holy Communions, Our Blessed Lord will be happy." He whispered something to himself and made a quick sign of the cross, then pointed to an easy chair. "Sit down—as usual I wish to make use of your kindness. I have turned some film and perhaps you can help me to sell it. But first you must listen to some music."

I marveled at his vitality. A man of more than fifty just back from a journey lasting nearly three months, mostly on foot, sometimes on horseback, into the mountains to visit the stations in his diocese—Oba-Oba, Popole, Ononghe, Fane des Roses, Dilava, and a dozen others—some of them high in the heart of the Owen Stanley Range, among clusters of miserable villages huddled against the cold of perpetual cloud cover, saturated all day in gray mist. The people in such villages are miserable savages, seldom, if ever, visited by Government patrols, eking out lives scarcely human. There are other mission stations on the coastal plain, more civilized, but separated by rivers and streams and stretches of swamp, everlastingly hot and stinking and full of fever.

He looked straight at me from under tangled eyebrows. "You know, I have not long." He made a wry face and tapped his chest. "The doctor says it is some trouble of the heart, nothing can be done." He moved swiftly across the room again to another table, set against the wall and covered untidily with books and papers and the paraphernalia of a man possessed of a cultivated but violently active mind. He shuffled through a pile of disc recordings and lifted one triumphantly. "This you will enjoy, it is marvelous, believe me."

On a smaller side table there was a record player sprouting wires like a piece of modern sculpture. He looked over his shoulder as he adjusted the controls, and grinned. "You like my apparatus. I have made this construction since you last came, it is very modern, you will hear, beautiful." He raised his eyes and lifted his hands in invocation, "Now you must tell me that you like this music."

I had not heard it before but knew immediately, from reviews I had read in musical magazines, that it was the Missa Luba, an arrangement of the Mass written by a Belgian priest in the Congo; a curious and sometimes exciting mixture of African rhythms and Western musical grammar. Some of it was clearly derivative and to me reminiscent of the Schubert Mass in E flat, and some of it hackneyed; but much of it was glorious and blood-curdling, with passages in the Sanctus and the opening of the Gloria in Excelsis marvelously uninhibited and primitive.

The Bishop crouched in his chair, leaning forward, eyes shining, wanting to sing with it, his voice croaking in his throat against the discipline of restraint. We listened for ten minutes and then he sprang up and went across to the machine and stopped it. "Some other time you must hear the rest." He looked at his watch. "We must go to dinner soon, but first I want you to hear something else." He searched around the room, moving piles of books and unopened packages, photographs, cassettes of film, a box of rosary beads from France, and found what he was looking for. He held up a reel of magnetic recording tape.

"Ah! Now you will hear something quite different, you must like this too, excuse me." He disappeared behind a partition into the alcove where he slept, and went on talking. "I have no place for my machines now so this one I have in my bedroom."

I remembered the homemade tape recorder that he had showed me on my last visit, and wondered at the range and flexibility of a mind that could cope with the spiritual and material problems of an active missionary bishop and at the same time could turn expertly to photography, film-making, musicology, and the building of audio-acoustic equipment. All of these things he used to help raise funds in Europe to keep the mission alive.

He reappeared from behind the partition, but his voice, singing, continued to come from the other side, and he grinned again at my sudden confusion and surprise. "The Sinatra, eh? . . . but yes, it is me."

He filled my glass as we listened to the song. It was something that I couldn't place, neither words nor music. A simple tune such as might become popular for a season or two as a song to be sung in cafes, or to dance to in the half-light of love, but not quite straightforward in musical syntax. And I realized that it must have been a primitive tune caught by the Bishop on his rounds and taken down as nearly as possible in conventional notation.

He saw the tentative awareness in my face and nodded. "Yes, it is a Fuyuge song, not possible to write in our notation so I have sung it into the microphone to preserve it—you like it?" I said I thought it lovely, and he smiled and said, "Then we will write some words for it and we will become famous." Just then the Angelus bell rang and we stood up to repeat Gabriel's greeting, while in the next room the high, cracked voice of the Bishop sang a primitive song of longing.[1]

I had an omelette after all, in the refectory with the priests and brothers, some of them resident here for a while at the head station, others in for a few weeks from the mountains and the coastal villages for spiritual or physical refreshment. And after dinner we gathered in the Common Room, some to talk, others to read the latest mail and magazines, some to play billiards on the half-size table with worn and faded baize.

George Canavan was there, playing cards with two of the Australian brothers who are in charge of the mission boarding school. The brothers were teasing George slyly about the misadventures of the previous two days, for the bush telegraph had spread the gossip all through the Mekeo country already. But the French priests and brothers would say nothing, being discreet.

The Director of Agriculture and the distinguished visitor had come for after-dinner coffee and were talking to Brother Bernard about rice-growing. For thirty years the mission has grown rice, mainly to feed the children in its schools, and the priests, nuns, and

[1] The Rt. Rev. André Sorin, M.S.C., Bishop of Port Moresby, died a few days later, of a heart attack.

brothers working on its stations. And for thirty years the same brother has been sowing the seed and harvesting the crop, going out at night with a lantern, like his peasant parents in Brittany, to see if the ears were ripe for the sickle or ready for the threshing floor.

"We grew three hundred tons this year," said Brother Bernard. "At thirty pounds a ton we saved nine thousand pounds on food bills for the schools."

Father Julian Efi Papu of Inawaia village was there, and I remember the film that the Bishop showed me of Father Julian's homecoming after his ordination, and his first Mass in his own village: how his brother had led the dancers, his fine, arrogant Mekeo face painted red, yellow, and blue, eyelids speckled with green and golden spots, bird of paradise plumes on his head, his body bare and glistening with oil and pig fat, a kundu drum in his hands beating out the naked pagan rhythms, hissing like a snake through betel-black teeth as he shuffled and jumped in a tightly packed phalanx of dancing men, honoring his priestly brother. And the same braves, still painted, receiving Communion from Father Julian, their school-mate, at Mass next morning.

Old Father Pinaud ambled over toward me, filling his pipe to tell me quietly that he had written more of his new book on the life of Mother Marie-Thérèse Noblet, first Superior of the Little Papuan Sisters, the Handmaids of Our Lord, adding that there would soon be sufficient evidence to introduce her cause in Rome. "For," he said, "she was, without doubt, a saint."

I had heard much of Mother Marie-Thérèse, and had several times listened to Father Pinaud speak of her, for her cause was dear to his heart and had become very much his preoccupation in these last years of his life. He had known her well and had watched fearfully at her bedside many times when Satan had possessed her in long nights of torment, seeking to destroy her soul and so prevent her from building up a granary of grace among the savages of Papua. For that was how the frail French girl saw her Little Sisters, a reservoir of Divine Love, an armory of faith, hope, and charity with which to oppose the devil and defeat him in the struggle for Papuan souls.

One is uncertain about unauthenticated holy women and I was glad to see, standing shyly in the doorway of the room, a genuinely holy man looking almost timidly in my direction. Father Pinaud, feeling that he had lost my attention, made gestures of resignation and moved away toward the billiards table. I crossed the room delighted and surprised to find that Louis Vangueke was on the island, for I thought him to be somewhere in the field and had not expected to meet him on this visit.

Louis Vangueke's father, dead these many years, was headman and chief sorcerer of the Ongofoina clan, and a man of great character. He kept the cold fear of Satan in the hearts of the Mekeo and Roro tribes so that when the first French missionary came in 1885 to gather these people into the arms of Holy Mother Church, the two men were adversaries, one representing God and the other the devil. The struggle between them lasted three years. One day I hope the story will be written for all to read, for it is full of astonishing incidents and amazing happenings.

At the end of three years the missionary, Henri Verjus, called the clans together on the plateau where the mission buildings now stand. A few hundred yards away, overlooking the sea, was a little hill where the missionary had said his first Mass in Papua. Now he was going to lead the clans to the top of this hill and there plant a great cross, and at the foot of the cross the leaders of all the clans were to break their spears as a sign that they accepted the Peace of Jesus and would fight no more.

But these people were among the most cruel, barbarous, wicked, unrefined, and treacherous of all the New Guinea tribes, and a dispute soon broke out among them as to which clan should have the honor of carrying the cross to the top of the hill. They took up the spears that were to be broken for a sign of peace and began to fight each other with them. But the sorcerer of the Ongofoina (father of Louis Vangueke) stood up and said that he would lay a great curse on every man present if they did not put away their spears and do as the missionary said: and the men were afraid and stood back from the cross and let the sorcerer and his clan carry it to the top of the hill. Every year since then, when the tribes gather to celebrate the anniversary of the founding of the mission, the procession to the top of the hill is led by the Ongofoina.

Soon after this Henri Verjus left Papua and went home to France to die in his mother's arms, a young man worn out with his labors; but first, passing through Rome, he knelt at the feet of Pope Leo

XIII and presented him with a chaplet of paradise plumes, signifying the surrender of Papua to Christ. The sorcerer's son was sent by the Bishop to study in Madagascar with the Jesuits, and he became the first Papuan priest. Now, a man nearing sixty, so frail and gentle that he seems almost pure spirit, he is a pastor among his father's people. Of himself he says, "When I think of the lowliness of my origins and the great graces that God has shown me, the words of Mary's Magnificat sing in my mind, 'He that is mighty hath done great things to me.'"

We talked for a while and I arranged to film a short sequence of Father Louis saying Mass for his people. But we talked more of preparations being made to celebrate the twenty-fifth anniversary of his ordination, and of the Jubilee Mass that he was writing, encouraged by the Bishop, using traditional song themes and dance rhythms of the Mekeo people.

Then George called me over to say that a Government trawler would be calling at the island in the morning. There was, he said, an officer of the Education Department on board who was going down the coast to the village of Manumanu. The trawler would leave him at Manumanu and stop long enough to pick up a public health survey team that had been working in the village; it would then go straight to Port Moresby. He thought it might be a pleasant and relaxing way of getting back to headquarters after the discomforts of the past two days.

I agreed, thanking him for the suggestion, and asked at what time I should be ready. He said that the trawler master hoped to leave before ten o'clock in the morning so that he could reach Manumanu on a rising tide. This would allow him to clear the bar and stand in close to the village to embark the medical team and its heavy X-ray equipment in sheltered water instead of standing off and having them shuttle back and forth through the surf in canoes, a hazardous business even in calm weather.

I said that I would like to go to the village of Chiria for half an hour before leaving the island, to talk to the girl who was running the women's club, but would be at the jetty by ten o'clock and would he please let the skipper know.

Then I said goodnight and went out into the moonlight, and walked across a patch of meadowland cropped short by dairy cows and pack-horses belonging to the mission, and climbed to the top of the hill where priest and sorcerer had together planted the cross of peace, overlooking the sea. A graceful stone crucifix now stands in its place, and there is a little chapel with a spire where the anniversary Mass is said each fourth of July. The white stone catches the moon's light, and in the curve of the chapel's indented side the sound of the sea whispers.

I thought of Henri Verjus and Father Louis, of the Bishop and Marie-Thérèse, and the hundred priests, nuns, and brothers who have died in Papua in this mission alone. In silence I marvel at the astounding capacity of man to imagine, to achieve, to believe. How like a God indeed—and yet in so many ways how uncomprehending.

After a while I felt chill, and fearing a bout of malaria went back to the mission guest house and took some tablets, then lay awake under a mosquito net listening to the shrill, incessant stridulation of cicadas streaming in through the shutters.

The Bishop lent me his war surplus jeep and his driver, Joseph, and we followed the winding wheel-tracks between the coconut palms along the beach until we came to the village, a mile or so from the mission.

Most times when I have passed through Chiria village the only sound and movement has been the sudden scurry of frantic hens and chickens from under the wheels of the vehicle, or the shuffling grunt of great black pigs wallowing in the dust under the houses; for the children are usually at school, the women in the gardens, and the men out fishing, or over on the mainland visiting, or fetching logs for new canoes. The few old men left in the village during the busy part of the day sit around smoking and yarning, and the old women chew betel nut and split palm leaves to make skirts, or spin bush fibers into thread.

But today was different. Alongside the car track that skirts the village on its way from the Government station to the airstrip, a group of Chiria men was busy building: not, as is usual, three or four members of one family engaged in some joint domestic undertaking, but twenty or thirty men, with wheelbarrows, shovels, and pickaxes and a truck full of stones, and the portable concrete-mixer from the Government station.

Joseph noted my surprise and grinned, "They are building the new co-operative store."

This in itself was not surprising, seeing that the old store, built some years ago in the middle of the village, had long been lop-sided and in need of new thatch for the roof. The unusual element in the scene was the single-minded determination with which every man was working. Nobody stood watching. No old and toothless elder, sheltering from the sun in the shade of the twisted flame trees, mumbled building-magic under his breath, or laid down the laws of tradition to guide the young men as they worked.

Joseph again supplied the answer. "The co-operative officer from Port Moresby is coming this morning in the trawler, and he will visit Chiria this afternoon to inspect the new store and to fix a date for its opening. It was decided four months ago, when he was last here, that a new store should be built, but the men have been busy fishing and making new gardens, and nothing has been done, so now they have to hurry because he is a good man and they do not wish to disappoint him."

The situation is a normal one. After ninety years of contact with missionaries and administrators the Papuan has not yet seriously accepted the Western sense of time. For the seafaring villagers of the coast, as for other Pacific island peoples, time has always been a fluid mathematic, a relative and flexible measurement marked off into divisions by the coming and going of trade winds, the spawning and the traveling habits of great shoals of food fish, the migration of birds, and the coming of monsoonal rains.

All human activity has been naturally ordered by the recurring incidence of these and similar events—the time for making new gardens and planting them; the time for long trading voyages; for visiting, arranging marriages, and keeping ritual feasts; for fishing, for making new canoes and mending old ones. These have all been fixed for generations without regard to the Gregorian calendar or the Australian Budgetary Year.

And into this pattern is inextricably interwoven the daily detail of domestic custom, and the ritual of traditional religious and magi-cal practices which we thoughtlessly call superstition or quaintness, or curious custom, although these practices are seldom more curious or less well-founded in local logic than our own.

The coastal Papuan therefore lives two lives, the pattern of one being ingrained by tradition, the other imposed upon him by the Australian administration and, to a lesser extent, the missionaries, each with their own separate calendar of significant dates. In consequence the villager who tries to please equally the elders of his clan, the Government officer, and the missionary, is in danger of becoming an induced schizophrenic. The solution of the romanticists (and until recently the tendency of the Australian Government) has been to leave the Papuan people more or less alone, and this could well be the right answer, since the natural life led by coastal Papuans is almost an ideal one so long as peace prevails and the Government is benevolent.

But the problem is complicated and confused by the stepsister relationship which exists between the Australian colonial territory of Papua and the United Nations Trust Territory of New Guinea, administered jointly by Australia as one territory. So long as this arrangement lasts the future of Papua is tied to the future of the Trust Territory. Consequently the ultimate status of the Papuan villager seems more likely to be determined by point-scoring political games played in the United Nations than by any amiable agreement reached between Papuans and Australia.

In any case the yearly commercial output of each Papuan, after eighty or ninety years of exposure to civilization, is a few pounds over and above his comfortable level of subsistence, and although this constitutes a very much higher standard of living than that enjoyed by tens of millions of Australia's most virulent critics it does not produce a solid foundation for political independence and economic self-sufficiency in this twentieth century.

Hard-working Australians, especially in the departments concerned with agriculture and co-operative enterprises, do their best to create and develop new sources of income for the villagers, but the main commercial crops of New Guinea are copra, coffee, cocoa, and rubber, already overproduced by other countries with more powerful political influences in the world of international commerce. This is largely the fault of nature and history, but it nevertheless seems clear that Australia needs to make some quite spectacular effort in Papua if it is to silence criticism, however hypocritical and unjust. Politics on the international level take no account of simple contentment.

Meanwhile the villagers of Chiria, on Yule Island, unaware of these nightmare problems that plague those who most wish to help them, do their good-natured best to please the district co-operative

officer from Port Moresby by building the new village store while
he is busy at the Government station auditing their account books.
And in spite of the haste, the co-operative clerk has found time to
gather the right kind of leaves for making magic, to speak over
them the appropriate charm, and to place them carefully at the
bottom of each post hole so that the success of the new store is
assured.

I had not time to stay and watch the job completed, or to interrupt the men with casual conversation, but hoped that I would
be able to come back for the official opening, for these are usually
pleasant and interesting occasions. Delegations come from villages
all along the coast with choirs and dancing teams. Government officials make honest speeches, and missionaries bless the new building, ensuring by prayer the efficacy of the magic charms laid in
the post holes.

I went to one such ceremony not long ago, and on that occasion
found that the program of entertainment which followed the official opening demonstrated quite clearly the three main influences
of Papuan village life.

The old people performed first. Decorated in traditional fashion,
and playing kundu drums, they sang the songs of their ancestors
and shuffled through tribal dances with an uncertainty that re-
flected lack of practice, forgetfulness, or failing memory. The young
people were intrigued and mildly amused, and the smallest children
giggled in little groups as they watched, then ran away into the
shadows to laugh aloud.

Then the middle-aged came into the ring with their mission-
educated children, neat in clean dresses and white shirts. They sang
hymns and Bible-narrative songs called Piravetas, brought to them
generations ago by Samoan pastors and catechists who worked on
the coast in the early days of missionary history in Papua. They had
hibiscus and frangipani in their hair and they danced the respecta-
ble and sterilized versions of the old Polynesian dances while their
men kept time with slow-strumming ukeleles. And apart from the
somewhat lugubrious hymns, their singing and dancing was accomplished and suitable for the occasion.

After them the younger men, led by lads from Government offices
in Port Moresby, and the local co-operative society clerks who had
been to school there, produced a jazz band of guitars and home-

made percussion instruments, with a double bass built from a tea
chest, a broom stick, and a single strand of rope; and after a self-
conscious start and tentative glances at the village elders, they took
charge.

To self-taught chords and simple rhythms they sang cowboy songs
and pseudo-Hawaiian love laments through their noses, while some
of the more impudent and adventurous girls, wearing Western frocks
and rebellious looks, danced bare-footed fox trots with each other
on the beach. Some of the lads from Port Moresby did the same,
dancing together with grotesque gyrations. But no boy or girl so
defied tradition as to dance together, although some of them went
quietly off into the night to keep assignations. But this is custom.

A motor horn sounded along the track and Joseph pulled over to
make way for the Government Land-Rover. It drew up beside us
and a lady got out. Then it went on, carrying the Director of Agriculture and his visitor to the airstrip to catch the plane back to
Port Moresby. I waved to them as they drove away, then got out of
the Bishop's jeep and joined the lady whom I knew to be the wife
of one of the Government officers at the station.

She carried a roll of posters under her arm. They were, she explained, Mothercraft Posters issued by the Department of Public
Health, sent to her to be passed on to the Chiria village women's
club. As the club was meeting this morning she had come to de-
liver the posters. We walked together through the village and saw
women making their way to the end of the single broad street that
runs between the two lines of plaited palm and thatch houses that
constitute Chiria. We joined them under the shade of a huge mango
tree where already a table was set up, covered with a clean cloth,
and on it a jam tin holding a bunch of brilliant orange marigolds.

Three chairs were placed on one side of the table for the officers
of the club, and woven grass mats for the members to sit on were
spread on the other. Some of the women had already taken their
places, and others were still coming or standing about with babies
straddling their hips, talking together and waiting for the meeting
to start.

All of them were neatly dressed. Even those in traditional costume, bare from the waist up, and tattooed on face, breast, and
arms, wore their best skirts of dyed and finely split palm fronds,
and had flowers behind their ears, and oil on their hair. Others

wore simple trade store or homesewn frocks, or clean grass skirts with brassiere tops. Most of them had babies or young children, all cleanly dressed in simple Western style.

The creation of women's clubs in the village has caught the imagination of women all over New Guinea, not only in places where there has been a long association with white people and some understanding of Western social structures, but also in areas where Westerners were unknown a few years ago. They help to meet one of the most vital needs of the changing native society.

In the traditional domestic structure of village life the influence of women, although important, is almost entirely confined to family affairs, and the part they play in the organizing of village and clan activities is usually indirect. The intelligence or character of a wife does not, as a rule, greatly affect the status of her husband among his fellow men, and in the old society it made little difference to a fight-leader, or a sorcerer, or a famous maker of canoes, or a celebrated dancer or story-teller, if his wife was as unsophisticated as the rest of the village women.

Today it is different. Native leaders who become involved in the wider worlds of social, political, and commercial activity that have been opened up to them find themselves spending more and more of their time working and thinking and living outside the familiar and secure framework of tribe and tradition. As they take an increasingly active and responsible part with educated Westerners in government, church, or even business activities, they begin to feel the inadequacy of their own unsophisticated social and domestic background. They realize the need for a private as well as a public framework for their new kind of life.

Among the most lonely men in New Guinea are those emerging leaders who live in two widely separated worlds—one peopled by administrators, politicians, executives, accountants, and technical specialists, the other represented by an illiterate and barefoot village wife. And one of the most regular disappointments of the Government officers who are responsible for the training of native girls in nursing and welfare work is the constancy with which they contract illicit liaisons with educated native men and become pregnant.

The women's club, in the village, provides part of the answer to this problem of providing educated women for educated men within the framework of the village and clan. If they do nothing else, they at least give the women some basic experience in the simple forms of modern social organizing, and open up new fields of activity for them that run, in some measure, parallel to the expanding activities of their menfolk.

Each club elects its president, secretary, and treasurer, one of whom needs to be in some degree literate so that she can deal with correspondence and keep the minutes book and accounts. The literate member, if there is only one as is often the case in semi-primitive areas, is usually appointed secretary or treasurer. It is generally more appropriate for the president to be a woman with some traditional status in the village as this pleases the older women, and allows them to feel that they can belong to the club without loss of personal dignity.

This does not happen to be the case at Chiria, where the president is the youngest member of the club yet has the solid support of most of the women of status in the village. She does not, in fact, live in the village at all, but keeps house for her widowed father, a retired Government clerk, who lives in a small cottage on the edge of the Government station.

She came along as we stood waiting for the meeting to begin, a shy girl, not yet twenty, dressed neatly in simple Western clothes, a brooch in her hair and shoes on her feet. Her name is Marie Thérèse, a favorite name on Yule Island. She was educated first by the nuns at the mission station, and later in a Government school in Port Moresby where her father worked before his retirement.

I felt that she seemed somewhat too diffident and retiring to make an effectively militant feminist, although the women ceased their chattering instantly when she called them to order and opened the meeting with a short prayer. A hymn followed, and then the treasurer called the roll and collected sixpence from each woman. She then announced the income and expenditure since the last meeting and reported repairs to the club sewing machine, the purchase of a ball for the village girl's basketball team, and the receipt of samples of material for curtains intended for a clubhouse yet to be built.

The secretary then reported that she had approached some of the men about building this clubhouse for women's activities, but that the men claimed to be too busy with the new co-operative store. She thought, however, that the Government medical officer

had spoken to the elders about the need for such a building to be
used as an infant and maternal welfare center, as well as a meeting
place for women's and girls' groups. She thought that if the older
women brought domestic pressure to bear on their husbands something might be done soon.

They used the local Roro language for their discussions and I
could not follow them, and when Mary said something quietly that
sent them all into fits of screaming laughter, making them rock from
side to side and push each other with their hands, I asked the
station wife beside me to explain the joke.

She said that Mary had already scored one notable victory over
those men of the village who looked askance at this organized female interference with traditional village life. She had, it seems,
introduced to the women the idea of having a village latrine, explaining that such an innovation would help to reduce disease and
sickness among the children. She had obtained a booklet on the subject from the welfare officer in Port Moresby, with specifications for
a suitable structure, and had read it at one of the club meetings.

Most of the women, believing implicitly that sickness of any kind
is the direct result of sorcery and not of malign bacteria and other
natural phenomena, doubted that the building of an edifice for exclusively practical purposes would achieve any miraculous effect
such as the lessening of sickness among their children; but they
thought the project sufficiently spectacular to serve as an announce-
ment to the men that the women were embarking upon a campaign
for the modernization of village life.

Accordingly they approved the project and empowered Mary
and her two fellow officers to approach the Government officer for
materials. So far the women had not trespassed upon the rights or
the authority of the men, although direct contact between the three
women and the Government officer was getting close to a violation
of traditional decencies. But when it came to the crucial question
of a site for the new structure a clash was inevitable, since the
allocation of clan land for any purpose is strictly a matter for the
elders.

The women, after suitable discussion, decided where the latrine
might best be located to serve the needs of the community, and the
woman whose husband held usufructuary rights over that portion
of land undertook to gain his permission to use it for this remarkable

purpose. When he flatly refused to be a partner to such womanly stupidity, not to say revolutionary nonsense, she wisely held her peace and went off to consult with Mary, who in turn discussed the problem with the Government officer's wife, who then took it up with her husband and the Government medical officer.

Soon afterwards the men of the village went to the mainland for some days to fetch logs for a new canoe. In their absence a gang of young women, under the leadership of the woman whose husband had refused his co-operation, gathered together and dug the hole. They worked in an atmosphere of inflamed excitement, aware of a sense of daring and a feeling of personal involvement in the making of history, seasoned with a lively fear of the consequences as soon as the men returned.

Meanwhile a second group of women walked to the Government station and returned, each carrying a precut plank of wood on her head. Their leader brought a packet of nails and a set of door hinges. The youngest girls and some of the female children were sent outside the village to gather kunai grass for thatching the roof. Mary moved from point to point, supervising.

By nightfall the building was ready for use.

Soon after dawn on the following day the woman on whose family land the monument stood emerged from her house and walked through the village to make first use of it. When she came out the women of Chiria felt that they had taken on a new importance.

When the men came back they were astounded and indignant. The man whose land had been used beat his wife brutally, while the rest of the village listened in silence to her cries. When he had done he came and stood in the village and delivered an impassioned oration, castigating Mary as a witch and a mischief-maker, condemning all of the women of Chiria as brazen and immoral, and calling upon each man to beat his wife so hard that she would never again venture to step across the boundaries of propriety. Finally he uttered a passionate rallying cry for volunteers to come and help him tear down the offending edifice.

The men stirred uneasily, many of them feeling that he was taking the matter somewhat too seriously. But some of them followed him and might have helped him to carry out his intention. But when they came to the place and saw Mary there with the Government officer, inspecting the new work, they stopped.

The Government officer turned and looked at the men with pleasure and gratification, and asked for the owner of the land to step forward, which he did, but sullenly. Then the Government officer shook him by the hand and congratulated him for being a generous and progressive citizen, and said that he would make known to the Number One Government Man in Port Moresby that this man of Chiria had done a worthy thing. It might even be, said the Government officer, that this man's name might be mentioned in the Native People's Session on the radio.

Nonplused, the man began to mumble about pulling the building down, at which the Government officer frowned, and pointing to a paper that Mary held in her hand said that it was a Government building permit signed by himself. The man knew then that he was beaten, for the power of Government paper is understood even in the most remote parts of New Guinea. He hung his head and stood dejected, knowing that the building was sacrosanct and inviolable.

Then the Government officer winked at Mary, making her blush, and he clapped the man on the shoulder and said that he was a true leader of the people, at which the other men murmured approval, and the man felt himself becoming important again.

It was a reference to this occasion that had made the women laugh while they were discussing the probable building of a welfare center.

When quiet had been restored the meeting of the women's club continued. Mary displayed the posters that the station wife had brought with her, and said that they, too, were to be used in the new building. She held up each one in turn, translating the legends and explaining their simple message of cleanliness in the home and village, the benefits of a balanced diet, and the protection of food from flies, and babies from mosquitoes.

Then she opened a children's story book and began to read from it, translating from English into the village language as she went along. The fifty or more women hung on her every word, and I went away without disturbing them.

A little later I swung my bags aboard the Government trawler *Leander* and waved goodbye to Joseph and to Yule Island.

Five

My fellow passenger was standing by the cook's galley in the stern. When I came aboard he looked up and said, "Come and have a cup of tea." He said it as though he were inviting me into a drawing room instead of onto the cramped, unglamorous after-deck of a coastal trawler; but Peter Livingstone is a man of gracious ways, with a family tree hung with colonels and fine ladies who have sat for fashionable painters.

His function in New Guinea, as a specialist officer of the Department of Education, is to create a native literature in the English language, for use in the schools. It is a task that calls for a sympathetic understanding of the native mind, a knowledge of educational and literary techniques, of publishing and printing, and of New Guinea folklore and legend. As the tea brewed he told me that he was going to Manumanu to visit an anthropologist who was living there among the villagers, and from whom he hoped to get interesting material for children's story books.

We could hear the captain speaking to the crew, and in a while the anchor came up. Then the engine room telegraph clanged and there was vibration as we got under way. We left the stone jetty and steered across Port Leo Bay, keeping clear of the low-humped point of land where silt from the St. Joseph River lays long-fingered underwater traps for ignorant mariners. Behind us, partly hidden by lines of palm trees, the unobtrusive office buildings of the Government station merged back into the deep green drop cloth of the overhanging hills.

On the northern shore the memorial chapel of the mission stood sharp and white against the green of the hill and the bright blue mantle of overriding sky. Further down the slope the Carmelite convent's red roof caught the sun and sent flashes of reflection across the water; I wondered for a moment about the silent, ever-prayerful women living there in isolation, cut off even from their fellow religious on the island. "A dynamo of prayer," the Bishop called them, these spiritual daughters of sixteenth-century Thérèse to whom the name New Guinea was unknown.

Behind the southern point, as we left the bay, the mainland village of Delena came into sight, clear in morning air not yet misted with the heat, so that the timber-framed house with its two stories and angular construction stood out sharply. Constance Fairhall of the London Missionary Society lives there, preacher and nurse and one of the founders of the leper hospital on Gemo Island, near Port Moresby.

To Protestant Sister Fairhall, active and efficient, a life lived in physical suspension and given up entirely to prayer and contemplation would most likely constitute an unthinkable idleness; yet had she lived four hundred years ago she might well have found a soulmate in Thérèse the Carmelite who, for all her supernatural and suspicious intimacy with God-in-the-Spirit, prayed, played politics, and ran convents with equal determination and dexterity, and firmly believed with Constance Fairhall that the only key to the complete life is ". . . to find Him, and find in following Him, a way of life which gives the answer to all our questions and the meaning to all life."

And it is perhaps ill-mannered and is certainly ungallant to refer to so individual a personality as "typical," yet like many of her other admirers I find it difficult not to see in her a synthesis of the scores of English people of the London Missionary Society who have left their imprint on the history of Africa and the Pacific islands during the past hundred years.

And there is no doubt whatever that along the southern coast of Papua, the imprint of the Society is not only unmistakable, it is dominant, except in the Catholic enclave with its bridgehead round about Yule Island and its main stream of influence running back into the high interior.

The London Missionary Society sent preachers and teachers to Papua in 1871, before the Catholic mission or any other outside influence had seriously impinged on the native people. Three years later the Reverend Dr. Lawes established the mission's headquarters among the villages in Captain Moresby's newly discovered harbor. It was the first white settlement in Papua.

When eventually, ten years later, the British Queen sent officials to annex Papua to her crown, and to establish an administrative capital at Port Moresby, Dr. Lawes and his colleague, the Reverend James Chalmers (called Tamate by the Papuans), were there to welcome the party, to introduce native leaders to the Government men, and to act as interpreters between them. The official ceremony of annexation took place on the veranda of the mission house, and the village children had long since been taught to sing "God Save the Queen."

It was a proud moment for Lawes and Chalmers, and for the other members of the London Missionary Society who were there to take part in the celebrations. Both men were already famous, not only in the Pacific as pioneer churchmen but throughout the Western world as explorers and geographical writers of international reputation; Chalmers, the explorer and friend of the tribes, and Lawes the scholar, already at work on a translation of the New Testament and the Psalms.

Queen Victoria spoke through the mouth of her naval aide-de-camp, Commodore James Elphinstone Erskine, Commander of the Australian Squadron of the British Fleet. Dr. Lawes, an impressive figure with fine full beard spread across his breast like a bishop's bib, repeated the official rhetoric in Motu, the language of the people.

On behalf of Her Most Gracious Majesty Erskine besought some four hundred naked and uncomprehending inhabitants of the Port Moresby villages to always keep in mind that, ". . . the Queen guards and watches over you and will not allow anyone to harm you . . . if they attempt to do you harm they will promptly be punished by Officers of the Queen."

He further informed them that the fact of being annexed by Her Majesty would protect them alike "from the encroachment of foreigners and the aggressive and unlawful actions of persons of whatever nationality." And perhaps to the embarrassment of the good Dr. Lawes he then made reference to the seeds of Christianity "which have already been sown by English hands, in the persons of the good and valiant gentlemen whom I am delighted to see present on the occasion." The six warships lying at anchor in the harbor gave substance to these utterances, but for many years afterwards it was the missionaries who played the most effective part in the advancement of the Papuan people.

Of Dr. Lawes it was said that "his name was used as a passport among the natives who know him as a good man that makes peace." And of Chalmers that, "strangers are asked if they know Tamate and if so they are treated with kindness. To many tribes who have never seen him he is known as a mighty sorcerer, and all like to inquire about him."

But in the end, when Chalmers had been almost thirty-six years a missionary in Papua, he was killed by cannibals in the gulf country, struck down from behind by a blow from a stone club, then beheaded, and his body dismembered and distributed among ten villages for eating. A younger missionary who was with him suffered the same fate.

An expedition led by the acting administrator of the time, young Judge Robinson, went in search of the murderers. It is said that they found ten thousand skulls but not those of Chalmers and his young friend, and that they set fire to the villages and shot down many of the savage tribesmen. For his part in this affair Robinson was severely censured. Next morning he was found dead at the foot of the flagpole at Government House, with a pistol in his hand.

Today there are few Papuan leaders of consequence who are not prominent members of the Church that was established among them almost ninety years ago by the London Missionary Society under Lawes and the martyred Tamate.

We left Delena far behind and headed into a playful southeast breeze, keeping a little to seaward but clearly in sight of the black sand beaches and patches of mangroves along the shore. Being empty, with nothing in her hold, *Leander* rolled abominably.

They are all the same, these coastal boats, almost without exception smelling of burning engine oil, rancid copra, rats, and mildewed bed coverings. The cockroaches eat your toenails while you sleep, and hide in the refrigerator during the day, usually behind the butter. The box-like dining salon, just large enough to hold four people uncomfortably, is always next to or above the engine room, from which it is separated only by a burning hot steel plate.

The cook is usually competent in two dishes, one consisting of incinerated meat of any kind, served submerged in a thick sauce of burned onion, flour, and Worcestershire relish; the other is a sweet made from egg powder, dried milk, sugar inadvertently mixed with tea, vanilla essence, and ash from the stove. And all small ships in New Guinea leak, have continuous engine failure, and roll alarmingly.

A black-hulled copra boat passed us, heading up the gulf, low in the water with the weight of cargo going to traders and plantations or mission stations along the coast: machinery, benzine, frozen foods, timber for building, roofing iron, clothing chosen from the mail-order catalogues of stores in Brisbane and Sydney, mail from Port Moresby and from friends in Australia.

Her scanty deck space was crowded with passengers going back to their village after visiting in the capital, for Papuans are habitual travelers and every family in the land has some relative temporarily in Port Moresby at work or at school, in the hospital or in jail.

A little later the captain rang for half speed and we guessed that we were getting close to Manumanu, so went forward and saw the village clearly in sight, perhaps not more than three miles away, though partly hidden by coconut palms along the foreshore. *Leander* wallowed forward slowly here, for the mud banks are treacherous and always shifting, and there is never enough water over them except at the top of the tide. Occasionally, with the rolling of the boat, the sun flashed on the unpainted iron roof of a building new since my last visit, and I wondered if it would be the church or the schoolhouse, both of which had badly needed reconstruction.

It was almost an hour before we let go the anchor in the river behind the village, and then the anthropologist came aboard, longing for a cold drink, for although he had beer in his stores ashore there is no way of keeping it cool in a grass hut.

Dr. Murray Groves, smacking his lips over the first cold beer he had tasted for several weeks, has an advantage over most other anthropologists working in Papua, since he spent much of his childhood in Port Moresby, speaks fluent Motu, and has many close friends among the people of the coastal villages. Papuans to him are not specimens, nor does he regard their ways as strange or uncouth.

He is a pleasant and easy companion, a generous source of information about the Motu-speaking people whose villages he has

lived in frequently, a good feeder, and a man of substantial figure
respected by the lean, spare Papuans. He was spending, he told
us, some months in Manumanu, recording details of many beliefs
and practices that are fast dying out.

Manumanu is a neat village with two rows of houses facing each
other across a wide main street, one row backing onto the beach
and the other onto garden lands and groves of coconut palms. Like
most villages on the coast it retains its traditional appearance in
almost every respect, except for the addition of a co-operative store,
a schoolhouse, and a church, these being apart at one end of the
village so that the main street looks much as it might have a hundred, or a thousand, years ago.

There are about two-score houses in the village, each of them
identical to the casual eye of the visitor. Set on posts, five feet or
so above the ground (about the height of the average Papuan
man), each house has a rough ladder leading up to a front veranda
that spreads the complete width of the house. This is where the
family sits in the evening. During the daytime those who are at
home usually sit on a platform under the house, away from the
sun.

The veranda is hung with fishing nets edged with shells which
act as sinkers. Fish spears, paddles, cooking pots, and baskets complete the decor. Under the house the canoe sails are kept, rolled
around the mainmast; in addition the ropes, unfired clay pots, and
fibers to be dried for skirt-making, or for spinning thread, or twisting into rigging.

The houses themselves are big oblong boxes with pitched roofs,
divided inside by half partitions which separate sleeping from living rooms. Walls of plaited coconut fronds, or sago palm bark, or
pandanus leaf. Roofs of sago leaf or kunai grass. Posts of mangrove,
floors of split black palm, all tied, without nails, with vines. Mats
to cover the floor and to sleep on. A sand tray in the middle of
the main room for the fire to rest on, to cook in bad weather, and to
keep warm at night. In almost every village there is a child with
ugly scars that came from rolling in the fire while asleep.

Families are compact, and relatives live closely together, sometimes married children with their parents until their own progeny
become too numerous; then they move and start a new home, but

usually next door or in the same clan grouping, so that people of consanguinity almost always live as immediate neighbors.

Dr. Groves, for his stay in Manumanu, had rented a village house from a family not immediately needing the space for its own accommodation, and he lived the village life as nearly as possible, making only a few concessions to luxury and convenience. He had, for instance, tinned meat and butter, and I had brought him a bottle of wine, for he likes a drop of claret occasionally. He had a kerosene pressure lamp so that he could work at night, and used an outboard motor to power his seagoing canoe and so saved himself time in routine traveling.

We had barramundi for dinner—a delectable, deep-fleshed fish. At seasons it runs in shoals along the Papuan coast and at these times the villagers of Manumanu eat it at every meal. Soaked in a creamy liquid squeezed from the flesh of a young coconut that has been scraped and grated with a seashell, then wrapped in a banana leaf and broiled on the embers of a wood fire, there is no dish of seafood in the world to better it.

Dr. Groves licked the last smears of fish fat and cream from his fingers and settled back with a sigh of satisfaction. We sat with him on the veranda of his house, Livingstone and myself, and Enno the village headman sitting with us because we were visitors. Along the street, on both sides, we could hear a low hum of voices punctuated now and then by sudden bursts of female laughter. Occasionally a pig grunted and shifted its bulk under the house, then snuffled as it settled down again in the dust.

We were discussing the *hiri*.

Not so long ago the Papuans of the coast, like most of the seafaring people of the Polynesian and Melanesian islands, made long trading voyages once each year, fixing the times of departure and return on a timetable set by the pendulate changing of the annual southeast and the northwest winds.

Some of these voyages ranged a thousand miles. Most of them lasted over a period of two or three months, or even more when the seasons were abnormal. They were highly significant events, dominating much of the calendar of activity throughout the year. Their arrangment affected the spacing and number of births in the village. On their material framework of preparation grew a complicated espalier of ritual, a set of formularies, and a mystical social system that became interwoven with the material and economic living system of family, clan, and tribe.

The actual details varied from place to place, dictated by geography, by the local pattern of winds and tides and ocean currents, by custom, and economic needs and ties. But all over the microcosmos of the Pacific these annual trading voyages have been, since the beginning of Pacific history, a basic incentive, like the challenge and inner compulsion that, in days gone by, sent Western men from Europe across the oceans to America, Africa, and Asia, and today fires them into outer space: the answer to the need of all men for adventure, and the desire to embrace elemental danger. The long ocean voyages of the Pacific islanders are a parallel. There is only one kind of human being; the differences are differences of time and knowledge and technology.

The practical incentive for undertaking a hiri in the old days was the annual food shortage and threat of famine during the dry season, when nothing grew in the gardens and the fish were far out to sea. Each year, at this time, the Motu men set out in fleets of great oceangoing canoes, called *lakatois,* to visit the villages of the Gulf of Papua, where regular year-round rains made certain a continuous supply of swamp-growing sago, beyond the needs of the local people. To exchange for this sago surplus the Motu men took cooking pots, manufactured by their women from a clay found only on their coast. The exchange gave them sufficient sago to tide their people over the period of natural famine.

Today, when every Motu village has its co-operative store, and trading vessels call regularly with cases of tinned meat and bags of flour, tea, sugar, and rice to be exchanged for copra, there is no longer any danger of seasonal starvation. And although a continuous exchange of social visits may still take place, the people can travel along the coast without organized effort as paying passengers on a trading boat. Consequently there is now no collective motivation for the traditional hiri.

But old customs die hard, and many of the Papuan people cling to what is left to them of their old culture and their identity as a distinctive people. They do not all find, in the church services and festivals introduced by missionaries, or the agricultural and economic experiments of the Government, a satisfying substitute for the completeness of their own traditional patterns, even when they realize that change is not only inevitable, but in most part desirable.

And the white man, however benevolent, honest, and ingenious in his attempts to raise the living standards and the status of the people who have come under his political jurisdiction, frequently holds the complacent but erroneous conviction that his own culture is at all points superior to that of the native. This is a danger by no means confined to Pacific relationships. There are distressing examples of this myopia among the greatest and most benevolent nations of this day and age.

But we were not discussing matters so profound as we sat on the veranda of the anthropologist's house in Manumanu this moonlit night. We were listening to Murray Groves and Enno talking about the hiri, and the attempt of some of the men of the village to revive it in the coming season. It was rumors of this activity, coming to Groves through Papuan friends in Port Moresby, that had brought him to Manumanu with tape recorder, camera, typewriter, and a sleeping mat, to stay for several months.

In the old days, said Enno, the preparations for the hiri began with the coming of *laurabada,* the great southeast wind, and they finished when the *lahara,* the sailing wind, brought the lakatois back from the northwest. This meant, said Groves interpolating, that the hiri, from the time of the first active moves to make preparation, until the eventual return of the men from the voyage, was in the minds of the Motu people, and affected their activities for almost nine months of the year. This one fact shows the size of the gap that is left in their lives when the need for the hiri is removed, and nothing put in its place.

Livingstone asked a technical question, and Enno called across the street to a man sitting with his family on the veranda of his house. There was an exchange of words to which all the village listened; then the man stood up and called to another man farther along the street, and the pair of them left their own houses and came and sat with us.

Livingstone offered them each a cigarette which they took silently, and lit with a stick taken from the fire, and Groves introduced me and we shook hands without speaking, as is the custom.

I recognized one of the men as Akea, who cares for Groves'

canoe and acts as his factotum when the anthropologist is working in these parts. Groves claims him to be the finest sailor and fisherman on this coast, handy with engines, and influential as a sorcerer. A twist in one eye adds color to this additional attribute. He has a sister married to a man in Hanuabada village close to Port Moresby.

The name of the second man I have forgotten, but will call him Tau, because every Motu village has a Tau, which simply means "man," and he won't object if he ever reads what I have written, since it is an honorable name.

I listened while they talked of the hiri, piecing together bit by bit the intricate picture of interwoven activities, the rituals and creative artistries, knowledge, skills, beliefs, and superstitions, and the complex of relationships that go to make an individual person part of a wider, living culture. And I thought how high a price we ourselves have paid, and are asking these people to pay in terms of personal diminution, for the privilege of material progress.

The first young gusts of the laurabada come in late April or early May to stir the tops of the coconut palms and send ripples racing across the shallow water of the bay. And some man, resting under his house smoking, or chewing betel nut, will hear the palm fronds suddenly click together in the wind; or sitting in his canoe out on the reef, waiting for fish, will see the surface of the waters stir and will think to himself, "Soon it will be the time of the hiri." And he wonders if any of the other men of his village are thinking the same thing, and if they are, then who among them might be planning to build a lakatoi.

The names of the village leaders, heads of families and clans, will pass through his mind, and he will resolve that in the time between the going down of the sun and the eating of the evening meal, when the people discuss the daily affairs of the family and clan, he will set in motion that discreet process of inquiry that elicits answers to unspoken questions and imperceptibly sets a people's creative forces in motion. And this he does.

By the end of a week the village knows that such-and-such a man is going to build a lakatoi to go on the hiri, and that his cousin, son of his mother's brother, is to be his partner in the enterprise. There is a feeling of relief in the village because a necessary decision has been taken and a cycle of events put into motion.

Henceforth, until the hiri is finished, the man who is to build the lakatoi is no longer called by his name, but is known as the *baditauna,* or big leader. His partner is the *doritauna,* in charge of the aftermast. Their wives no longer speak to them directly, but through a third person, nor do they refer to them by name; and man and wife sleep at opposite ends of the house. The baditauna and the doritauna become persons set mystically apart, dedicated, like priests of the temple in old Jerusalem. The man Tau, sitting on the veranda silently smoking while we talked, was baditauna, perhaps the last man on the coast to bear that title and to lead a hiri from Manumanu.

Groves had his tape recorder going, anxious to record each detail of the hiri complex of mysticism, magic, practical activity, purpose, and achievement. Anxious, even more than many of the village men, that it should all be carried out in traditional detail, for in many instances the anthropologist and student, with access to the records of the earliest researchers, has more accurate knowledge of these details than have the villagers themselves, relying on the fast-fading memories of the oldest members of the clan. And the story of the hiri is this.

In the days and weeks that follow the first coming of the southeast wind, other men may decide to build a lakatoi and join the hiri; in any case the same activity is going on in other villages, some planning one lakatoi, others two or even three or four, depending on the number of people in the village. Eventually they may all join forces and sail as a fleet, for the sake of friendship and safety.

Each baditauna and doritauna picks a complete crew for the voyage, so that each lakatoi has two crews. Among them are two men responsible for the mast, another two responsible for the sail, and other pairs to look after the anchor and its cable. Together they prepare the four great logs that will be hollowed out to form the hulls of the lakatoi. The mast men go into the bush to mark suitable trees for cutting later on.

In August the building begins. The two leaders no longer wash themselves or cut their hair. Much of the normal food of the region is now taboo to them. They keep their own company.

When the four hulls have been made and lashed together the sorcerer is called, and with the root of a wild plant and the parings of the claw of the giant cassowary, together with the bony snout of a garfish, he makes a little fire, and with the smoke he fumigates

the gunwale of each hull like a priest censing a newly dedicated
building. Then he takes small squares of banana leaf, and in them
wraps the leaves of the same wild plant from which he took the root
to make his incense, and these he places in the slots where the cross-
members of the lakatoi hold the hulls together.

Then the builders lay decking across the four hulls, leaving
an overhang all around so that they are well protected from the
weather, and when this is done they build, in the middle of the
deck, a square with walls of plaited leaves like a house without a
roof. Then a covered lean-to is set up at each end of the lakatoi as
a shelter for each of the crews, and as soon as these are ready the
two leaders go on board and live there until the voyage is completed. Each of them takes with him a young boy of his family,
usually a son or a sister's son, and this lad is his servant and pupil
until the hiri is finished, and is called his *iduha*.

In the old days, before canvas became commonplace in the
Pacific islands, the two great sails of the lakatoi were made of palm-
woven mats, stitched together and shaped like a giant crab claw,
about twenty feet from top to bottom and ten feet across at the
widest part. The women plaited the separate strips of matting, and
the men sewed them together and fashioned each sail, binding its
edges onto an outline of rope made from bark fibers said to be
stronger than any hemp or manila, although this is doubtful.

I saw this old way of sail-making some years ago, on a small
island down the coast, and although there was no comment from
Enno, Akea, and Tau when I spoke about this and told them how it
had been done, they regarded me with more evident respect from
then on. They, themselves, have always used canvas sails, and it is
unlikely that they have seen a traditional sail being made.

When the decking is laid and the masts have been stepped, the
two leaders send their two young servants to the top of each mast to
hang the clan badge, usually a cone shell decorated with a tassel of
split leaves, and suspended on a cord of fine fibers that have been
twisted together between the palm of the hand and the maker's
thigh. These badges are called the *pepe*, and they hang at the mast-
head throughout the voyage, and when the lakatoi comes home
and the journey is done they are taken down and hung from the
ridge pole of the man's house, above the veranda, so that everyone
will know that he has been the leader of a hiri.

Some of the men, not greatly active in the building of the lakatois, are busy at this time making armshells. These will be used during the hiri as currency for specialized transactions, like the purchase of logs to make a new canoe or as payment for pigs and dogs for eating at ritual feasts; or as tokens of good faith before negotiating marriage between a girl of a gulf village and the son, or nephew, of a hiri voyager.

The armshell makers sit in the shade with their tools and materials: a cone shell, a flat piece of sandstone and a cylinder of the same material about as big as a gardener's scythe stone, a pot of water, and a tapping stone that is used as a hammer. With these they fashion inch-wide armbands, and grind them smooth inside and out with the sandstones so that all trace of coloration is removed, and the finished armlets are pure, calcareous white.

And while the men are active in these various ways the women are busy making pots to be exchanged for sago, so that everybody in the village is occupied in a creative way in a common enterprise upon which they all depend for their well-being and continued existence.

As the weeks pass the laurabada blows more constantly and gains strength, and the gentle breezes of June and July change into the gales of August which rage sometimes for days on end and bring driving, almost impenetrable, rain. And giant gray-green seas come rolling in across three thousand miles of ocean and make even coastal sailing dangerous, and a misery of discomfort and sickness; work almost ceases and the people stay indoors, and there are sudden sharp bickering arguments and domestic fights.

Then, in September, when the wind eases and the rain stops, work begins again and the lakatoi is quickly finished. When it is ready for sailing the men build a temporary platform that protrudes over the bows of the great ship, and the nubile girls and young men of the village go aboard and dance on this platform while the crew sail the lakatoi out into deep water for trials. So the village children also become involved.

When the trials are completed and all adjustment made there is a pause, and day by day the leaders and the crew study the weather, trying to decide when all the signs point to a safe sailing date. The baditauna and his partner use all the spells and prayers they can remember, chewing either betel nut or wild ginger and spitting out the juice; and they call upon the spirits of ancestors for guidance and help, as men have always done when setting out to face the unknown.

This choosing of a departure time is crucial to the success of the hiri, and in making his decision the baditauna needs the help of all his instinct and knowledge, and of all the tribal magic and supernatural help. If he leaves too soon he may find himself far at sea when a late gale sweeps down, and a drenching rain, and waves that batter the lakatoi and sweep over it, breaking down the protective walls that protect the pots so that they are all tumbled about and smashed.

Or, if their departure is delayed overly long, the season of the southeast wind could come to a premature end and leave them becalmed between two villages, with no breeze to take them on or to bring them home again, their trading incomplete and their food running out. Traditional these voyages might have been, but certainly not routine.

When, with the aid of incantations, spells, formulas, and precautionary rites the time for departure is agreed upon, the wife of the baditauna takes the pots that she has made and stacks them neatly in the middle of the walled-in portion of the lakatoi, where they will be most protected from the elements. Then comes the wife of the doritauna, and after her the wives of the crewmen and their near-relatives, who bring their pots and stow them within the four protective walls, so that in the end there are several hundreds of pots aboard the lakatoi.

They sail at the end of September, or if the season is a late one, early in October, and when they are gone the wife of the baditauna goes to her house and hangs a long cord of twisted vine from the rafters. Every day thereafter, until the lakatoi returns, she ties a knot in the vine to keep count of the days. On every tenth day she ties a bigger knot.

And until her husband comes back she does not wash herself or cut her hair. Neither dare she let the fire in her house go out or the lakatoi will most certainly be lost; so whenever she goes to her garden she leaves a girl at home to watch the fire and keep it burning. And the wife of the doritauna observes these conditions also; and the two women may only visit each other, and not the other women of the village.

After several days of sailing, if the weather is good and the wind remains fair, the lakatois reach the first of the villages of the gulf country, and when they come close to the village the two leaders and their serving boys jump into the sea and wash themselves. Then they cut their hair and shine themselves with coconut oil, and the members of the crew put on clean clothes. Then they wait for the elders of the village to visit them.

When the elders come aboard the baditauna gives a present to the village headman, either an armshell, a pearl shell, or a shell necklace, and this man then becomes his trading partner. The doritauna and the other members of the crew then choose trading partners and give them presents of shell ornaments. When this ceremony is completed the villagers go away, and in a little while a group of young men comes to the lakatoi with a pig, which is killed and eaten by the crew.

In the morning the pots are carried ashore and set out in rows close to the village. The owners of the pots then go to the beach and collect short sticks that have been washed up by the tide, and breaking each stick into two pieces, they put the two parts of a stick into each pot.

When this is done the villagers come to inspect the pots, and although every family is concerned, and will acquire pots in exchange for sago before the visitors depart, the village people do not negotiate directly with the men of the hiri, but only through their chosen trading partners, who are called *taruas*.

The tarua chooses the pots required not only by his own family and relations, but friends for whom he has agreed to act, and as he chooses each pot he takes out one-half of the broken stick, and so a tally is kept. For every pot chosen by the tarua the village family pays a banana leaf sack of sago weighing about eighty pounds.

Not all the pots may be exchanged at this one village, nor the required amount of sago collected to take home, and the men of the hiri may now sail on to another village. But, if things go well at this first village, they will stay for several days bartering armshells for logs, repairing their lakatoi or replacing its hull with new ones, exchanging objects of adornment, arranging return visits, or discussing intervillage marriages and other matters of mutual interest.

During this time the active women of the village go to the swamps to make the sago from the pith of the sago palm, and the men who have negotiated to supply logs for canoes go to the hills and cut them, and float them down the river to the village.

So the men of the hiri continue to visit and trade along the coast for about two months, until in late December or January the wind begins to change to the northwest and their thoughts turn to home. Then the lakatois are reversed so that they sail eastward, back from the gulf.

While they have been away, their women in the home village followed every detail of their activity through the interpretation of dreams and innumerable relevant signs and manifestations that have kept them in a ferment of doubt, conjecture, and anxiety for fifty days.

The sorcerers have been busy interpreting dreams in which fire, water, stones, running dogs, and sick pigs have been the most significant symbols. In addition any itch, twitch, or tickling of any part of the body has contained a hidden extrasensory message from the men of the hiri, needing immediate deciphering and elucidation by sorcerers, and old people with special gifts of divination.

Then, on the fiftieth day, counted according to the knotted vine hanging from the rafters in the baditauna's house, the women and girls and little children climb the headland to watch for the lakatoi returning.

From then on, day after day they keep constant watch, and each day doubt and trepidation mount, and the sorcerers are kept busier than ever interpreting signs, until at last a young girl gazing steadfastly out to sea gives a gasp and points an uncertain finger at an infinitesimal speck on the hazed horizon; and an excitement runs through them all, and they know that the men are coming home.

The women run home, and the wives of the hiri men hasten to wash themselves and cut and oil their hair and put on their best grass skirts, five or six layers of them, and deck themselves with leaves stuck into the armbands, and necklets of dogs' teeth and pendants of cowrie shells. And the other women, and such men as are left in the village, prepare food and kill pigs for a feast of welcome, and clean the village and decorate the dancing drums.

When hours later, the lakatoi comes to anchor a little way from the shore, the men clean themselves, and after a decent interval their wives come out in canoes to greet them. And each man gives his wife one bag of sago to take home so that some of it might be used for the homecoming feast. Then the baditauna and the doritauna wash again in the sea and put on their best clothes, and decorate their faces with red dyes and scent themselves with aromatic shrubs. Then they bring the lakatoi to the beach, and the children gather around to watch while the women welcome the men with a dance and lead them into the village for the feast.

It was late when we finished talking, and most of the other people in the village had long since gone to sleep, and the only sound was the sighing, monotonous beat of the sea dropping onto the beach and sighing back through the sand as the tide ran out. The Southern Cross cartwheeled down onto the horizon and a million stars shone in the black-cloth sky. Enno looked sad and Akea as inscrutable as ever; and Tau, the baditauna with his back against the wall, and his eyes closed, seemed to have left us on some voyage of his own far out beyond the edges of time.

Six

It is dangerous to wake a sleeping person, for while he sleeps his spirit leaves his body and goes walking about the world, and if you wake his body while his spirit is away he will die immediately. So when I opened my eyes slowly in the morning, aware of whisperings coming from the doorway, and saw three young Papuan faces peering around the doorway at me, I knew that they were debating whether or not I was sufficiently awake to be disturbed, or if my spirit was still wandering elsewhere.

Livingstone was snoring quietly in a well-bred manner, looking distinguished even in sleep. Our host was up and had gone out of the house. I walked to the door and saw him standing in the sea washing himself, native-fashion, with a towel around himself for a lap-lap, for one never sees a Papuan naked once he leaves childhood behind.

I dressed, then walked with the children through the village to call on the medical team, camped in the village rest house. They were finishing breakfast and packing their X-ray gear and other equipment, so I stayed to take a cup of coffee and exchange news. They said that they were going aboard the *Leander* during the morning and would leave at high tide for Port Moresby, having finished their work along this stretch of the coast.

They had been traveling for a month, making a tuberculosis survey in all villages between Yule Island and Port Moresby, using the portable X-ray equipment, making skin tests, and giving vaccinations. It was part of a systematic survey, they said, covering the whole of New Guinea.

The Government, helped by the missionaries, provides New Guinea with what is probably the most comprehensive free medical service in the world, and although some of the activities of the

Health Department are not clearly understood by the villagers, and others often violate custom and traditional belief, it is generally accepted that medical care without magic and liturgy is a curious but necessary part of the white man's way of life.

But when, for instance, clinical investigation or treatment requires that samples of blood or milk or urine be taken, people are reluctant to come forward, even in sophisticated areas. In remote parts of the country it is sometimes impossible to get such samples, except from orphaned children, because everybody is certain that in surrendering these samples the patient is literally delivering his life into the hands of the stranger.

The basis of the public health system is a chain of about seventeen hundred village aid posts where native orderlies deal with the daily home-doctoring needs of village people, and refer serious sickness or accident to the nearest missionary or Government medical center. The orderlies also supervise village hygiene and are supposed to visit neighboring hamlets to check on health and sanitation. Some of them are marvelously efficient and effective. Most of them are reliable. A few, inevitably, are lazy and dishonest.

At key points all over the country there are regional hospitals. Some of them are crude and horrible and are soon to be replaced. Others are new and have cost millions of pounds to build and equip. All are staffed by doctors and nurses from Australia, and have schools attached to them for training native orderlies, nurses, and technicians. The bigger missionary groups also have hospitals staffed by trained people from various parts of the world. In addition, teams of specialist doctors, surgeons, and nurses from Australia come to New Guinea two or three times a year to work at the regional hospitals.

In between the two extremes of village orderly and high-cost hospitalization, the New Guinea villager has a wide range of medicare to call on. It includes infant and maternal welfare for practically every family; a medical emergency service that makes almost daily use of aircraft to bring the seriously sick or injured into the main medical centers for urgent attention; there are settlements for leper and tubercular patients, a system of medical patrols that covers the whole country, and full-time malaria eradication units whose job it is to rid the country of this disease within the next few years.

Yet in spite of this the life expectancy of the average New Guinea native is thirty-four years, and of the estimated eighty thousand babies born each year, a third are dead within twelve months, and only three out of five reach five years of age. The greatest killers are ignorance and supersitition aided by malaria, pneumonia, dysentery, and tuberculosis; and it is the debilitating effect of endemic malaria that makes most of these other sicknesses fatal.

"Control malaria and you will double the expectation of life, halve the infant mortality rate, and double the population in seventeen years." This is but one *cri du coeur* among many that punctuate the speeches, essays, reports, and assessments of doctors and administrators who year after year insist that until the "curtain of disease is finally lifted" in New Guinea, no person in the country will ever be more than 8o percent healthy.

This is a difficult truth to impose on the villagers of the Papuan coast in spite of ninety years of Christianity and Western teaching. They have seen penicillin cure frambesia in a few days, and aspirin dispel headache in an hour. They will take malaria tablets in good faith when the aid post orderly gives them out, and are not above going to the hospital with a broken leg. But there is not the slightest doubt in their minds that death is caused solely and deliberately by an act of sorcery, and although the white man's medicine may well alleviate sickness of all kinds, it cannot prevent death if death has been willed by an enemy. They believe, therefore, that the only defense against sorcery is the employment of countersorcery.

I saw Akea walk past, coming from the beach where he had been working on Dr. Groves' canoe. He seemed uncommunicative and withdrawn and hardly acknowledged my greeting. He was carrying a small, string-woven bag in which Papuan men sometimes keep tobacco and other small personal belongings. Ten minutes later, as I came back through the village and passed Enno's house, I saw Akea go inside, and as I wished to speak to Enno and was also curious to know why Akea was being taciturn, I went up onto the veranda of the house and looked inside.

The wooden window shutters of the house were closed, and the only light inside came from the door, or filtered in thin beams through the plaited walls, so that the little tableau in the back of the room was almost lost in gloom. But I could see Akea leaning

over a reclining child while Enno, and a woman I took to be his
sister, looked on anxiously. The three of them, sitting on the floor beside the child, not speaking, told a silent, simple story.

Akea is a sorcerer of high repute. Enno is the village headman,
accepted as such by the Government and missionaries alike. The
child is sick.

A little later Enno will go to the village aid post to get some
malaria tablets for the child, but in the meantime he is making sure
that the evil being worked against the child by some unknown
enemy of his household will be canceled by the magic of Akea.

Enno feels very deeply about this because he and his family have
long been prosecuted by someone, unknown, who is causing sorcery
to be worked against them. Enno's wife is already a patient in the
tuberculosis hospital on Gemo Island, near Port Moresby. Enno himself is a sick man. On top of all, the medical team just leaving the
village has told Enno that his child has malaria, and this may be
true; but somebody is willing these things against Enno, otherwise
they would not happen. His sister sits beside him silently watching
Akea gently massage the child's stomach.

Akea is masticating a root of wild ginger, and there is a faraway
look in his twisted eyes. In a while he bends over the child and
blows softly on her stomach, then resumes the gentle massage. Enno
watches, looking troubled. Then Akea suddenly leans forward and
places his lips to the child's flesh, and sucks strongly. Then he pulls
back swiftly and turns away, spitting and retching loudly.

Relief and satisfaction fleet over the woman's face. Enno looks up
with wide eyes, questioning. Akea spits again and nods, then covers
the child with a bit of blanket. He takes from his mouth a small
stone and shows it briefly to Enno and the woman. Then he puts
it into his little bag and gets to his feet. Enno goes into the darkest
corner of the room and comes back with an armshell which he gives
to Akea. The woman nods approval. Akea has been paid. The child
will get well.

I went back down the ladder.

It would be unjust and ignorant to accuse Akea of callous dishonesty and deceit, or Enno of superstitious ignorance and simplicity. For although a sorcerer may well be an evil man, taking de-
light in works of wickedness, he may just as well be a good and
clever man, and a worker of protective magic, and a healer; and al-

though he may appear to practice deceit by suggesting that he has withdrawn a pebble from the child's inside, it is reasonable to believe that the stone is understood by everybody concerned to be a symbol of the sickness rather than its actual cause. Akea himself has absolute faith in these rituals and their efficacy.

And even if Enno and his sister may not believe implicitly that Akea has taken a stone from the child's stomach and so cured her sickness and prevented death, they do believe, without reservation, that with his rituals he has frustrated the wickedness worked upon the child by an unknown enemy.

To dismiss the power of sorcery, or its effect upon the people of New Guinea whatever their level of education, sophistication, or Christianization, is ignorance. It would be just as foolish to deride the power of prayer, suggestion, or faith.

There was the case of the woman of Hanuabada village who fell sick, having been bitten by a snake placed in her path by a sorcerer. Her relatives took her into her house and called a healer who worked diligently over her for a long time, using all his magic, but she seemed certain to die. Then the village medical orderly, being conscientious as well as a little puffed up with the importance of his position, and jealous for the reputation of his profession, sent word to the doctor at the hospital, and the doctor sent an ambulance and had the woman brought to him. Then, when he had heard the story and examined the woman, he gave her injections and put her to bed between sheets in a beautifully clean and antiseptic ward.

Next day her relatives came and saw that she was no better and that she would most surely die; and going back to the village they spoke about it among themselves, and were troubled. So at night they went back to the hospital when all of the doctors had gone, and the night staff of white nurses was busy, and they took the woman back to the village. And in this they had the help of Papuan nurses and orderlies who knew that the woman was suffering from sorcery and that she could not be cured in the hospital with white man's medicine, but only in the village, by magic.

When they got the woman home they laid her on her sleeping mat, and her husband's sisters and other women of the family sat around her, gently stroking her body with their hands while they whispered the healing prayers, some of them belonging to the past and some taken from the mission prayer book. And their sorcerer sat at her feet and wove spells. And in the morning she got up and went about her work.

There was a great argument as to who cured the woman, the sorcerer or the doctor at the hospital. The villagers had no doubt whatever, and the doctor was certain that his anti-snake bite serum had worked the cure. The missionary in the village thought that the woman would have died in the hospital because she could not believe that she would get better without the rituals of the sorcerer, while on the other hand the sorcerer might not have saved her had she not received the antidote at the hospital.

My retinue of children rejoined me at the bottom of the ladder, coming from Enno's house, and we went on through the village together. Two women were making pots, sitting in the shade under their house, and another was showing her small daughter how to split palm fronds along the rib, and lay them out in fan patterns to dry in the sun; afterwards she would teach the girl how to make skirts with them.

Some small boys came running between the houses, calling out and laughing, and carrying little homemade outrigger canoes with cloth sails made from worn shirts. My retinue deserted me and ran off with them to the beach, leaving only two small girls who still followed, shy and big-eyed, making cats-cradle stories with a long loop of twine woven from hibiscus bark. They call the game, "making with your fingers."

At the end of the village I crossed a stile into the school yard. The little girls would come no farther but stood, their eyes following me and their fingers busy with the string.

Not wishing to disturb the lesson I avoided the schoolhouse and kept along the edge of the compound, but could still hear the high-pitched, sharp young voices chanting multiplication tables.

Fife vunsa fife,
Fife toosa tscn,
Fife dreesa fitteen,
Fife vorsa tsventi . . .

The young Papuan teacher, looking out from over the half-wall of the woven-palm schoolhouse, saw me and smiled, but made no other sign, knowing that the children would immediately lose in-

terest in the lesson and start whispering and giggling if they knew
that I was listening to them. In any case Livingstone would be paying an official call during the day and I would go with him, and
they would sing for us.

In a corner of the compound three men were quietly at work re-
building the church, and I remembered having seen the sun flash
on the new roof as we had approached in the *Leander* the day before. I stopped to admire the new work and to talk to them for a
while. One was the Missionary Society pastor, a Papuan from a
village on the other side of Port Moresby, while the second man
was a Manumanu villager and a deacon of the church.

Beyond the compound, Groves and Livingstone were watching
men prepare new garden land for the seasonal planting of bananas
and yams. There were thirty or more men at work, some clearing
away old growth and burning it in heaps, others turning over the
ground with digging sticks.

They worked in rows of eight or ten men, each with a pointed
hardwood stick some six feet long and two inches thick. Every man
drove his stick deeply into the ground; then the whole row levered
the earth over in a long furrow, uttering shouts of encouragement
to each other. Then they moved backward to start a new row.

I knew that Groves was studying each detail of the customs and
traditions of the Manumanu people, holding these villagers to be
the last custodians of paganism on this coast, and that Livingstone
was also interested for his own professional reasons, and not wishing
to disturb them I continued walking alone, and came across a man
planting a banana sucker.

First he made a deep hole in the sandy loam and into it put a few
leaves tied together at the stems, and over them he whispered what
seemed to a prayer or a short song. Then he stood the banana sucker
in the hole and slowly covered its roots with soil, at the same time
continuing with his quiet singing. And I supposed that he was singing the songs of his ancestors, reciting their names, together with
his own, after each song, just as some Christian sects add a doxology
at the end of their hymns and prayers.

Then I went back through the village, noting the fall of the light
and the ground plan of its layout in case I should later decide to
send a film unit to make some record of Manumanu life, and the

customs that have been extinguished in most other Motu villages and are fast dying out even here.

A group of men came from under a house and walked down to the beach carrying a fishing net. I stood back, knowing that if I passed in front of them they would catch no fish that day. An elderly man, leader of the family genealogical line, carried the head of the net, followed by the other men in single file, and when they came to their canoe they stepped forward one by one to deposit their part of the net on the deck, then stepped back, because no one may step in front of the net while it is being carried.

A family paddled quietly by with three new cooking pots and a basket of fish and crabs on the deck of their canoe. I called out to them and the man answered, saying that they were going to a village upriver to trade the fish and the pots for yams and other garden food.

I went on board the *Leander* and took some steaks and dairy butter from the refrigerator, and something to drink because the village well water is brackish and hard on stomachs accustomed to the reticulated water of the towns or the clear water of highland streams. I took these things back to the house in the village as exchange to our host for his hospitality. I also took some tobacco for Enno and the other elders as a sign of respect and friendship.

That evening after dinner we sat on the veranda again, and Dr. Groves told us of the hiris that he had seen in past years, only one of which had followed traditional rituals in every detail. They had taken eleven hundred pots on that voyage, made from clay that the crewmen of the lakatoi dug for themselves in accordance with the old rules.

Then he explained in detail the pot-making rituals, describing the varieties of pots and their uses, the methods used to dry and fire them, the significance of the designs etched on the rims, and the magic employed to ensure that the pots wouldn't crack during the firing.

On the beach at the end of the village a group of lads were singing to the accompaniment of a ukelele and guitar. The song was a popular one, a remembrance of the days when the white man's war came to New Guinea and Papuans discovered for the first time that there were such people as Americans and Japanese, and that civilization could bring disruption on so much larger a scale than any-

thing they had known before. Thousands of Papuans were recruited
into labor companies and other military and naval units, and hundreds of families were moved away from their villages for their own
safety, or to make way for strategic installations.

The men in these units grew homesick, missing the tightly woven
family life of their villages, and found the monotonous diet of
canned meat and rice no substitute for traditional village food. One
of them, in his misery, wrote the song that has since become a popular folk song all over Papua:[1]

> *Raisi mo ianina lalo hesiku*
> *Dahaka bama ani bama moale*
> *Dina vada be dihomu do bainala*
> *Sinagu baina nanadaia dahaka e nadu*

> (I am tired of always eating rice,
> What shall I eat to be happy?
> It is evening and I will go to my mother
> And see what she is cooking)

There is not much left, even in Manumanu, of the old music or
the dancing of premissionary days, although the season of the
dance is still observed. It comes after the harvest, when there is
food to spare for ritual feasting, and at that time the young men and
girls are out each evening, practicing their dances. But they are not
the same dances as those which horrified the missionaries when they
first came among the Motu people.

These early missionaries made an issue of traditional dancing,
refusing church membership to any who continued to have any connection with the arrangement or performance of dance festivals
which were, in the historical and social structure of the people, an
essential and all-important element. From the point of view of
Christian morality and Western social practice the missionaries had
no other choice, since the Motu dances were for the most part un-
equivocably orgiastic and primarily designed to give sexual pleasure.

Dr. Lawes said that the Motu dance was a "carnival of licentious-

[1] There are several versions of this song. This one was given to me
by Mr. Oala Rarua.

ness and sensuality . . . it lasted from three to four months during which time all work (except that absolutely necessary) was given up and the people gave themselves up to lust and immorality. The meaning of the dance, the *raison d'être* for its existence, was fornication. The young men kept tally of the girls they had connection with, and reckoned them up at the end of the season."

There is still dancing on occasions, but today's occasions are likely to celebrate the opening of a new co-operative store, the visit of a senior personage from Australia, or the election of a village council; and if opportunity for sexual pleasure is sought on such occasions, it is not achieved with the same license or facility.

The singing stopped, and Livingstone yawned and said that he would go to bed. Dr. Groves asked me if I would like to travel with him in the morning to Port Moresby. He would, he thought, start before dawn and travel by canoe, using the outboard motor. He would take Enno to visit his wife at Gemo Island and to get further medical advice about his little daughter. We could be in Port Moresby by eight o'clock, before the southeast wind came up, and the sea would be calm all the way.

Some of the men, he said, were out fishing for barramundi and might have a catch that could be taken in and sold. It seemed a convenient plan, so I went into the house to pack my box.

Seven

We waded barefoot out to the canoe in shallow, warm water that was scarcely lapping, so low the tide, and no wind blowing. Stars were still hard and bright in the sky, but on the beach and in the village behind us everything slatey and gray, though sharply etched in the clear, cold air of predawn. The hull of Groves' canoe felt cold and damp to the touch, like something dead. I shivered, and zipped up my wind jacket.

Two men from the village brought barramundi from their own canoe farther along the beach, carrying the fish on sticks thrust through the gills, and stowed them in the hollow hulls of our canoe. No one spoke. We were like a company of players discovered as the curtain goes up on a dark stage, moving about silently and mysteriously.

The canoe was double-hulled, decked over like a raft, and bare-masted. Akea stood midships, near where the outboard motor hung poised over a slot in the decking through which it could be tilted into the sea. He directed the action of each one of us, not speaking, but making quick, clipped gestures with head and hands, moving where needed to make things quicker.

Enno emerged from the blackness of the village and came aboard, his sister carrying the child. Enno himself had the big net bag that all New Guinea women carry, and in it food and presents for his wife at Gemo Island, his cooking things, some betel nuts to sell or give for presents in exchange for hospitality, some fish wrapped in leaves and tied with strands of vine, and a few hands of green bananas. Fresh garden food is hard to come by in the urbanized villages near Port Moresby.

Akea's two young nephews were the crew; the older boy to steer with the great-bladed paddle, the other to sit on the bow

and keep watch. Later, Akea would put out fishing lines to troll
and the boy would watch them as well. Akea himself would stay by
the engine.

Dr. Groves came aboard yawning, spread a grass mat on the decking and lay down, covering himself over with a blanket, for it would
be cold once we started and he had made this journey so often that
he would not want to see anything before we reached Port Moresby
in about four hours' time. He settled down hopefully to sleep.

Livingstone was staying behind in Manumanu to finish his work,
but two other men of the village came along for reasons of their
own, and sat on the fore part of the deck. One of them helped pole
the canoe out into deep water. Then Akea started the engine with
a swift pull of the cord and it caught immediately, and we headed
out to sea along a pathway of moonlight.

Given good conditions there is no better way to travel long sea
distances, point-to-point, than by power canoe. Sail offers more
entertainment and exhilaration when the sea is easy, the wind fair,
and time inconsequent, and there is great excitement to be had in
riding a wild southeaster in big seas; but then one gets wet to the
earholes and this is done, voluntarily, only for sport.

To cover distance in good time and in reasonable comfort regardless of wind and sea, I prefer power canoe to anything. And the
best time to travel is early morning, preferably before dawn. Once
the sun gets up there is no shade on a sailless canoe. Also, at this
time of the morning, the sea is usually smooth between the beaches
and the outlying reefs, unless there is an exceptional wind, and then
one stays at home and does not travel at all.

Akea signaled with outstretched arm, telling the young steersman
to pull around a point, until he had lined up the high palm tree in
the village with the southern point of the bay, and this, he knew,
would bring us to a small gap in the mud bank and let us through;
for although the canoe is shallow-drafted and can ride in two feet
of water, the tide was at its lowest and outboard motors are easily
damaged.

So we went quietly, at half speed, while the lad in the bow
watched for rocks and coral outcrops. At the mud bank Akea slowed
down almost to a stop and the two men slipped overboard and
stood to their waists in water and led us through the gap; then,
when we were through, they hauled themselves aboard and settled

down to sleep. The motor roared and we were away, heading southeast down the coast to Port Moresby.

At this time, between night and daylight, the sea leads its secret life and is most alive and most alone; it seems not to concern itself with those that sail upon it, but concentrates on simply being. It loses its malevolence, its frightening power of destruction, its violent angers, its deceit, its superficial beauties that are compounded of the sun's light and the sky's reflection. At night, when the sun is on the other side of the world, and the sky is remote in its own detached majesty, the sea becomes herself. The great unchanging ancient womb of creation and of time.

Now, in her nakedness, she is most beautiful; skin-smooth like fluid black marble, and mottled with deep, underlying swirls of fish-skin silver and dark gray, ever-moving, never still, living, moving, making beauty continuously; never, not even in its most tempestuous and tremendous overpowering anger, whipped by wild winds, is it more vitally alive.

Akea sat still, watching, looking ahead, not stirring; the two boys like black statues; the two men and Murray Groves sleeping; Enno and his sister sitting apart, silent. I watched the eastern sky for the first faint stirrings of dawn. The engine hummed in its own isolation.

We went on for an hour, then passed Redscar Point, where in daylight a long landslip of red rock, sloping from the headland's top down to its sea-beaten base, has been remarked upon by voyagers back through centuries; by night this landmark comes up suddenly, a black bulk standing head and shoulders above the palisade of palms that stretches almost continuously along the foreshore.

There is a village just behind this point, but we saw no light. It was still dankly cold.

Suddenly Akea pounced and grasped the trolling line, calling to the steersman at the same time, but softly so as not to wake his master, Groves. The youngest boy watched wide-eyed and apprehensive as Akea pulled the line in hand-over-hand, straining with one foot against the framing pole of the canoe. There was a flash of silver some fifty feet astern, and a kingfish jumped and twisted once on the end of the line. But it had no chance against the finger-thick cord and the steel hook baited with lily root, and the pull of the canoe.

He brought it alongside and dragged it up on deck, breaking the fluent dappling of the sea surface into a myriad of quick-winking eyes that swiftly fell behind and were lost. The big fish, all of fifty pounds, thudded and flapped with its tail along the deck as Akea dragged it to safety before unhooking. Its skin was sea-sheened, black, blue, deep green, with a flash of violet-pink along the belly. Akea dropped it into the hollow hull for safekeeping. It would bring him six or seven pounds in Port Moresby, and of this he would give something to Enno and the boys; that is, if Dr. Groves didn't need the fish to give to friends in Port Moresby as a gift.

The sky lightened imperceptibly, and suddenly the palisade of palms on shore became separate trees and the color of the water changed to gray, and back behind us in the west a tinge of pink lit the underside of a single cloud. High up, five frigate birds soared out to sea on angular pinions.

The sun appeared and lit the eastern sky with the colors of a ripe mango, yellow and gold and red; then it was broad daylight, and the sea green and sullen, with a long swell.

We caught another fish; so now Akea would make a profit, and Dr. Groves could still win favor with his friends.

An hour more and we began to converge on the big fishing canoes coming in to Moresby from the far reef where they had been all night. The day was now well on, almost eight o'clock and the sun climbing; soon it would become unbearably hot out on the sea. We turned toward the land and the low hills that encircle Moresby, but instead of steering straight for the harbor entrance turned into a narrow neck of water running between the coastline and an inshore island.

It rose almost straight out of the sea, the top of a submerged hill, barren of trees, covered only with a thin growth of anemic kunai grass, almost yellow from lack of sustenance and moisture; a bare, desolate, inhospitable, high-peaked lump of land, less than a mile square.

Gemo Island. A place for lepers and people with tuberculosis. This is where we would land Enno to visit his wife. We entered the narrow neck where the waters meet when the tide is running. When you stand on the island, high up on its single hilltop, you can see this meeting of the tides, as Sister Fairhall did twenty-five years ago when she started the hospital on Gemo.

Sitting alone in her house, the only white person on the island, she wrote to a friend back home.

"Here the tides meet . . . I am hoping that
at Gemo the tide of suffering and superstition
may meet the tide of healing and love."

Miracles are what you make them. The resident Government officer at Port Moresby went with her to look at the place chosen for the leper hospital. He remarked, "What a barren spot." The lieutenant governer, Sir Hubert Murray, paid a visit and said that he wouldn't work there for five thousand pounds. She herself wrote to her friend saying that it was "a barren, rocky place to look at."

The Government land commissioner said that the land belonged to twenty-nine different Papuan owners and they would never agree to sell or lease it. The owners came to her and said, "If you are going to make this hospital for us we will give you the land without conditions, for fifty years."

This was the first miracle. They have never stopped.

For many years now Gemo has been known as The Island of Happiness, yet it has never lost that look of desolation from a distance. Even today, when I know it so well, I am amazed how a place so arid to the eye can really generate so much devotion and love.

I remember when I first went there, long after it was founded, and Sister Fairhall had gone to other work in the mission although her name continued to be associated with Gemo as it always will be.

I had been invited by the tuberculosis doctor to go with him on one of his biweekly visits, and as we traveled the three miles of harborway between the customs wharf at Moresby and the island itself, I watched it take shape; even as we approached the Gemo jetty, and could see the people waiting for our launch to arrive, it had more the look of an uninhabited island harboring a few castaways than of a widely known medical center.

There were three white women working on the island then. Sister Phillips was in charge of the hospital and mainly concerned with the tubercular patients. Dora Durell nursed lepers, and Miss Jenny looked after the bookwork and a hundred other things. There were two Samoan nurses, and the rest of the staff was Papuan.

It was Dora who met us that first day. We could see her waiting on the jetty to meet us, her white uniform shining out among the brown skins. As we came closer I could see her more clearly. Tall and young, just out of her twenties, she stood with her feet planted firmly apart and hair flying untidily in the wind. When I stepped onto the jetty she stuck out her hand and said, "Welcome to our happy home."

She had a cheerful, forthright voice, and a handshake like a man's. She swung her arm around to take in the cluster of shabby huts and tin sheds huddled under the flank of the hill. "It's not much to look at, but it's all our own." There was a suspicion of defensiveness behind the bravura.

Then she turned to the doctor. "Sister Phillips is ready for you in the X-ray room."

I stayed for several days on Gemo, in the little room kept for visitors, on the side of the hill overlooking the hospital. Tiny brown ants swarmed over my hairbrush to feed on the residues of natural and artificial hair oils and when I brushed my head in the morning they raced all over my scalp. Insects, probably cockroaches, ate the binding of my bedside book and nibbled at toothbrushes. Geckos squeaked, and chased moths and flies across the ceiling most of the night.

During the day the three women left me alone to walk around and talk to people as I wished. In any case they were too busy to look after me.

I met Tau Boga the schoolteacher, himself a leper, though only a young man, newly married. He had a small hut perched high on the side of the hill, hanging over the sea, divided into study and bedroom, both kept as neat and tidy as a monk's cell.

He had two assistants teaching the very young children, while he himself took the older classes and all the lepers. I was surprised how affected I was to watch a young girl, perhaps thirteen years old or a little more, with fingers already eaten away by leprosy, intent on writing verses in English to Tau's dictation, the pencil held awkwardly between twisted digital stumps.

Afterwards I sat with Tau and talked about his life on Gemo Island and about his hopes of a normal life when he was cured, as seemed certain in a year or two. And he told me how, as a lad, he had wanted to do something for his own people and had decided to become a schoolteacher, and had done well at the Government teacher-training school, not only in his studies, but at sport, especially cricket.

And when he became a teacher he married a Hanuabada girl and they had a child, but before it was born the telltale marks had appeared on his face at the bridge of the nose, and the horrible headaches and nausea. When he came to this part of his story Tau looked down, ashamed.

"I did not want to live when they told me. I thought to myself, all is finished for me. I did not want to go on. When I came here I wished to die.

"Then, after a little while, I saw the Sisters always busy helping the people, and the orderlies and nurses working hard even though many were more sick than me, and Gemo Island did not seem so ugly, and I thought to myself that I too could help to make it more beautiful if I would stop thinking about myself and do something good for the other people.

"So I begin to walk around among the people, and I see the children growing up with their future dark and unknown. Like me they are thinking that there are no more opportunities for them. So I have encouraged them that there are opportunities for everyone. I tell them that they are not neglected by the community, because I am a Government teacher and I have come to teach them.

"At first they do not believe that I mean true with them until they see me sweep out the schoolroom and write lessons on the blackboard by myself. Then they come, and together we learn to be members of this community, and of our country and the world.

"I teach them that each one of us has a work to do for New Guinea. I believe that I have opened for them a new page in their life. The page of hope."

Tau went back to his classroom, and I took the hillside path from his house and came down to the beach again, and walking between the hospital buildings saw Toparua the pathologist leave the tin shed he called his laboratory, and cross to the tuberculosis examination room with a dish of slides.

Toparua is a medical orderly, trained to use the microscope to look for "snakes" in specimens of sputum. He comes from Buka Island in the Solomons where people have such fine-boned faces when they are young that many boys and youths are as beautiful as women, with almost transparent nostrils and earlobes, and fragile, delicate temples. And these people of Buka are jet black so that you cannot see them at night.

I followed Toparua into the examination room, past a group of patients clustered around the door in the shade of an arthritic frangipani tree. Dr. Wigley lifted his head and smiled. He was looking at lung X-rays with Sister Phillips who made notes as he spoke. Toparua put down his slides and went out, and Sister Phillips said a silent "Thank you" with her lips as he passed.

The doctor tapped one of the X-rays and made a discouraging face. The Sister looked glum and waited for him to speak.

He looked at me and said, "This one is probably cancer and, as usual, too late for us to do more than palliate."

I waited for him to go on.

"There's not much that we can do for lung cancer even in civilized countries where people go to a doctor when they suspect that something is seriously wrong. Here, in New Guinea, when people feel they are going to die, they avoid the doctor in case he sends them to the hospital. If they're to die they want to die at home so that when their spirit leaves the body it will not get lost in strange surroundings."

He turned and spoke to Sister Phillips.

"He'd better be seen by the surgical team, though I doubt if they'll operate."

Then he looked at me again.

"They all smoke from an early age, uncured native leaf, prepared trade twist, or imported cigarettes, and all inhale deeply." Dr. Wigley has few reservations about what he calls "the sinister relationship between tobacco smoking and the liability to develop lung cancer." He finished reading the X-rays, and stood up to begin the examination of patients under treatment.

Sasa, the Samoan ward sister, came in and took her place beside the doctor. She picked a case card from the filing cabinet and handed it to him, then called out to the group around the door.

"Kikeri." She sounded like a girl calling to her brother. "Kikeri, will you come now?"

Sister Phillips, collecting the X-rays on the other side of the room, looked around, smiling with motherly affection at the young man who came through the door.

Dora Durell had already told me the story of Sister Phillips and Kikeri: how, six months ago or thereabouts, she had been on a medical patrol through the villages, and looking through the huts for sick people, hidden away, had come across Kikeri lying in the dark, in filth, ill, alone, and unable to move through weakness and pain.

She had been appalled and surprised, for although Papuans are superstitious about sickness they are, as a rule, gentle and solicitous with those who are ill. Stepping out of the hut into the bright sunlight she called to a group of men sitting under a tree close by, and asked them why nothing was being done for the sick man.

They shrugged and made no answer, so she went and stood over them and spoke to them strongly in their own language. And one of them said, "He is a stranger from across the river. He came this way five days ago, traveling to Port Moresby, but fell sick and we let him rest in this house because the owner is dead, and it is empty."

She scolded them, saying that they should be ashamed to treat a visitor to their village in such a manner. The men looked embarrassed and annoyed, and their leader said, "He is not of our people and does not speak our language, neither has he kinship with us through marriage, and if we interfere the sorcerer who has made him sick will be angry with us."

Sister Phillips shook her head sadly and called for her folding stool, and when the young boy who was her special carrier had opened it out she sat down among the men, and taking her Bible read to them, in their own language, the story of the Good Samaritan. And afterwards she expounded the meaning of the story.

Whether their hearts were touched, or they considered it sensible and expedient to get rid of this powerful white woman together with the sick stranger without further embarrassment, and for the sake of peace, they made a stretcher of sticks and an old blanket and carried Kikeri down to the river and put him in a canoe, and took him to Gemo, sailing and paddling for two full days.

He soon recovered from the pneumonia that would have killed him if, as he said later, God had not sent Sister Phillips to find him; and he seemed likely to be cured of the lung infection that kept him still on Gemo; but he didn't want to leave the island, and had asked if he could stay on as a medical orderly.

So Sister Phillips had undertaken to train Kikeri herself because she had found him and he was, as it were, her personal responsibility. They fitted in the bookwork during the evenings as often as possible, although she was already giving Bible study lessons at night to Rea, the pastor-patient, and also spent much time in the wards after dark, especially when people were dying.

One becomes accustomed to meeting remarkable people in New Guinea. It may be that this beautiful and cruel country, geographically accessible, but historically remote, offers to both male and female Quixotes an escape from the unreality of a civilization dominated by impersonal powers, in which even the minimum means of self-expression and achievement are to be had only on application to the right authority, and with the presentation of the right credentials, social, academic, or political; and where the word "Love" has purely private connotation.

In New Guinea the work to be done is beyond the capacity of impersonal powers, and the material rewards are so small that the challenge is willingly left to those who simply want to achieve, to create, to express, and to identify themselves with the ebullient evolution of the human mind, body, and soul; and among such people, faith, hope, and love are, in fact, the substance of daily life even if not known by those names.

Sister Phillips had said as much, but in better words the night before, as we sat talking over a late cup of tea. Looking down at her hands and speaking with simple truth, she said, "I always felt that I wanted to be a missionary, even when I was quite young. As a girl I used to collect money for the Missionary Society and when, at the end of the year, I handed in eight shillings and five pence, they gave me a book called *Derona—The Story of a Young Papuan*. And when I had read it my mind was made up.

"And I can honestly say that I've never regretted the step that I took when I offered for missionary service. In the truest sense of the word it is a grand life. Some people say that we have to give up too many things and make too many sacrifices, but we don't really, because whatever we give we get back a thousandfold from the people with whom we work, in their love and affection, and in our own sense of something worthwhile accomplished and created.

"And when we see the people we have taught going into the far places of their own country to spread the gospel and help the sick, and to concern themselves with the welfare of strangers, that is our greatest reward."

I watched her now, in the examination room, a mother-figure, ample, strong, plain of face and faith, uncomplicated; looking with unspoken love and deep compassion on her patients as Dr. Wigley examined them one by one. She smiled with him when he was able to give praise for progress made; nodded her head in agreement when he urged patience and discipline; showed concern when he was disappointed by a patient's failure to improve.

When the doctor had finished his examinations he went to the wards to see those too sick to get up for his visit: two old people near to dying, but also three small children immobilized in plaster casts and lying helpless on their backs like beetles turned over. These are in the special care of the Samoan nurses, Sasa and Poia, who lavish such love on them, and are themselves so gay that other patients visit their wards when they need cheering up.

I left the doctor and Sister Phillips, and went on past the tuberculosis section, and along the narrow strip of muddy beach to the leper hospital where I had business with John Korabo. I found him sitting on his bed busy with needle and thread, making the sail of a model lakatoi that I had commissioned for my godson who would sail it in Sydney Harbour.

He looked up and grinned and nodded toward the other end of the ward, and I saw that he had finished the hull and the outrigger, and had painted them pale blue and red, and put them to dry near an open shutter. He seemed excited, and stopped sewing for a moment to speak.

"Tomorrow, in the morning, we will try it in the water and set the sail."

He picked up the sail and began to sew again, each rough, half-inch stitch taking almost a minute to make. Then Sister Durell came and stood beside me, watching him work, until I could bear it no longer and said "Goodbye," and turned away. She walked with me to the doorway of the ward.

"This is a wonderful thing for John. He has not long to live, and doing this work for you has made him very happy. He feels that he is needed, and that he has something to offer."

She looked sad for a moment and I suddenly realized what strength is needed to live the sorrows of so many people.

"It would almost break your heart to see some of these leper lads taking pains to do things with their hands, like tying a Scouting knot so that they can gain a proficiency badge; sometimes it takes half an hour to tie one knot." Then she brightened up.

"You'll see us this afternoon in all our glory—we're having a parade to celebrate Papua Day."

She had told me earlier of her own coming to Gemo. How one day, at school in England twelve thousand miles away, she had listened to a visiting missionary talk about Gemo Island, and had decided then and there to become a nurse so that she could go to work on the island.

During the rest of her school days, and in the years of her training in England as a nurse, she corresponded with Sister Fairhall who then lived on Gemo Island, and through her letters lived its life and created for herself a picture of the place and its people, so that she felt that she almost knew them by face as well as by name. Then when she had passed every examination she presented herself at the office of the London Missionary Society and said, "I am now ready to go to Gemo."

So she left the family home in suburban London and came by boat through the Mediterranean and Suez, called at Colombo and then Sydney, and passed through the beautiful Whitsunday Passage of the Great Barrier Reef, and so came to Port Moresby and Gemo Island.

"It was a wonderful trip," she said.

I thought of the climax to that long voyage. The inevitable disappointment she must have felt as she stood in the wheelhouse of the little launch that took her across to the island on the last stage of her journey. Seeing, finally, out of the sea haze the dun-colored, dusty, barren, arid island take shape, with its cluster of ugly huts and unkempt sheds, and the people waiting on the jetty like dumb survivors of some unknown catastrophe.

When I had asked her what she felt, she had replied, "It was just like coming home."

Toward midday the excitement and the activity began to build up all through the hospital wards and in the huts where the staff lived—children being washed and uniforms pressed, flags being shaken out, things borrowed and made do. Men and women I had become used to seeing as orderlies and patients, wearing old pants and singlets or their nursing uniforms, suddenly appeared in full Scouting rig, spotlessly clean and neatly pressed.

Somewhere a trumpet sounded, and a second later echoed back off the side of the mountain. A whistle blew, and gradually almost everybody on Gemo converged into the bare open space between the church and the Sisters' house and the sea, and began, with much chattering and pushing and changing places, to form up into troops.

Then they set off, with Sister Durell in the uniform of a Girl Guide leader at their head, followed by flag-bearers, bugler, and drummer, up the track behind the hospital, through the dusty dead kunai grass, up onto the bald stony pate of the mountain where the wind made the flags flap madly and all stopped for breath. And far down below, the sea surged slowly over the world to unknown places. They marched twice around the mountaintop and then down again, Sister Durell, Tau Boga, and his children, Kikeri, John Korabo, Poia, the old leper nurses (themselves lepers), and the orderlies from the tuberculosis wards; children too young, and men and women too old for Scouting elsewhere, but all in uniform; Boy Scouts, Girl Scouts, Sea Scouts, Brownies; almost the whole of Gemo. And at the end of the line, Toparua, the pathologist, carrying the little boy whose legs were in plaster, his white teeth shining in a wide smile out of his jet-black face.

I turned away weeping. Surely, in the whole wide world of Scouting, there is not and never has been a troop so odd and so marvelous. Only the very bad tuberculosis cases could not go on the march, and Sasa stayed with them and led them in the singing of marching songs until the troop came down from the mountain; then they joined all together in the recital of the promises and the saluting of the flag.

That night there was an impromptu concert outside the Sisters' house, with a band of guitars and ukeleles. Muri, one of the medical orderlies, danced a Kiwai dance and clowned it outrageously for the benefit of the children who rolled on the ground in agonies of ecstatic laughter. And Sasa and Poia taught the young girls and boys some dances of Samoa. And John Korabo sung a cowboy song while Toparua accompanied him on the guitar.

I sat on the veranda with Sister Phillips, and while I watched she told me a story.

"We had a patient here once," she said, "who stayed for five years, and was cured and could leave. We had a farewell party and there was much singing and hand-shaking and smiles of happiness—and a few tears. And in the morning the boat came and he went away.

"When he had gone it seemed different here on Gemo, and difficult for us all to settle down again straightaway. There were little jobs that he had always done, and now we had to find other people to do them. We missed him.

"Then three days later, he came back. Naturally we were surprised, and I asked him why he had come. He shook his head slowly and said, 'I didn't like it out there. I was alone. And a little afraid. So I came back. Because here there is a great umbrella of prayer, and I feel safe and sure.'"

Next day in Port Moresby I had sought out Dr. Wigley to thank him for arranging my visit to Gemo Island, and as he talked about it I began to understand more clearly what I had seen.

"Outsiders sometimes criticize our standards and our methods without understanding our problems. They just don't realize that we are dealing with people who think that sickness is a matter of magic and witchcraft, that it is something you can't fight, something that is going to make you die."

He looked impatient and a little testy.

"Shiny hospitals and modern clinical methods are fine, but they are not everything, and we have to give our patients much more than medicine. First we have to take away their fear and superstition, and with good sense and encouragement give them confidence in what we are trying to do, and help them to believe that they can get well."

Then he smiled.

"The women of Gemo are fine nurses, none better, and they do good work with what we give them in the way of drugs and equipment. But what matters most is the simple fact of them being there on the island, dispensing faith and affection which are more valuable in this case than all the medicines in the pharmacopoeia."

When I left him I went to the airways office and dispatched John Korabo's lakatoi to my godson in Sydney.

PART 2

One

Tourists, cruising the South Seas in luxury liners, stop for a single day at Port Moresby and there, as the travel brochure so simply puts it, they see "groups of bright, happy, stone age islanders, indolently whiling away the time, sunning themselves in chattering, gossiping groups."

Two miles out of the town, eastward, the visitors find a complete village of people who live on canoes. Here they can take photographs of Mekeo men with beehive hair styles, and of tattooed women wearing grass skirts and necklets of dogs' teeth. But they must pay, otherwise the models will turn away and refuse to be photographed. Then, because Port Moresby has nothing much more to offer except a beautiful cemetery of war graves, they take a bus ride into the hills, going as far as the road reaches in a matter of an hour or so.

Here they stand and look at New Guinea; a tangle of twisted limestone ranges lying like a massive dinothere asleep in the jungle. They take more pictures but it is all too big to fit into the aperture of a camera. And when they get back into the bus they tend to be silent, glad to be away from this stupendous and terrifying solitude. (There is a hotel a little way down the road.)

But the solitude is only apparent. In these mountains that form so fabulous a barrier between the narrow coastal plain and the high upland valleys of the interior, there live a hundred thousand people of the Goilala, the inland Kerema, and the Kukukuku tribes, of whom it has been said by officials who work among them, that they are "feared by neighbours and famed afar, even in these primitive lands, for their treacherous savagery, for their skill with bow and otherwise as bushmen, their forays for plunder and their murderous raids," and that "their general reputation includes killing as a means to win prestige among their fellows, and killing for the sheer joy of it."[1]

This is the name enjoyed today by tribes who live within an hour's flight of Port Moresby.

In the thin early morning sunlight I walked across the tarmac toward the Cessna. Fifty yards away airline officials and cargo boys were busy around the four-engined aircraft from Sydney, unloading, refueling, and loading again for the northward flight to Lae, on the other side of the island.

I, too, was bound for Lae, but in the Cessna and by a devious route, looking for locations among the mountains where we might film some of these savage people and so show them to delegates sitting in the United Nations Trusteeship Council in New York, debating the issue of self-government for the people of the Territory of Papua and New Guinea.

There were three of us, the pilot, an airfield inspector from the Department of Civil Aviation, and I. The inspector, a thin and freckled young man, intended to look at mountain airstrips, most of them made recently and not yet opened for general traffic, one of them still under construction.

Our pilot said that he was the only man in the country permitted to land on two of these airstrips, so remote, unknown, and makeshift are they. He had, he said, during their construction been dropping supplies to the patrol officer in charge of the work, and so knew where to find them and how to approach for landing. The inspector was to look at these strips and determine if they could be opened for general traffic.

We taxied out onto the strip and took to the air like a gnat, swung for a few seconds in a quivering arc, then straightened out and followed northwest above the coastal plain, keeping a course parallel between the Owen Stanley Range and the Coral Sea. After fifteen minutes we passed Manumanu village and in the hazy distance ahead could see the low lump of Yule Island sitting offshore. But before we reached it we turned north and headed into the

[1] Comments from the trial judge and government field officers in the case of Womeni-Nanagawo; heard at Kerema in the Gulf of Papua.

mountains, making for the pass that would let us through into the Goilala country, and the airstrip at Tapini.

Pointing into the mountains, we flew at the huge barrier of flat-bottomed cloud that, most days, lies along the top of the range, piled up by the trade winds to a height of sometimes fifteen thousand feet or more. But because it was early morning the clouds had not yet merged and settled on the mountains in a solid mass as they do later in the day. Then they hide the ground under a thick gray blanket and make landings impossible, because the only navigational aids are on the main air routes, and localized flying is done entirely by sight.

Now, it being not yet eight o'clock, we could weave among the huge thunderheads of cumulus cloud, seeing a pathway clear between peaks at each turn, the pilot looking above, below, and behind as he banked, not wishing to get trapped in this majestic maze where only local knowledge and an infallible memory are guard against the dangers. So, for safety's sake, most mountain flying is done in this early part of the day.

In a while the clouds thinned a little and the landscape opened out below. We could see fine yellow-red threads leading along many of the mountainsides, marking where the French missionaries from Yule Island have spun a tenuous network of bridle tracks up into the hinterland.

These are the narrow clambering ways by which the bishops of the mission, through these past eighty years, have made their annual pilgrimages, visiting each mission outpost every year, covering the tortuous circuit on foot and horseback in three flagellating months, to encourage their priests, hear their confessions, and celebrate Masses with high ceremony in districts where homicide is habitual.

Then suddenly we went into a funnel of cloud between two peaks, and emerging, found ourselves above a strange sight—a great cruciform church with a tall clock-tower crowned with a silvered steeple, set on the brink of a mountain pinnacle with the Bishop's track coming up to it on one side and going down deeply into the dark of a jungle-covered ravine on the other. And beside it another building almost as big, but without a spire; and this I knew to be the school.

We passed close enough to see that the clock in the tower showed

ten minutes to eight, and a swarm of small brown boys poured out
of the school building and spread over the playground, running
about excitedly; so we made one circuit of the steeple out of courtesy before going on our way. The name of this mission station is
Ononghe, and it is, like many of the other stations in this area,
situated with a Gallic aptitude for the fine dramatic gesture, on the
edge of an abyss.

We flew on, the altimeter showing seven thousand feet, and the
mountains on either side rising above us another two thousand or
thereabouts. A bridle track came climbing out of a valley and
leveled out along the ridge beside us, so that we were flying
parallel to it and could clearly see people walking along and pointing at us, perhaps half a dozen or so of them, going in our direction
toward the Government station at Tapini.

Ahead of us a great flat face of mountain walled off the end of
the valley in which we were flying, and it seemed that if we stayed
on course we must smash into it; but suddenly just when the
stomach contracts and the passengers' hands run with sweat, another narrow valley opens off to the left. The pilot banks into it
sharply, and you look across an enormous gorge into a little green
cul-de-sac with a cluster of timbered buildings at the far end, and
a few white markers that outline the landing strip.

The Cessna swoops steeply down like a predatory bird across this
great gorge, almost clipping its lip as the wheels touch just beyond
the ledge. The aircraft bumps and rumbles along the runway, disappearing for a moment into a dip, then struggles uphill against
the grade to stop outside the subdistrict office. This is the Tapini
strip and the Government station, center of civilization for the
Goilala people.

We could only stay a short time, long enough for the inspector
to take a walk along the strip for a routine check. The Government
officer, knowing that he was due, had a score of prisoners from his
jail at work on the strip, some planting grass roots on bare patches
to bind the soil, and others cutting the grass where it was long,
swinging at it singlehandedly with thin strips of sharpened steel
called serafs. This is the main occupation of prisoners on out-
stations, and where the crime rate is low the Government officer
sometimes finds it difficult to keep his strip in order.

I went into the office to see if there was any mail or messages for the patrol officer at Woitapi, our next calling point, less than fifteen minutes' flying time away, but two or three days' walk along the mission tracks, depending on the weather.

A map on the wall, stuck all over with colored pins, intrigued me, for I could think of no activity or administrative program which could be carried out from Tapini in so many places at once, and when the Government officer came back with the inspector I asked him what the pins indicated.

He said, "They represent the locations of murders committed in my bailiwick within the past five years—fifty-five of them reported and investigated. I imagine that there have been as many others unreported." He waved his hand vaguely in the direction of the airstrip where the prisoners were casually cutting grass. "There are five down there awaiting trial, and I'm going out next week to investigate another couple of rumors."

He sat on the edge of the table.

"Our problem in a primitive area like this, of course, is to get something going in the way of agricultural or community development that will keep them interested and occupied and give them something else to do besides chopping each other to pieces whenever they feel annoyed."

This is only one aspect of the problem. Another is the vexed question of finding appropriate punishment for murder in a community where this particular crime carries no stigma, where going to jail is, more often than not, regarded as achieving distinction, and where death by violence or any other means is accepted fatalistically.

In a very considerable part of New Guinea it would be an unusual family that did not include one murderer, or murder victim, among its members or close relations, and the Government is reluctant to hang people for actions not considered among themselves to be unusual. It prefers to make each murder trial an occasion to explain, ceremonially, the civilized theory of the sanctity of human life and the right of society to defend its members from private or unofficial violence.

So, when a primitive villager is found guilty of willful murder he is formally sentenced to death by the judge; but the sentence is then commuted and he is given a jail sentence of from two to four years which is served on a Government station. And here he is led to discover a new kind of existence.

For the first time in his life he gets fed regularly without personal effort and quickly puts on weight and achieves a shiny skin. His sores and skin diseases are attended to. He learns to keep clean, and to speak Pidgin English or Police Motu which, by itself, opens up a vast new world of knowledge and information. Where the facilities exist he is taught a trade, usually carpentry or one of the building trades. His social horizons are enlarged and he becomes an avid gambler at card games. When his sentence has expired he may get a job as cook-boy to one of the Government men, or as an interpreter, or even achieve the status of a truck driver.

If not, he returns to his village with a background of practical education, enhanced prestige, new possessions, and new ideas. Quite often such a man becomes a progressive element in his community; but sometimes he finds that village life has become intolerable and he pines for life on the Government station and so commits another crime so that he can go back to jail.

It was on this airstrip at Tapini that the Minister for Territories himself, visiting from Canberra, received a deputation of Goilala people who wished to protest against the white man's complicated system of law enforcement and justice.

They said that it was inconvenient and irritating, and in their opinion a waste of time for people like themselves, whose lives were fully taken up with domestic and tribal affairs to be forced to come to the Government station time and time again to repeat the same story about the same incident, and to answer foolish questions put by strangers about the actions of the accused and the deceased and the witnesses, relative to events that happened months previously; and then the upshot no more than a man going off to jail for a year or so to be fed up like a favorite pig, given a knife to cut grass, and then sent home again to his village. It was, they said, putting people to a great deal of trouble for nothing.

This head-on collision of different logics based on different immediate needs and beliefs explodes into conflicts of misunderstanding all over the wide field of social and domestic education, wherever modern man meets the primitive.

The Goilalas think it stupid of us that we defer to a team of highly favored witch-doctors who perform a tedious and elaborately dull ritual of inquisition whenever a man is murdered. They are at one with old Israel in maintaining that to claim an eye for an eye and a tooth for a tooth is more practical, expeditious, and emotionally satisfying than any meticulous search for motive or extenuation.

They are well aware of, but not disturbed by, the fact that the habit of arbitrary revenge is self-perpetuating; but until the Government provides a substitute diversion that requires a state of law and order for its successful undertaking, they see no reason to relinquish their own well-founded customs in favor of ours.

It is a dangerous and meddling impertinence to stamp out old customs, even if they include casual murder, without giving the deprived an opportunity and incentive to develop new ones. And to do this successfully demands an intensive study of the local requirements.

There was the case of the Goilala rats.

One day a lady came from Port Moresby bringing some illustrated posters. She belonged to the maternal and infant welfare service and she wished to sew the seeds of Modern Mothercraft among the women of this isolated and backward area.

The posters showed in a graphically clear way that dirt breeds disease. That mosquitoes make people ill with fever. That flies contaminate food and so make babies die. One poster showed a rat nibbling at stray scraps of food left lying about the house by a village slattern. A complementary illustration showed a good housewife collecting into a single heap every food scrap in sight, presumably for disposal. A feature of the layout was one fat and arrogant rat dramatically dominating a corner of the poster.

The people of the Goilala like rats. Rats form an important part of their diet which is otherwise low in protein, and they spend much time hunting for rats to eat. It had never previously occurred to them that one could, as it were, raise rats domestically for food by collecting all available food scraps into one place, thereby saving the rats the labor of scavenging and, at the same time, developing a simple habit-pattern in their feeding that would make them easier to catch.

The people were grateful to the Government for sending this lady to show them such a simple and effective domestic trick. It did not cross their minds that she had meant to teach them how to eliminate one of their principal sources of food supply. Such a thought is inconceivable among people who lose many of their old people and young children by death through starvation at certain seasons.

The airstrip inspector came back to say that he was ready to leave and go on to Woitapi, so we got back into the aircraft and flew on again, like a lonely and determined bird, across a continuing confusion of mountain crags and razor-edged ridges. And looking down it seemed impossible that there could be, in this tangled landscape, a patch of flat land big enough to turn into an aircraft landing place, however makeshift.

But ten minutes after takeoff we dropped nonchalantly over the lip of a ridge and looked into a little gully, blocked off at one end by the inevitable mountain but clear at the other, giving an open approach. And in the bottom of the gully we could see a red-brown scar in the earth, swarming with little black dots like an ant bed that has been stirred with a stick.

The pilot muttered, then banked the aircraft and circled over the approach, and as we turned we could see the black dots ebbing swiftly toward the edges of the strip, so he turned once more and throttled back almost to stalling point so that the Cessna seemed to flutter down clumsily, like an uncertain butterfly landing on a windblown flower.

As soon as the wheels touched the ground the Cessna bumped roughly on the uneven surface of the strip, and there was tenseness about the pilot's face as he urged the aircraft quickly up toward the patrol post—a cluster of grass huts on the edge of the jungle where the strip comes to an end. And as we raced along we were chased by fifteen hundred screaming, near-naked savages with matted hair and mud-spattered legs and arms, who charged in upon the aircraft with their arms held high above their heads, leaping and jumping and yelping with wild excitement. For this was the first time that the big bird had landed among them.

They came after us in a mass, and as we lost speed they caught up and surged toward the Cessna in a swirling whirlpool of humanity, not understanding that the first man to approach the aircraft from the front, before it stopped, would be decapitated. I felt frightened.

Through the window we could see the young patrol officer

gesticulating frantically and shouting instructions to his native police to keep the crowd out of danger, but although the policemen struck out with sticks and fists they were overwhelmed and carried on the crest of the crowd toward us, struggling to keep their feet, and command of the situation. The pilot swung the Cessna around roughly until the nose pointed away from the mass of men, and cut the engine quickly so that the propeller tick-tocked to a sudden stop.

Immediately they were upon us, beating the fusilage with their hands, pressing their faces against the window and screaming meaninglessly with excitement—a thousand or more men making a noise that drummed inside the ears and skull like the roaring of sea surf when a swimmer is tumbled under it. And when the pilot opened his window to shout them back the sound that burst in upon us struck the drums of my ears with a sharp pain, and nothing that I had heard before could compare with it.

I knew that we need have no fear of active violence, yet there was something fundamentally fearful about the primitive intensity with which these excited, unkempt little mountain men, near-naked and dirty, with misshapen faces, looked up at us with wild, staring eyes, their heads held back and mouths shouting hoarse, inarticulate cries as they beat upon the aircraft with their hands; and we immobilized inside.

Few of them wore clothing of any sort—only a girdle of pandanus leaf wrapped around the waist, drawn down between the legs and tucked in at the back. Their skins were dry and cracked and caked with mud, their gums stained blood red, teeth black with betel nut juice. Their features, ugly and sullen in repose, seemed madly angry in their excitement.

We sat there, in a caul of aluminum and perspex, unable to get out, the pilot fretful over the safety of his plane, watching the patrol officer push his way through toward us, and after him, a quiet, slow-moving, sturdy man in rough and worn khaki. The shouting crowd parted to let this man through and he spoke to them, smiling as he passed. I had not seen him before but recognized him as the missionary priest Père Gremaud because I know his brothers, the one at Yule Island and another in Port Moresby, both also mission priests. And they are all much alike. Now I noticed that many of these screaming primitives wore crucifixes and medallions around their necks, indicating that they are part of Père Gremaud's flock, and some of their children were probably among those we saw running out of the schoolhouse when we flew around the church tower at Ononghe.

For fifty years the missionaries have worked here, patiently trying to teach these people the "Peace of Jesus" that Henri Verjus first established down on the fever-ridden coast before the beginning of the century. Their bridle tracks radiating from Yule Island into the mountains have been, until now, the only thread connecting the Goilala with our civilization. Their churches, perched on precipices, and their village schools have given these people their only inkling of a different and more rewarding kind of life than the one they know.

Until the Government station was opened at Tapini a few years ago the Australian administration had no way of providing health and education services, or of keeping law and order in these parts, except through the missionaries. Now, this new airstrip brings Woitapi, in emergency, within fifteen minutes of Tapini where there is a Government doctor, hospital, and school.

The shouting stopped and the men drew back a little and watched while patrol officer and priest let us out of our captivity. The pilot stepped down and eyed the mass of men with professional hostility and asked that a police guard be placed around his plane, and as soon as the formal niceties were observed he excused himself and, walking slowly around, tested every part for possible damage.

The inspector took surveying gear from the aircraft to check levels on the work already done, and to peg out other sections for excavation or filling. The patrol officer went with him, and Père Gremaud and I walked together across to the hut and sat on the rickety veranda.

He looked up at the sky and said that the clouds were settling down early on the mountains and that if the inspector had much work to do we might not get out today, but would have to stay over until tomorrow. The pilot was watching the sky too, and in a while he called a policeman and asked him to bring some heavy logs to which the aircraft could be tethered. Then he joined us on the veranda and called to the cook-boy to make a cup of coffee.

Most of the men had gone back to work, but some of their leaders still stood around the Cessna, whispering to each other, while others, including a few women with net bags of sweet potato hanging across their backs, came as close as the policeman would allow, and crouching down tried to determine the sex of the machine, still believing it to be a bird. Then, prompted by her companions, one of the women placed a heap of food in front of it and stood back and waited to see if it would eat.

I asked Père Gremaud if he thought that the strip would speed up the process of civilizing the Goilala people, and he grinned and said that this was something he didn't know, but he did know that instead of walking for eight days to visit Yule Island for the next retreat he would now be able to travel in comfort and be there in less than an hour.

Two very old men stood apart from the rest, one of them, toothless and bent, leaning on a long, crook-handled bamboo cane, the mark of his chieftainship. He was, said Père Gremaud, the owner of the land now being converted into an airstrip, and the leading chief in this part of the Goilala. The other ancient wore a wreath of cassowary feathers and nothing else, and carried a small string bag containing charms and materials for working magic, being the local sorcerer and rainmaker. Together they regarded the plane with the blank sagacity of important people who can find no explanation for phenomena that occur, but who need to appear cognizant for reasons of prestige. Occasionally they whispered together, venturing tentative opinions without committing themselves. Later they would take the credit for the day's events.

We had our coffee, then walked down the strip to watch the work and to find out how long the inspector would be. The tribesmen were laboring vigorously, excited and stimulated by the arrival of the aircraft, seeing in its coming a justification of their months of labor. Some groups stood on a bank, levering out the high sides of the strip with long and pointed poles; others shoveled the mullock into roughly constructed troughs made from oil drums cut lengthwise and tied to long handles so that they could be carried on the shoulders of two men like stretchers. As the troughs were filled other men ran with them across the strip and emptied them upon the ground to build up the lower levels.

The pilot stopped to discuss technical matters with the inspector and the patrol officer, and Père Gremaud and I walked a little way and stood on a hill overlooking the scene. We saw the brown-red scar of earth against a vast and vivid background of green, the hundreds of men moving about and the sound of their singing, the tiny yellow plane and three young white men clustered around a tripod. And nearby, a makeshift compound of long and low grass shelters to house the workers who had come from distant villages.

What did it mean? How do we justify our laboring to lead these people out of their own life-pattern of individually directed violence, conditioned by environment, into our own confusion of impersonal and illogical enmities and hates, and our up-to-date brand of intertribal warfare waged on a scale undreamed of by these simple primitives? Should we, perhaps, be more modest in the assessment of our particular kind of progress? And is the so-called sense of duty which we assume toward these people genuine and magnanimous, or should we admit that we are simply driven to it by history and pride?

Père Gremaud looked up at the sky and held out his hand. There were a few spots of rain and he said, "You won't get out of here today with your plane." I thought he sounded a little smug.

It rained gently until late afternoon, then cleared, but ragged clouds hung on the hillsides and it was too late to go on. Meantime we cooked a packet of deep-frozen meat that we had brought with us, and vegetables from the patrol officer's garden. And the inspector went to his plane and brought back a bottle of rum so that the afternoon passed pleasantly.

At four o'clock the patrol officer switched on his radio to listen to the national news from Sydney. Through the usual screen of static and atmospheric interference we heard the young man in the studio unemotionally reporting border warfare somewhere in Southeast Asia.

A group of near-naked Goilala women belonging to the cook and his assistant came creeping in through the back door of the hut and stood huddled together, toes crossed and arms folded over their breasts, close-hugging themselves as they listened, uncomprehending.

Four of them gazed mutely at the radio, wide-eyed with awe. Two others whispered surreptitiously, one of them guardedly tracing with a finger the passage of the voice along the aerial wire outside, down into the house and so into the machine. The other woman followed the descent with her eyes, then drew her breath and turned her head away swiftly to hide her face from these mysteries.

The two old men, chief and rainmaker, appeared at the door to grin and listen. This is white man's magic. Sorcery of such high order that our seeming indifference confuses them. In their community the Spirits are all-powerful and must be treated with respect, and continuously placated. When the radio is turned off they sigh and go away shaking their heads.

Two

I was very cold, and slept badly. From a daytime temperature of well over eighty the thermometer had dropped more than forty degrees during the night. My bed of saplings had a thick canvas tent-fly for a mattress and there were three woolen blankets to cover me, but I was still cold. I should have spread a thin layer of kunai grass between the saplings and the tent-fly to keep out the damp that rises from the ground. At five thousand feet above sea level it is nearly always cold at night, even this close to the equator.

Soon after daylight, while we were having breakfast, two young men came to say that their father had died during the night and that they must bury him and could not work on the strip today. Whenever the weather turns suddenly cold, many old people die in the mountains, for they are weakened by malnutrition and greatly susceptible to influenza and pulmonary diseases.

We took off at seven o'clock and crossed the main range, out of Papua and into New Guinea, through a pass at ten thousand feet, leaving behind the Goilalas and coming over the country of the Kukukuku people, where there is another newly established patrol post and airstrip called Kainteba.

Patrol Officer Tom Steen, a slender young man of studious bearing in spite of soiled shirt and shorts and heavy walking boots, seemed pleased to see us. We had brought mail, and although most of it was official and would mean nights of dreary statistical desk labor under an oil lamp, there were also letters from Australia. In any case we were his first visitors for many weeks, and the pilot had thoughtfully brought him two loaves of fresh bread as a gift.

The airstrip at Kainteba has the steepest gradient of any strip in New Guinea—at its sharpest one foot in seven. There is a high hump in the middle so that if you stand at one end you cannot see an aircraft on the ground at the other. Apart from that it is fairly average and neither more nor less dangerous than a score of others similarly situated.

The airstrip inspector climbed out of the Cessna and, looking around, sighed. It was clear at mere sight that if he applied all the laws of his department to the airstrip at Kainteba it would be closed immediately as failing to meet any of the elementary standards of aviation safety. Yet he knew that it could not be done without official embarrassment all around.

The Australian Government has said that it hopes to bring the whole of the territory under administrative control by the end of 1964. Whatever the fine definition of "control" might be it certainly requires that a Government station should be established within reasonable reach of every section of the population, if only to maintain law and order and to provide speedy help in times of urgent necessity.

We walked across to the patrol officer's grass hut for a cup of coffee, Tom Steen and I together. The pilot and the inspector came behind, slowly, pointing out to each other possible improvements to the airstrip, noting how the mountains, crowding in, caused wind chutes that made landing hazardous under some conditions. They realized, as they talked, that the work of improvement called for professional technicians and heavy earth-moving equipment, not an uncertain work force of jungle primitives armed with digging sticks.

But there are no roads into these places. The airstrip site is chosen by a patrol officer after he has walked for weeks in these wild, upended desolations, and there is no other way into them except by walking. The airstrip is makeshift. It can be nothing else until proper equipment can be brought in, and it can only be brought in by air. So the problem revolves upon itself in a cycle of frustration and compromise that will only be broken when the Australian Government or some even higher and more affluent authority decides that the Kukukuku and other isolated groups in New Guinea are to be civilized regardless of cost.

There is of course the possibility that these almost impregnable mountains might one day soon become so strategically important (lying in the arc of Southeast Asia) that the Kukukuku will have to be resettled elsewhere to make room for the installation of some of the complex machinery of our own kind of intertribal fighting.

The coffee was drunk quickly and the inspector and the pilot went out again to consider the strip. Tom called his house-boy and asked him to fix a bed for the inspector because he would need to stay for a day or two to make some kind of survey. Then he filled my cup again and asked if I had any special reason for coming to Kainteba.

I said that I was always looking for new locations which might illustrate phases of development in New Guinea. In addition I wanted to follow up a story that, for me, had begun a few weeks again in Sydney. He looked surprised and uncomprehending. I said, "The Queen versus Wendo of Didima." He said, "Oh," and began to make more coffee.

It is unlikely that Queen Elizabeth has heard of Wendo or, for that matter, of Didima, which consists of five grass huts huddled on a narrow strip of stamped red earth, on a ridge in the high middle of New Guinea. And, presumably, she doesn't know what Wendo is no longer at Didima but is in jail at Kerema, even though she is technically responsible for his welfare, having inherited the obligation from her great-great grandmother Victoria who, in 1884, had promised that she would guard and watch over all of the people of Papua.

But it was in the Sydney *Morning Herald* quite plainly, under the heading, "Proceedings Listed in the Law Courts Today." And there were three periwigged judges keeping the Queen's promise, aided by learned advocates and junior council, clerks, shorthand writers, and all the paraphernalia of the law, discussing legalistically whether or not Wendo of Didima a Kukukuku, and others, had been illegally found guilty of participation in the willful murder of twenty-seven men, women, and children of the neighboring village of Yaba.

No question arose of whether or not Wendo and his friends had committed the crime for which they had been tried and found guilty by the judge in Papua—the facts were indisputable. But whether or not they had been found guilty by a proper following of the precisely established processes of British law—that was the question exercising the Queen, through her judges and council in the High Court of Australia.

Wendo himself, cutting grass on Kerema airstrip, was not aware that he and the Queen were in dispute over this or any other matter. He had quite enjoyed the murders, although the trial had been distinctly a bore and utterly confusing. But I had gone to the court and had been fascinated by its procedures. Then because Didima is but a mile or two from Kainteba I had taken the opportunity to call in and see the kind of country in which these events took place, but more importantly to see Tom Steen, who had been a member of the patrol that had come to arrest Wendo and those of his friends who had accompanied him to Yaba, two days away from Didima, openly and without much subterfuge, to butcher the inhabitants of that village.

After the arrests and conveyance to the jail at Kerema, Tom had come back to establish this patrol post among the Kukukuku people, and to build the switchbacked airstrip, as an earnest gesture of the goodwill and best intentions of the Government.

He got up and went to a new steel filing cabinet. It looked oddly out of place in this rough bush house built of unplaned timber, with plaited walls of pandanus leaf and a roof of kunai grass, and cluttered inside with the furniture and accessories of a newly established outback patrol post.

While he searched in the cabinet I looked around and made a mental inventory of galvanized iron carrying boxes, ropes, axes, shovels, gasoline lamps, bags of salt for trading, a radio transceiver, cases of tinned food, boots, rough cupboards made of packing cases, packets of nails, gun cartridges, an Australian flag pinned to the wall, a photograph of the Queen, and two guns slung under it; and in a little alcove his bunk covered with a skin rug, and a side table with books and family pictures.

He found his diary covering the period of the Yaba investigation, and thumbed through it, looking for a sketch map of the area. He found it and brought it over to me.

"Here we are now, at Kainteba." He put his finger on the spot. "A little way north, up here just across the border as far as we can tell, is Didima, and all around us are the other villages that were involved, seven all told not counting Yaba which is down here to the south, about two days easy walk.

"Didima is the village farthest from Yaba, no more than fifteen miles as the crow flies, probably less, yet the men of Didima had never before been to Yaba, which shows how isolationist they are, and how discouraging and difficult the country is to traverse."

He left the map with me and went back to his chair under the flag, and for a while we went over the story together, myself asking questions where I couldn't follow the sequence of events, and he looking up his notes to refresh his memory, or staring up toward the roof while he thought back on particular incidents.

While we were talking a Kukukuku man and two women came and stood at the bottom of the steps, looking up into the house. The women carried bags of vegetables, and one had a baby on her hip. The man was unarmed, having left his bow and arrows at the edge of the station, hidden in the grass; he would pick them up on the way back, being forbidden to carry weapons onto the station, but not daring to travel without them.

They stood without speaking until we looked up, and then the man's eyes flickered from the food to Tom, and Tom nodded, but no word passed. This is one of the earliest stages in contact and pacification—encouraging villagers to come into the station with vegetables for sale.

He drew my attention to ugly sores on the child, and then called to the house-boy and told him to buy the vegetables with giri giri shell, and afterwards to take the group to the medical orderly to get treatment for the baby. It would, said Tom, almost certainly be a case of yaws, and a few shots of penicillin would clear it up quickly. Then the medical orderly would acquire an easy reputation for making magic and more people would come to the station for treatment.

The interruption reminded Tom that he had other visitors, and he excused himself, saying that the inspector might want to talk to him on the airstrip; so I said that if he would leave the diaries I could, with them and the other information he had given me, spend a useful half hour filling out the Yaba story. So he brought the diaries across, then went out quickly and left me.

The Yaba story is a simple one, motivated largely, like most primitive killings, by resentment, jealousy, and the desire for revenge. In fact, the planning and carrying out of the Yaba massacre provide practically a textbook illustration of the pattern of traditional intertribal killings in New Guinea.

The trouble is that there is never any real starting point. The

Kukukuku, like other mountain tribes, are a fragmented people, split into hundreds of small hamlet and clan groups of less than fifty individuals, sometimes twenty or even fewer, and with a history of interclan feuding that goes back for generations. They are pathologically insular and independent, but partly nomadic, so that the seeds of new feuds are being continuously sown over a wide area.

But the Yaba story can conveniently begin with a man from the village of Mambanya, which is closest to Yaba of all the villages concerned, who came one day to visit a marriage relative at Didima; and they sat around the fire and talked.

In the evening the Didima host cooked mareta, a pine-like fruit which turns blood-red when cooked and looks like a thick crimson stew. A medical officer once told me, on patrol, that it appears to have a narcotic or alcoholic effect on those who eat much of it.

During the evening, while they were eating, the visitor from Mambanya remarked that his leg was sore from a spear wound received in a fight, some time ago, between men of his village and some men of Yaba. He described the fight and said that some of the Mambanya men had been killed, and that the Yabas had taken possession of a piece of Mambanya land that had many good areca nut palms on it, and some mareta trees, and a stream where eels could almost always be caught.

In the morning the visitor and his host went to another village where the story of the fight was repeated, and there was much rough talk about the troublemaking people of Yaba, and somebody said that they should gather some men together from villages round about and go to Yaba "to eat pig."

Now this phrase is used as a kind of naïve doubletalk to mask a more sinister suggestion, and to those who know what is behind the invitation it can mean, "Let us go to Yaba and kill them all," while to the timid and those who for one reason or another do not wish to be involved, it can simply mean that a routine pig-buying expedition is proposed.

During the next day or two there was much movement between the seven villages, some of the men staying at other villages and talking long into the night before returning to their homes the next day.

Wendo was one of the Didima men who took part in some of this talk, but he was not an important man or a leader and only became,

as it were, the personal opponent of the Queen because he happened to be first on the list of witnesses at the trial. Thus, for-
tuitously, do some people become either famous or infamous.

His story was that he was sitting quietly by his fire one morning,
round about this time, when some other members of his clan passed
by, saying that they were going downriver to a village known to
the Mambanya people, where they could buy pigs.

They had some of their women with them to carry food for the
journey, and this seemed sufficient evidence that the mission was
to be a peaceful one, although sometimes the presence of a few
women in a raiding party is a calculated subterfuge designed to
allay suspicion.

So Wendo joined the expedition, and reaching the neighboring
village of We-a found men of the seven villages, including some
of the headmen, assembled together and talking about the expedition to buy pigs.

The next morning they all set out, about forty grown men (the
exact number never came out at any of the court proceedings),
four boys, two young and unmarried women, and some wives—a
formidable party. All of the men carried bows and arrows and axes,
and some had knives as well. And they all wore their traveling capes
of beaten bark, that hang from a topknot of hair and reach down
beyond the buttocks, and are worn to keep out the rain which sometimes continues in the mountains for days in a steady drizzle.

They walked for two days, camping along the way, and on the
second night built their shelters within easy walking distance of
Yaba village.

In the morning it was wet and cold, but before sunrise the leading man of the Mambanya group, he who had the aching leg and
whose name is Kaiwetika, woke them all up and addressed to them
a formal invitation in these words, "The Yaba people have been
killing us at Mambanya, will you all come down with us and eat
pig?" There could now be no further doubt about the real purpose
of the expedition.

The men picked up their weapons and the women their string
bags, and the party moved on to Yaba, coming in sight of it just before daylight, which is the accepted time for a surprise attack. Then
leaving the women and small boys on a little mound close by, the
men moved into the village, taking with them the two bigger boys

who were to be given their first practical lesson in tribal murder-ing.

There were six houses in the Yaba village, and the raiders divided into six groups and came and stood, one group outside each house, and called out to the people inside that they had come to buy pigs.

Now they could not simply break into the houses and slaughter the people inside before they woke up, because the Kukukuku houses are carefully constructed in such a way as to make this im-possible; in fact, they are built precisely to cope with this kind of situation.

The high, conical roof reaches down almost to the ground, and its framework of lathes forms a cage that has only one narrow en-trance into it, about eighteen inches wide, which is hidden by over-hanging thatch.

This entrance leads into an interior walkway that surrounds an inner room where the people live. The walls of this room are four or five feet high, and the only entrance is on the opposite side of the house to the exterior door; and it can be blocked off with wooden slats.

This means that anybody entering a Kukukuku house must bend down to come through the exterior door, then walk around the nar-row corridor fully exposed to attack from over the top of the inner wall, before coming to the inside doorway which is blocked. Visitors, then, whether friends or foes, must stand outside and declare them-selves before coming in.

So the raiders did this, and called out that they were from Didima and other villages, not making mention of Mambanya, and that they had brought axes, salt, giri giri shell, razor blades, cassowary wing-feathers, and lap-lap cloth to exchange for pigs.

Some of them, including the headman from We-a, also said that they had brought "talk" from the Government and had authority to give a Government "hat" to the leading man of Yaba, and to shake hands on behalf of the Government as a sign that fighting must cease; and they added that when this was done they could all sit down together and eat pig.

It is difficult to know exactly what transpired, but the people of five houses, men, women, and children, came out, and the raiders lined them up, explaining that the Government did it this way to count the people in each village. And each Yaba man was held by two of the raiders.

In the sixth house there were two brothers, Hapigau and Watama, with their four women and two children, and the older brother was suspicious and called out, "Are you white men that you come at this hour and ask for pigs?"

And he picked up his bow, and an arrow, and looking out saw his friends standing in line and the leader of the raiding party haranguing them. So, whether in anger and ill-temper, or with deliberate murder in his heart, he fired an arrow and hit one of the raiders in the head.

Then the leader of the raiding party gave a signal by striking a piece of timber with his ax, and the massacre began, men being struck down savagely with axes where they stood, or shot in the stomach with arrows, and women hacked down, or shot as they ran away.

The Yaba men in the sixth house barricaded their door, but the raiders set fire to the house and stood back waiting for them to run out.

In a while, when their skin began to burn, the two men made a bolt for it, followed by the women. The men came out first and ran toward the river and the shelter of the high rushes, and although the raiders fired at them with arrows, and hit them several times, they escaped and lay hiding. But the women, handicapped with children, were caught and killed with ax blows.

When everybody in the village was dead the raiders ransacked the houses and then withdrew, and after singing a victory chant a little way along the road, they visited the people of Mambanya to assure them that they could now reclaim their trees and their eel waters; then they made their way home to their various villages.

That, in substance, is what appears to have happened.

Later that morning a young man named Pungai-Wagabu came to Yaba from yet another neighboring village to visit his aunt, one of the women of Yaba, by name Naga. He picked his way through the carnage until he found her, chopped about the head, with her skull split, and her suckling child lying dead a few yards away.

He went into the bush and brought long sticks, and going to his aunt's house he pushed them through the roof thatch until they rested on the inside wall, and so made a burial platform upon which he put the bodies of his aunt and her husband, with the baby between them, for this is the burial custom of the Kukukuku.

Then the two men who had escaped, though wounded, returned, and with Wagabu's help they made platforms for all the bodies. Then they smashed the cooking pots and bows and arrows and other personal articles belonging to the dead ones as a mark of respect, before going home with Wagabu.

It was a month before the "talk" reached the Government station at Menyamya across the main range to the north, and then the Government officer, busy with other things, could not come but sent a small police patrol under Constable (First Class) Gaigo, himself a Kukukuku, to investigate. Nine days later Gaigo returned and told what he had seen. A village deserted, one house burned down, and twenty-seven bodies laid out on burial platforms.

The Government officer spoke on the radio to his headquarters on the coast and reported what Constable Gaigo had told him, and the news was relayed to Port Moresby; and from here directions were given that two patrols should set out immediately—one from Menyamya in the north because it was closer to Yaba than any other Government station, and the other from Kerema on the south coast, because Yaba is in the Kerema administrative district. Tom Steen came up with the party from Kerema. They followed the Tauri River and came to Yaba in two weeks, by which time the massacre was two months old.

Climbing up the outside wall of the house in which Naga lay with her husband and child, and looking through a window made by Constable Gaigo on his earlier visit, they saw two bodies, almost reduced to skeletons, but showing such signs of violence as cleft and broken skulls; and between the adults a glutinous mess that bore no relationship to anything.

The two parties joined forces to establish a camp, and set about rounding up the suspected murderers and likely witnesses, most of whom had taken to the bush as news of the patrol seeped through to the villages. A plane came out from Lae to drop supplies, and when it looked as though the search would be a long one, Tom took a party of carriers and police over to Menyamya for additional supplies.

After a month they had collected thirty prisoners and witnesses, and while the officer in charge of the expedition, Assistant District

Officer Carey, remained to round up other suspects and witnesses, and to conduct coroner's investigations, Tom Steen led these prisoners and witnesses down to Kerema.

It was an eventful journey. Many of the carriers were reluctant volunteers and gave trouble, dumping their loads on the side of the track and making off into the jungle. There was also much sickness among them and progress was slow. Heavy rains brought the rivers down in flood so that they were held up for some days at the Tauri crossing, being unable either to bridge or ford it because of the force of the water coming down from the mountains.

Arrangements had been made by radio for the party to be picked up by a Government trawler at the mouth of the river, so that the prisoners could be taken to Kerema by sea for the last stage of the journey. But when the Kukukuku men saw the ocean for the first time many of them panicked and had to be bound and carried in canoes out to the ship.

Meantime the officials in Port Moresby had decided that a permanent patrol post should be set up among the people of the Didima-Yaba area, and Kainteba was selected because it had just enough flat land for a temporary airstrip and had been used for the airdrop of supplies from Lae. A young patrol officer was sent up from Kerema to start the post, but was drowned trying to swim the river.

When all the prisoners and witnesses had been collected and brought to Kerema, a judge came out from Port Moresby.

Wendo was the first of the accused to be cross-examined by the prosecuting counsel. When asked what part he had played in the massacre he replied, "It was raining and I stayed in the camp near the fire. I did not see anything."

His friend, Yamigoto, went one better, saying, "While the killing was on I ran to a house and went inside and sat by the fire because I was cold."

One after the other the accused denied taking any part in the murders, for the Kukukuku are fine liars.

"I was afraid and ran away," said one of them, "and I saw nothing."

A fourth said decisively, "I had to build a house so I left and went home."

The man who was the headman of his own village, and who had

pretended that he was empowered to speak to the people of Yaba on behalf of the Government, washed his hands unctuously of the whole affair saying, "I saw a man chase a boy and kill him, but I turned my head away because I thought that, being a headman, I should not see such things."

Another, even more hypocritical, declared that he had recognized a distant relation among the men of Yaba lined up for slaughter, and felt so sorry for him that he went down to the river and stayed there weeping with compassion.

But some, not willing to belittle themselves in their own eyes and in the eyes of the world, readily admitted to their part, so that a man named Danamo said, "I saw Akwaiabu hit a man with an ax, and I held another man and killed him with my knife."

And Kaiwetika, who because of his sore leg had started the whole affair, acknowledged that he had shot an arrow into a Yaba man, but added cautiously that he did not have his ax with him, and that the man was finished off by somebody else, so that he could not fairly claim the victim.

Several sought a middle course, acknowledging that killings had, indeed, taken place and that they were present, but that their own contributions were on a minor scale; so that a man named Yapmato could say, quite casually, "I was standing by the fire drying myself, because it was raining, and a man said to me, 'Have you come to kill men of Yaba or to sit over a fire?' So when I saw a young boy come running I shot him through the neck with an arrow. But he was only little."

Another claimed that he was on the outskirts of the melee and taking no part until a young lad ran between the legs of the fighting men and came toward him, so said the man, "I chased him and killed him with my knife, and then went up on the hill and watched."

All this came out at the trial held at Kerema twelve months after the event, and although there was a great deal of conflicting evidence, and the memory of much detail had been fogged, and the principal witnesses had become bored with the whole matter and gone quietly off home, the judge nevertheless felt that he could justly convict Wendo and twenty-six others.

Another five were found not guilty on the grounds of insufficient evidence of identification, and it was generally thought that there were probably others who had not been charged at all because they could not be found.

It seemed a just and fair termination of the matter from a legal point of view, and a welcome end from the Kukukuku point of view to twelve months of utter and incomprehensible confusion and inconvenience, during which time they had been key figures in a coroner's inquiry, a magistrate's hearing, and a sitting of the High Court of Papua and New Guinea, while at home in their villages the whole life cycle of gardening, food gathering, and ritual feasting had been disrupted.

Those found guilty were sentenced to four years in corrective custody, a decision challenged by the defense counsel and so referred to the learned judges in Sydney. Those found not guilty were taken back to their villages where they still brood on the mysteries of the white man's ways, and the fearful wonder of the great salt water that begins at the edge of the world.

Three

I put my notebook away and went out into the sunlight to join the others. There was a fourth man with them, short, wiry, and tousle-haired, dressed like a laborer. He introduced himself as Father Fournier from Yule Island, recently arrived at Kainteba to start a mission station and a school. We talked for a few minutes about mutual acquaintances in the mission. Then the pilot asked me if I was ready to move on. We took off, leaving the airstrip inspector behind.

A small group of Kukukuku stood at the side of the strip and watched us go. They seemed like the lonely remnants of some prehistoric race watching with dull and uncomprehending eyes the busy and inexplicable activities of invaders from another planet.

The Cessna climbed quickly, the pilot weaving between peaks and pinnacles with the insouciance of a man driving a car through familiar city streets, skirting so close to mountainsides that the bark pattern of trees could be clearly seen.

After ten minutes or thereabouts, at nine thousand feet, we slid through a pass with peaks towering away on either side, and looked on the northern fall of New Guinea, range after range dropping away to the edge of the Bismarck Sea and the earth's equator. We had a half hour flying now to Menyamya, the Government sub-district station and main center of operations among the Kukukuku of the northern fall.

If anything, the country is more savage and bare on this side than it is on the southern fall. It looks even more cruel and unyielding, the shapes more grotesque and unnatural, more oddly juxtaposed than any others in this curious land.

The air is full of gusts and cross-currents and eddies, downdrafts and upward winds that fill the valleys and curl up over ridges in invisible waves, so that the aircraft, flying close to the contour of the earth, seems to ride the wind like an excited horse, soaring over sharp limestone lips as a hunter leaps a stark stone wall, to plunge forward again and swoop down long slopes.

It is exhilarating if you like this kind of excitement and dynamism, but I hate it, and long to be down on the ground again, and wonder how my guardian angel likes tagging along behind, hanging onto his halo. And how long my luck will last. Of the many single-engined aircraft in which I have ridden like this, four have crashed within the last fifteen months in the mountains of New Guinea. I am too timid for this kind of existence.

Down below Aseki comes into view, a tiny settlement as far to the north of the main range as Kainteba is to the south. But access from the coast is easier on this northern fall, and alongside the airstrip is a solid wooden house with a garden around it, and two good school buildings close by. And at the top of the strip, on a little hill, a new Government station is being built.

Lutheran missionaries live in the house beside the strip, a man and his wife, Germans as are many if not most of the Lutheran missionaries in this country. For years they have been the only non-natives in an area that contains about ten thousand people. The school beside the house is staffed with New Guinea teachers trained at their college on the coast.

This is difficult country and the people are hard to pacify and bring to a state of tractability. For fifty years white men have been trying to make friends with the Kukukuku, crossing this terrible country with exploratory patrols or prospecting parties. Time and time again white men have quietly boasted that they have established a good understanding with the mountain men, and time and time again these same white men have been treacherously ambushed and attacked. Some have escaped with arrow wounds, and others have been found in deserted camps with their heads smashed in by stone clubs. There are men still working in New Guinea who carry scars of old wounds received from the Kukukuku when they were young men patrolling or prospecting in these mountains.

Sitting up here in the Cessna, remote from the fantastic unrealities of modern politics, I think of the many men who sit in the council rooms of the United Nations and mouth words that are prepared for them thousands of miles away in their chancelleries.

When they speak of self-government for the people of New Guinea they use phrases that have no meaning in these mountains. Their appetites for trivial political victories blind them to reality. As my grandmother used to say, "Their eyes are bigger than their bellies." One such man said to me in New York, when tiredness and whisky had loosened his tongue, "I have been saying these things for so long that I almost believe them."

The Kukukuku have had self-government for generations, but they kill each other viciously and without excuse. They murder children and babies with less compunction than they massacre adults, without sentiment. Even so they are not yet ready to face today's world: they would be staggered by the magnitude of our depravity. Before they can fully imitate modern man they need to learn a little more. It would not be fair to pit their bow-and-arrow level of development and mentality against the prospect of annihilation by modern methods. It would be cowardly and in-human to give them self-government—as it was in the Congo.

We left Aseki behind, and for a while the country remained wildly rugged. But gradually the mountains began to fall away a little and the landscape looked smoother and more rounded, with fewer jagged outlines and palisades of sharply eroded rock, though the ridges remained razor-sharp and fell away sheer.

Then the horizons grew wider and the valleys more open, and instead of matted jungle the landscape became a long, untimbered vista of green-grassed kunai slopes, showing where year after year the land had been burned bare by incendiary hunters, and leached, so that nothing but thin, sickly kunai grows there any more.

In one of these open and untimbered valleys is Menyamya, established in 1950 as the first Government base to be set up among the Kukukuku of the northern fall.

The Government officers who came in to build the station had to fight their way in and for a long time were living in a state of siege. Even now it is still an outpost with a strictly limited area of free movement around about. But compared to Aseki and Kainteba it is a metropolis and center of civilization, having a courthouse and jail, a once-weekly air service to Lae, a church, boarding school, and a small hospital. It also has the ultimate mark of New Guinea ur-banism—a resident white woman who is not a missionary but the wife of a Government officer.

I once met a labor recruiter on the Sepik River who told me that
he had worked out of Menyamya several times, and had taken
"lines" of Kukukuku men to work on coastal plantations, and on the
docks at Lae, and in the gold mines at Wau. And he said that he
never had trouble with them, and that the Kukukuku themselves,
and their employers, had been entirely satisfied.

I thought that he must have been very lucky and asked him how
he had managed to get into the area to recruit laborers, seeing that
all the country round about Menyamya was officially classified as
uncontrolled territory at that time, and only hand-picked officers
of the administration and highly experienced missionaries were allowed in.

He said that the Government had tacitly approved of his going
in to recruit, believing that if primitives can be brought out to
work and live for a while among sophisticated people of other tribes
they quickly become impressed with the material advantages of
this new way of life.

Then, when they are returned to their villages at the end of their
working term, they become advocates of the new order and help to
break down resistance and suspicion and antagonism against the
administration. In our own society this is known as "social orienta-
tion."

The recruiter agreed that the Kukukuku are universally reputed
to be an odd lot, given to sudden, deceitful, and vicious treachery,
but he thought that if treated fairly and frankly they are easy
enough to get along with. He admitted, however, that those around
Menyamya are not especially co-operative.

He thought that there was a reason for this more-than-average
antagonism and suggested that it might be traced back to something that happened during the early days of contact, for the
Kukukuku have the habit of keeping count of old scores that need
to be settled before new business is undertaken.

There was, he said, the story of the young patrol officer, inex-
perienced in dealing with such people, who burned down a hamlet
and shot the people's pigs as punishment for some crime or slight
against the Government's authority; most probably a minor fight
in which a man was killed, or maybe two.

Not long afterwards, this group of Kukukuku sent the patrol
officer a parcel neatly wrapped in leaves and tied with orchid fibers.

He opened it and found a collection of severed hands and feet that had been removed from members of a neighboring clan. It was, he said, a sign that the people did not intend to have their ancient ways amended by any meddlesome stripling even if he did represent the Government.

The same man told me that climbing the track that leads from Menyamya into the mountains, and coming close to the big cave where the people of Menya village put their dead and smoke-dried elders, he found himself suddenly looking into a tree in which a Kukukuku sat staring down at him, bow raised to shoot and an arrow strung back tautly in the bamboo string.

He is an unemotional man who does not frighten easily; but he said that he went cold, and his hair lifted on his scalp, and he remembered his dead mother. Then just as he raised his gun to save himself, his mind told him that the man in the tree was dead and dried, and that he had been placed there by his family and friends because he had been a mighty fighter and would be happy sitting in ambush with his bow raised, ready to kill.

After that trip my friend went back to work on the Sepik River because (he said) "I can get along with live savages, but dead ones scare me."

We circled over the Menyamya station to announce ourselves, then slanted down smoothly to a perfect landing. It seemed almost civilized.

I walked across to the subdistrict office to pay my respects and found that the assistant district officer was away on patrol, but a motorcycle came chugging along the strip and stopped beside me. The young man straddled across it introduced himself as Clarrie and said that he was the medical assistant, and asked if we were going to Lae because, if so, he had a couple of patients who should go without delay, and could we take them, please?

I said I had dropped in to look at his hospital, but as for taking patients to Lae, well that was the pilot's business and not mine. So we consulted the pilot who said, suspiciously, "How many?" When it turned out that there were three adults and a child, he shook his head and said, "No, I wouldn't have enough fuel to take that load to Lae."

Then Clarrie explained that they were Kukukuku people and

very small, and one of them was a woman and weighed less than a hundred pounds, and the child was sick and weighed practically nothing so that actually he could call it about two and a half people.

He sat astride his motorcycle looking silently at the pilot with soft appealing eyes so that the pilot shrugged and said a reluctant "all right," and turned away to adjust the rear seats. As he went he looked back over his shoulder and said, "But please hurry up, I don't want to get caught up there with a load of Kukus." Then as Clarrie bent down to start the motorcycle the pilot winked at me and shook his head affectionately in Clarrie's direction.

There are 128 medical assistants employed by the administration, most of them coming to the territory with a background of experience as hospital wardsmen, male nurses, first-aid and ambulance men, or sick-bay attendants in the armed services.

Many of them are self-dedicated to medical work and might have been doctors and surgeons if their parents had been able to support them through college and medical school. As it is, most of them have made themselves capable medical practitioners largely through years of field experience and private study.

Without them it would be impossible for the Government to run even a partially adequate medical service, for they do most of the general administration of the Department of Public Health, and practically all of the medical work in the field, away from the main stations. The pioneering of medical services among newly contacted primitives is entirely undertaken by the medical assistants.

The hospital at Menyamya is at the end of the strip, away from the main station buildings. I rode down on the back of the motorcycle, clutching the medical assistant by the shoulders because he seemed a carefree driver and the strip is bumpy along the edges, and he was in a hurry to get his patients ready for the flight to Lae. When we reached the hospital he called an orderly and told him to get the patients and their belongings, and take them along to the Cessna. Then we had a quick look around.

The hospital buildings, though built of bush materials, are neat and clean—two wards, an office, dispensary, and operating room. It is the practice to use familiar materials for station buildings in the early stages of contact and to stick to designs that are locally conventional. The first Government officer at Menyamya built his office in the circular shape of a village headman's house.

There are flower beds outside the hospital, and the grass is cut short like a lawn and edged with whitewashed stones. Inside the wards it is dark, with only the daylight filtering through the plaited walls, and the flicker of a fire in the middle of the dirt floor. It is like the inside of a native house except for the beds.

In the female ward there was a station woman, wife of one of the policemen, waiting to be delivered of a child, and a bush woman lying huddled up under a blanket with her face hidden. She had hookworm and was very sick. And there was a little girl, no more than eight or nine years old, with her head heavily bandaged. An orderly had found her abandoned in the bush just a few hours from the station as he came back from a medical patrol. She had been hit over the head with an ax or a heavy bush knife, and her skull had been laid bare.

Clarrie thought that he would keep her at the station if he could find a policeman's family to adopt her, and later would teach her nursing. She might, he said, be a good beginning to welfare work among the women of the district.

The men's ward was crowded with patients and their friends, sitting around the fire in the middle of the floor, smoking and chewing betel nut. A party of them had arrived that morning and he had not yet discovered which one of them was the patient. There were two small boys with them, who came from the mission school on the station. The men had collected them as they came through, to act as interpreters. Probably the boys were nephews of one of the men in the party. They would all sit for a while, talking, and sooner or later would say why they had come, and which one of them wanted treatment.

Every patient in the hospital had two or three friends or guardians staying with him, sleeping on the floor close to his bed, or near the fire, for no clan will permit one of its members to stay unguarded among strangers. And each family or clan group would have brought its own food to cook and eat, fearful of sorcery if anyone else prepared their meals. Even the policeman's wife had a younger sister with her as guardian, although the hospital is only a few hundred yards away from her own home and husband.

When we came out there was a man standing on the lawn leaning on a stick. He had a small boy with him, no more than ten years old. The boy had a bag of food slung across his shoulder. The man had a wound in his side, low under the armpit, covered with a pad of grass wrapped in a fleshy leaf and bound on with strands of fiber that encircled his chest. The wound was suppurating and made moist runnels in the dust that covered his ribs. He looked as though he had come a long way to seek treatment. He had brought the boy to cook for him and be his messenger.

Clarrie went across to him and had a quick look to see if the man needed immediate attention, but it seemed unlikely that he was in urgent need of help. So he called an orderly and asked him to take the man into the examination room and get rid of the bush dressings and clean the wound for inspection. He would, he said, be back as soon as he had got the other patients away on the Cessna.

As we drove back along the strip he shouted above the noise of the motorcycle, telling me that the man had an arrow wound and could be dealt with here at Menyamya. It was, he said, almost routine. Dozens of men came in during the course of the year with arrowheads embedded in their flesh, or jammed in knee or shoulder joints, or between their ribs.

A man had gone back to his village only yesterday who had come in three weeks ago with two inches of arrow jammed under his kneecap. He had come down from the mountains, walking for three days. It was incredible how much pain these people could stand—presumably they simply took pain for granted as some inevitable part of human existence.

When a man gets hit with an arrow in a tribal fight his first thought is to run away as fast as he can; otherwise he will be finished off with a blow from an ax. But it is difficult to run quickly through thick bush with a long arrow sticking out of your body and getting caught up in the high grass and vines and creepers. So the best thing to do is to break the arrow off close to the wound.

More often than not, if the wound is only in the flesh, the arrowhead rots away in time, and although the wounded man might feel sick for a while such wounds are seldom fatal. But if the arrow is wedged in a knee joint or under the jawbone, or in the spine, it sets up painful complications and so handicaps the man that he becomes helpless and may be left to die.

We rode the motorcycle back along the strip and dismounted beside the Cessna. The patients who were going to Lae were already there with friends and relations. The central figure in the group was a short, middle-aged man, gaunt and bony and worried-looking. He held in his arms, pressed tightly to his chest, a small boy so thin and wasted that his legs were no thicker than my two thumbs, and his breast as hollowed-in as a soup plate. He lay in the man's arms like a dead fledgling.

Clarrie shook his head. "I'm afraid they came in too late for me to do anything with him. He's suffering basically from malnutrition, but has dysentery, which is bad, and probably pleurisy. They may be able to do something in Lae, but I don't have the staff here to give him all-day attention."

There were two women in the party, standing close to the man with the sick child. One of them was dull-eyed, almost idiot-looking, standing pigeon-toed, her hands clasped over her private parts. She looked incredibly filthy and moronic. Her only clothing was a tattered sporran of withered grass. Her breasts were like little old leather purses that had been lying out in the weather for ages. A bag of sweet potatoes hung from her forehead.

The other woman, similar in appearance but more alive, spoke earnestly to the man with the child. She seemed a woman of character and was, most likely, his sister and the boy's aunt. Half a dozen men stood by, watching them. They wore their bark cloaks and had pig tusks through their noses, and wore little aprons of grass fore and aft.

The other patient for Lae was a man with a fractured jaw. He stood alone, looking arrogant.

The pilot looked up at the sky, anxious to get away before the weather changed, and Clarrie motioned to the patients to get into the plane.

The men who stood near the family group moved forward and each touched the man with the child, gently, and without speaking, then stood back. And the sister, if such she was, made a final speech to him, then turned to the ugly woman and spoke brusquely. Then she, too, went and stood apart and watched.

We put the man with the child into the seat behind mine, and the woman in the seat behind the pilot, but she slid off and crouched down on the floor in terror. Then the pilot turned to the man with the broken jaw and motioned him to get in also, so he came forward and got in, trampling over the woman. We strapped them in. The man with the child trembled like a frightened animal as I fastened his safety belt. The pilot attended to the other man but there was nothing we could do with the woman except leave her where she was. The stink of them, unwashed since they were born, and smelling of sweat and sickness made me feel momentarily ill, but the drama of the situation kept my stomach taut.

Clarrie gave me a note to pass on to the doctor at Lae. Then the pilot slammed the doors shut and tested the locks. The engine started and the aircraft inched forward jerkily over the rough ground. I looked around at our passengers. The two men sat rigid, staring at the pilot and me. The woman was motionless, sitting in a little pool of water.

I made a happy face at the men, but there was no response. Then I raised my thumb and looked encouraging; they watched me, then turned to each other and slowly did the same, but with uncertainty as though not clearly comprehending whether or not this was part of a necessary ritual.

When I turned to wave goodbye to Clarrie they cautiously imitated me, and to test them I patted the top of my head and they did the same. So after that I stayed quite still so as not to confuse them. But when the pilot revved the engine to its maximum before take-off I put my fingers in my ears from force of habit, for the noise in these little aircraft is deafening when they do this, and suddenly remembering the passengers I looked around and saw that they, too, had their fingers in their ears.

When we left the ground the men looked at each other dumbly, and as we banked they clutched at the arm-rests, but neither made a sound. And in a while their eyes began to move more freely and they took quick glances at the peaks of the mountains as we passed between them, and soon they seemed to relax; but the woman was sick.

We escaped from the mountains and came out over foothills that slope down to the coast. The long thin road that leads from the gold mines of Wau to the port of Lae winds across this rolling landscape and goes past a house and farm buildings that belong to Mick Leahy, one of the first settlers in these highlands.

Mick was gold-seeking in the Kukukuku country in 1931 and was attacked by the tribesmen, and in the melee was almost killed when a stone club cracked his skull. His brother shot the man who struck the blow, but himself got an arrow in the lung. They drove the attackers away, killing some, but other prospectors were less lucky, and lost their lives to the savages. Mick made a small fortune from gold, stayed in New Guinea, and settled down to raise cattle in these foothills, in sight of the mountains where the Kukukuku nearly killed him.

And now, to me, flying in the tranquil sky above his farm and the fences that enclose his cattle in cleared pastures, everything seems suddenly peaceful and secure as though we have emerged from a strange place into an atmosphere of familiar elements; away from the restless air that eddies and swirls among high peaks and unreal landscapes, and the danger-laden solitudes of this savage land we have just left. It requires an effort of recollection to remember that it is only yesterday that we left Port Moresby.

We came, in a little while, over the wide valley of the Markham, one of the great waterways of New Guinea. The valley is twenty miles wide, and more in parts, and rich with the silt of thousands of years. The villagers who live in it are commercial farmers who grow sweet potatoes, peanuts, and garden vegetables, using tractors and other mechanized farm equipment which they own communally.

They share the valley with Australian settlers who farm alongside them, growing their own peanuts and buying the village crops for processing and marketing. And in the hills on the other side of the valley, toward the coast, there are villages where the people grow coffee and raise cattle.

These New Guinea people of the coastal lowlands are affluent by Pacific standards. Their special status as wards of the United Nations also gives them an awareness of the outside world and where they stand in it. Lately they have developed a strong commercial and political consciousness, and see the bright light of progress shining on their horizon with its promise of some kind of national status in the near future.

As yet they lack adequate leaders to show them the way and to define their aims. Their best men are themselves still in the kindergarten of modern politics.

When we had crossed the Markham Valley the pilot called up the airport at Lae to report our approach and ask for a clearance to land, for although the town has only two thousand people there are up to fifty aircraft movements in and out of its airport each working day.

Our passengers from Menyamya were quiet. When we came in sight of the town I turned around to the men and pointed down, and said, "Lae." They looked blank. I might just as well have said New York or London or Paris. It would have meant as much to them.

When we landed there was an ambulance waiting to take them to the hospital, and a medical orderly to escort them. I went across and gave him the note for the doctor, then stood back and watched the ambulance drive away.

I don't know what happened to them after that because I went looking for Somu Sigob.

Somu is an elected member of the Legislative Council of Papua and New Guinea. He represents the Markham people and all the other coastal and lowland people of the New Guinea mainland. The "civilized" highlanders who live in the huge valleys that open out westward beyond the Kukukuku country have their own representatives. So do the people of the New Guinea islands which lie to the north and east of the main island.

I found Somu sitting on his bed in the hotel, drinking a beer. He looked lonely, not like the political representative of more than half a million people heading toward self-government. The trouble is that he is a pioneer politician in a country that has no history of local politics. Given the background and the lessons of even a single generation of political experience Somu might feel more confident about being one of the most prominent leaders of an emergent people. As it is he feels that he has been thrust onto the political stage untrained to play more than a stopgap part.

The experience has destroyed men with more in their favor than Somu has, but history must be served by all kinds of men, including martyrs.

Somu used to be a policeman. In his day he has walked over a great part of New Guinea, the right-hand man and trusted confidant of many a young patrol officer working for the first time among primitives. The soles of his feet are half an inch thick.

Because of his loyal and efficient service, and his good bearing, he was chosen to go to London in 1953 to march in the coronation procession of Her Majesty the Queen. Then, in 1962, already advanced in New Guinea parochial politics because of such prestige, he was taken to New York to attend meetings of the Trusteeship Council as an "adviser" to the Australian delegation.

He poured me a beer, and I asked him how he had liked being in America. He looked worried and said would I mind if he spoke in Pidgin because he could not express himself well in English. This is not true. He speaks English well for a New Guinean who had his schooling before the Government insisted upon the language being taught in mission schools. I told him so, but said also that I had no personal objection to Pidgin and would be able to understand him.

He thought for a while, and sipped his beer. Then he said, "I used to think that we New Guinea people would be better off under the Americans than under the Australians because the Americans are very generous people and have a lot of money, and when they do something they do it big. I thought that if they ruled us they would give us all the things that we need to make our people live well and be happy. But now that I have been to America I do not believe this any more.

"The American way of life is good for the American people but not for us. We New Guinea people are lazy. We do not like to work. It is not natural for us. But the American people, they work hard all the time and they drive everybody fast so that they make a lot of money, and then they can buy lots of things.

"In New Guinea a man lives in his village and he has a grass house and a garden with taro and yams and sweet potato, and his children run about and play in the sun and in the dust. We are happy. If the Americans came to rule us they would make us work and we would soon die."

These are the kind of disillusionments that worry Somu Sigob since he has become a politician.

We had another beer.

Somu was a good policeman. He achieved the rank of sergeant-major, which is as high as any New Guinea man has yet reached in the service.[1] He showed considerable courage and resource when working among primitive peoples like the Kukukuku. There were

[1] The current "New Deal" in New Guinea allows for the creation of a police training college, which will give to members of the constabulary "every encouragement and opportunity of rising to commissioned rank in the service." (the Minister for Territories).

times when he was scared, but he always knew instinctively what to do because the issues were basic, and if there was ever any doubt the patrol officer could resolve them with a simple instruction.

But now the issues are not clear. Somu is no longer facing anything as simple as a savage with a bow and arrow. He is facing ideas that he can only vaguely understand, and he doesn't know if the men who put them forward, in Moresby or Canberra or New York, are friends or enemies. And neither do they. And there is no patrol officer to say, "Shoot," or "Don't shoot." In such a situation courage and resource are likely to give way to doubt and dismay.

Somu put down his glass and searched around for his wallet, and when he found it he took out a photograph of his new wife and her child, his son. His first wife was a village woman. The new wife is young and well-educated and speaks English with an American accent. Somu, who is forty-three, does not like being away from her, and for this reason, among others, finds his political duties irksome at times.

In his own village at Finschhafen, on the coast a little north of Lae, he has cocoa trees, coconuts for copra, and some coffee bushes. He is president of the Native Local Government Council in his area, and a member of the District Advisory Council.

Sometimes he is strongly tempted to retire from the confusion of national politics. The idea of going back to the village to live as a man of solid local consequence appeals to him. It fits the pattern of life as he understands it. Yet he does not wish to appear ungrateful to the white men who are helping him to become one of the leaders of his people as they move proudly into the promised land of self-determination.

At the same time he also feels that because he is always working with white men in the Government, and continually making visits to Port Moresby, and sometimes to Canberra and New York, he is losing touch with the people he is supposed to represent; and it is true that some of his people feel that Somu is no longer concerned with their problems but with his standing among the white men.

Life has become very much of a problem to Somu and to others like him who have become, largely by chance, the first generation of new leaders in Papua and New Guinea. They live like men who have stopped belonging. They shuttle between two worlds, one they have left and one they have not yet reached. They constitute a historical sacrifice that has to be offered, and the thought frightens some of them.

Somu has many good qualities and one outstanding gift. He is an imaginative rhetorician with a fine natural flair for histrionics. Whether speaking in his own Yabin tongue, or in colorful and descriptive Pidgin, he "talks good," and people listen with admiration, and are impressed.

Even with his limited English he can make a pretty point as when, later in the evening after we had dined and were speaking about the future of New Guinea and the place of the white man in the new order, he said, "You white people have taken men like me and made us the key to your own future in this country. If you turn us one way the door will be open for you. If you turn us the other way you will be shut out." It was only talk. Somu is a loyal servant of the Australian Government.

Four

Lae is the terminal port for the air service between Australia and New Guinea. Nearly five hundred miles farther to the northeast, on the extreme tip of New Britain in the Bismarck Archipelago, is Rabaul. A feeder air service links the two towns and the flight takes a little over two hours in fine weather. There is nothing between them but water and thinly populated jungle. Rabaul is the biggest town on the northern side of New Guinea. It has a non-native population of about four thousand, most of whom are either Australian or Chinese.

The modern history of this northern part of New Guinea, which is Trust Territory, closely duplicates the history of Papua, where Moresby came surveying in 1873 to fill in the map by finding the harbor that he named for his illustrious father. After him came the missionary, Dr. Lawes, with his Samoan evangelists. And then the British trader.

On the New Guinea side a Captain Simpson came, in 1872, also surveying for the British Navy. He charted the great harbor where Rabaul now stands, naming the outer expanse Blanche Bay after his ship, and the inner part Simpson Harbour after himself. One can only assume that his father was not a high admiral. A Methodist missionary, George Brown, arrived in 1874 with Fijian pastors and teachers as his companions, and after them came traders. But in this case the traders were German and not British.

At that time neither the British nor the German governments seemed much interested in claiming any part of New Guinea, seeing neither political nor economic advantage commensurate with the costs of developing communications and defense. In any case both nations were busy about their African possessions.

In Papua there was no enthusiastic encouragement of private

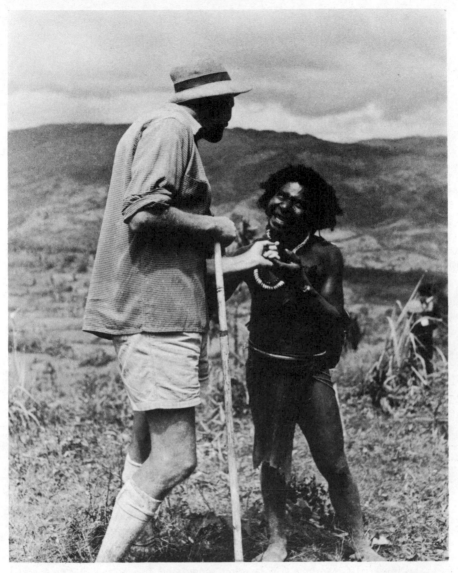

[1] The author saying goodbye to Avarabuni, a young man of the Duna people who live in the far western highlands of Central New Guinea. Much of this area has only lately been explored and many thousands of its people, still living in the Stone Age, have yet to have their first contact with the outside world.

This picture was taken at the end of an exploratory patrol that lasted for three months, during which time many previously unknown clans were found, among them that to which Avarabuni belongs.

Avarabuni came to the patrol camp with an arrow sticking in his back. It was removed by the medical assistant accompanying the patrol and in gratitude Avarabuni returned next day bringing a side of pig to present to the leader of the patrol, in return for which he was given a steel ax.

Avarabuni joined the patrol and attached himself to the author as a personal guide, remaining with the party until it reached the patrol post from which it had set out. He was the first of his clan to visit a government settlement.

[2] The curious natives of the Papuan village of Hanuabada three times witnessed the raising of the British flag in official ceremonies of annexation.

The first occasion was on April 4, 1883, when a police magistrate was sent from Australia by the Queensland Government to formally annex the southeastern part of New Guinea and call it British New Guinea.

The Imperial Government in London repudiated this action of the colonial Government, but in the following year, stirred by bitter resentment and protests from the colonists, changed its mind and sent a naval squadron to Port Moresby, instructing its commander to declare a protectorate over the territory. One of the ships of this squadron, H.M.S. *Harrier*, arrived some days before the other ships of the squadron, carrying a deputy commissioner of the Crown who, misunderstanding his instructions, drew up a proclamation and raised the flag.

When the main body of the squadron arrived, its commander decided to ignore the premature raising of the flag and to perform the ceremony again, which he did on November 6, 1884, from the veranda of the house of Dr. Lawes of the London Missionary Society.

The head chief of the villagers, appointed by the missionary, was presented with a walking stick, in the head of which was inset a silver coin bearing the effigy of Queen Victoria. The ships in the harbor fired a *feu de joie*.

[3] Pot-making is exclusively a woman's activity among the coastal Papuans, and the processes are formalized with minor ceremonies and rituals that have become traditional.

It is an annual activity, undertaken a little before the trading season, when the men take advantage of the trade winds to go on long sea voyages, during which they exchange the pots made by their women, for sago, pigs, and timber for canoe-making.

Pot-making extends over a period of weeks and all of the village women take some part in it, collecting the clay, gathering firewood and dried palm-fronds for firing the pots, sun-drying and baking them.

Wholesale pot-making is usually the monopoly of one village in each trading district, that village having easy access to suitable clay deposits. In such villages the women make hundreds of pots, each bearing a traditional clan design and the woman's personal mark.

[4] Men and women of the Mekeo tribes of Papua dressed for a ceremonial sing-sing. The men's faces are painted bright yellow and lined with red and blue. Each man holds in his hand a top-knot of feathers which, when the dancing begins, is fixed on top of the head by means of a pivot so that it bobs back and forth with the nodding motion of the dancer's head, and in time with the beating of the kundu drum which each man beats as he dances. The aureole of head feathers are tail plumes of the bird of paradise, and the necklets are of dog's teeth. Dog meat is regarded as a delicacy among these Mekeo people.

[5] Most of the Papuan people, regardless of the influence of the government and the missionaries, live out their lives according to a ritualistic pattern of behavior that links them directly to their ancestors.

Each daily action is accompanied by its traditional ritual and invocation, and no important community activity is engaged upon without the participation of a specialist, or especially appointed intermediary, who performs the necessary magic appropriate to that activity.

In this picture the village specialist in "garden magic" is working the traditional spells, and asking the blessing of the village ancestors, before planting the first of the new season's yam crop.

[6] The extreme ruggedness of the terrain and the primitive state of the people have delayed the making of practical motor roads in the New Guinea highlands; consequently, most of the developmental work is carried out from Government stations, whose only physical link with the outside world is an airstrip perched precariously on top of a ridge or laid in the bed of a narrow valley.

The airstrip at Tapini, only eighty miles from Port Moresby (capital of Papua and New Guinea), is typical of scores of highland airstrips, suitable only for light aircraft, which provide the only means of intercommunication between Government stations and headquarters.

[7] Young men and boys from Kukukuku villages near the Government station at Menyamya visit the district office on the edge of the airstrip.

The Kukukuku are among the most warlike of all the New Guinea tribes, feared by the coastal people upon whose villages they swoop from time to time, burning down the houses and dragging off victims whose bodies are eaten and whose skulls are kept as trophies.

[8] A Kukukuku warrior with black-palm bow and cane-bladed arrow. These hunting arrows are razor-sharp, and will penetrate several inches into a man at fifty yards or more. Note the girdle of human bones.

[9] When Mikael, the mission teacher of Alakasan, was murdered by fellow villagers led by his own son, his friend Tengbun tried to save him but was himself
attacked.

The handle of the ax, wet with Mikael's blood, slipped from the murderer's
hand, but the blow still left a deep scar in Tengbun's forehead, and there is another, deeper scar, in his back, and bewildered, abiding sorrow in his heart.

capital into the country; in fact, Government officials and missionaries together made it clear that they regarded commercial pioneers
as undesirable. They concentrated, in partnership, upon turning any
accessible Papuans into loyal and decent subjects of the Queen,
preferably Protestant.

There may well have been a climate of justification for this
attitude, created by an unsavory record of blackbirding and labor
exploitation in other parts of the Pacific, shared by Australian and
American plantation interests; but the attitude became, in time,
almost traditional and still persists.

But the Germans established a commercial emphasis from the beginning. They were not particularly concerned with civilizing cannibals but they did want to find and develop a regular and plentiful
supply of coconut oil; and this is precisely what New Guinea offered. Consequently the German Government supported commercial entrepreneurs and encouraged missionaries to pacify and
civilize the natives so that commerce could be carried on efficiently
and peacefully. They seemed to have no national or religious bias
in this and gave British Protestant missionaries the same encouragement as they gave their own Lutherans and Catholics.

So the two areas, separated by then unscaled mountains, miles
of ocean, as well as by politics, developed in quite different ways.
And Australia, having inherited them as a single patrimony, now
has the problem of dealing with them as one, while critics stand
on the sidelines and cry out, "Colonialism must end," and "Give
New Guinea self-government."

We fly, now, along a volcanic arc that starts somewhere west of
Java and runs through New Guinea and out into the ocean beyond
the Solomons. One is seldom beyond sight of an active volcano,
and eruptions are almost commonplace.

The great Dutch sailor, Abel Tasman, tells how in the middle of
a calm and clear night his ship suffered so violent a shock that
every member of the crew fell out of his hammock. It was an un-
dersea earthquake. Many ships have disappeared in these waters
with nobody knowing why.

But William Dampier, reformed buccaneer and friend of Robinson Crusoe, gives one of the most precise descriptions of volcanic
activity on the New Guinea coast in his account of the voyage of

1700, during which he named New Britain. He describes how one night, passing along the coast, he "sighted a great fire bearing north-west by west, blazing up in a pillar, sometimes very high for three or four minutes, then falling quite down for an equal space of time; sometimes hardly visible, till it blazed up again . . . and I knew it to be a burning hill by its intervals. The island all night vomited fire and smoak [sic] very amazingly, and at every belch we heard a frightful noise like thunder, and saw a flame of fire after it, the most terrifying I ever saw. The intervals between its belches were about half a minute, some more some less . . . the largest made a roaring noise and sent up flame twenty or thirty yards high; and then might be seen a great stream of fire running down to the foot of the island, even to the shore."

Louis de Bougainville, in the following year, complained bitterly of incessant rain in these parts, saying ". . . one tempest comes on before the other has gone off, it thunders continuously, and the nights are fit to convey an idea of chaotic darkness."

Then the noble Joseph de Bruni d'Entrecasteaux, searching for his vanished countryman, the circumnavigator La Pérouse, passed through Dampier's Strait in 1793, railing against the rain, scorpions, and alligators; but he may have been in a particularly querulous mood, being ill, for he also noted in the log that the wine was sour and the flour rotten. The poor man was sick with scurvy, his legs swollen and covered with ugly black spots. He was aiming west for Java, fresh food and rest, but died before he got there.

According to present-day statistics it rains 180 inches a year at Lae. It is no wonder that Bougainville and D'Entrecasteaux were depressed. I feel the same, for we battle through a wall of gray rain, and the aircraft engines groan like beasts in labor as we beat our way up through the deluge.

The plane is an old Dakota, the pack horse of New Guinea. Without it there would be practically no progress at all. But this one being twenty years old, or more, leaks. A young Chinese girl returning from a vacation in Sydney to her home in Rabaul, and dressed with meticulous simplicity in linen, wriggles as a trickle of rain seeps through the hole left by a loose rivet and makes a puddle where she sits.

The slim Chinese boy beside her changes places and mops up the moisture with a white handkerchief. They are both so neat

that they seem to have been cut out of paper. Their lips move and
I catch the click-clack of Cantonese as they speak.

Two nuns sit rigid, looking ahead without expression. One of
them is Sister Annette, a holy martinet who runs the maternity
hospital at Paparatava, near Rabaul, and has trained scores of New
Guinea girls to take charge of maternal and infant welfare centers
all over the territory.

A New Guinea lad sits alone looking lost and a little afraid. He
has the appearance of a highlander, low forehead and flattened
nose but bright, intelligent eyes and a squat, rugged strength. He
may be coming over to Rabaul to go to the Government technical
school. The other passengers are Government officers and planters,
and a group of visiting cocoa experts escorted by a senior man
from the Department of Agriculture at Port Moresby.

I am sitting beside Bill Race, a short, squat, white-blond Eng-
lishman with a completely pink face. He looks compassionately at
the Chinese boy and girl, feeling for them in their discomfort. Then
he giggles because he is a simple man at heart and finds it difficult
to be continuously serious, and the Chinese boy's ardent efforts to
be both gallant and comfortable strike him as amusing.

Bill Race is a medical assistant, and he has been on vacation. He
has been to England and then to the Continent. He looks out of the
window of the aircraft and is silent for ten minutes or more. Then
he draws my attention to a cluster of hollow-coned volcanoes. Two
of them are smoking in a lazy, desultory way. It is three years
since any of this group erupted, but they make a fine sight even
as shapes in a landscape.

We have passed over Dampier's Strait and are flying along the
center line of the sausage-shaped island of New Britain. The sky,
the land, the rim of sea stretching away to the equator, are black-
gray and bedraggled. We run in and out of squalls and the Dakota
bucks a little. The Chinese girl frowns and huddles closer to the
boy who is solicitous. We have another 250 miles to go and it will be
like this all the way, for the wet season has set in. The pilot tries to
avoid flying into the worst of the cloud, but it will not be a smooth
flight.

Bill Race nudges me excitedly and points down. I lean across him
and look out but can only see sodden landscape. He seems surprised
that I am so obtuse. Perhaps he is pointing to Kandrian, where he

was stationed before he went on vacation. A beautiful place when
the weather is fine, but subject to phenomenal rains, being in a
narrow bay that is open to trade winds and backed by high mountains. A Government man who was stationed there told me that he
once measured fifteen inches in a day and night of rain. I wonder
how Bill Race's bride will like it.

No doubt she will find it strange, coming from Hamburg with
its population of over a million, to Kandrian with a white population of six. And Bill says that she is nervous about the natives. Also
she does not speak English. Neither does Bill speak German.

He courted her by mail, he writing in English and she in German.
It was one of those pen-friend affairs until he took his vacation
and went to Germany to meet her. Before that their courting was
complicated by the language problem.

Fortunately, New Britain has a large number of German missionaries and there was one stationed near Kandrian. When the letters came from Hamburg, Bill took them over to the mission and
the priest read them to him. But sometimes when a letter came
the priest was away on patrol among the villages, three or four
days' walk from the station, and Bill would have to set out after
him to get the letter read.

The priest became interested in the courtship and the correspondence, and sometimes forgot that the letters were addressed to Bill
Race and just sat reading them to himself, ejaculating every now
and then, *"ja ja, das ist sehr schön,"* or, reproachfully, *"nein, nein
mein liebling,"* or even, with an air of surprise, "ah so!" and *"wunder-
bar."*

Then Bill would get impatient and say, "Excuse me, Father, but
what does she say?"

This embarrassed the priest who would then get flustered and
apologize and try to explain what she was saying, instead of just
reading out the whole letter.

And the matter was complicated further by the fact that the
priest could not speak English anyway, but only Pidgin which,
though a satisfactory and even colorful medium of practical expression, is extremely limited in its abstract range; so that "I love you"
can be translated no more emotionally than *"mi laikim yu."* Nor
are there any words of endearment that permit an embellishment
of these basic phrases, and "I love you my darling because you are

so wonderful" can never become, in Pidgin, much more evocative than "*Mi laikim yu bolong ologetta yu i gutpela tumas.*"

So Bill Race decided to go home to England and see his father, after which he went to Germany to see the girl, and they went touring together around Europe in a small car and, according to Bill, got along very well without being able to speak each other's language.

The first time I met Bill Race was out in the Solomon Islands at a place called Wakunai, which in those days consisted of a patrol officer's house, a kunai grass Government office, and a medical center set apart on a gentle hillside overlooking the Pacific Ocean.

The medical center, planned, designed, built, and directed by Race, occupied an area of some twenty-four acres, and included, in the clinical block, male and female medical wards, a maternity section, children's wing, and infant and maternal welfare section with a postnatal clinic, and an operating theater.

The educational block contained classrooms for student medical orderlies, nurses, and infant welfare workers, as well as a recreation room and lecture room.

An admission center, examination rooms, out-patient department, and dispensary constituted a third block, with a street of staff cottages making an enclosure on two sides of the whole combined center.

At the top of the hill, overlooking everything and with the ocean as a backdrop to its outlook, Mr. Race had built his own house, making a total of sixty buildings, neatly laid out and intersected by laneways lined with young kapok trees, clipped archwise to make long connecting corridors of shade.

None of the buildings contained a stick of machine-cut timber in beam, rafter, or roof-tree. And not a nail or screw had been used, or even a saw employed in the carpentering. The building materials came out of the surrounding bush and the only tools used were axes and knives. And the builders were Bill Race, the medical orderlies and nurses, and such patients as were ambulant and able to lift or carry.

The total cost to the Government for the whole project, said Mr. Race trying not to sound triumphant, was twenty-five pounds.

We looked into the maternity section where two women sat on their beds nursing babies. Mr. Race beamed as he crossed the ward toward them and reaching the nearest one leaned over and made motherly clucking noises at the sucking child, who took no notice. He turned to me, preening, and said, "Aren't they lovely."

I thought that he seemed excessively proud until we got outside and he explained that the women came from an inland village which he had visited while on medical patrols during the year, and that they were the first of their tribe to have their babies in the hospital.

The operating theater was a grass hut with fly-wire windows all around and a rainwater tank outside, an enormous luxury. It was furnished with a lightweight metal inspection table and a glass-fronted cabinet full of surgical instruments. When I said that I supposed they were used by visiting surgeons, Mr. Race looked hurt, and said with a somewhat haughty inflection that there were no visiting surgeons; and I realized that I had been unwittingly offensive and dull, and that Mr. Race did his own surgery when circumstances made it seem necessary.

"I'm not a butcher," said Mr. Race defensively. "But there are times, in places like these, when it is not possible to get a patient to a doctor, and drastic measures are needed to save a life, and it's part of my job to do what I can in such cases."

I kept silent, waiting for the breach to heal.

"I cut a bloke's leg off the other day," said Mr. Race after a while, modestly looking down at the floor. Then he added, "The boys helped me."

Looking at the surgical saw and other instruments, I felt suddenly sick.

"He was felling timber in the bush and a tree fell on his leg and smashed it, and when he came to me gangrene had set in. He would have died in a day or two, and we had no way of getting him to a surgeon, so I did the job."

I hesitated before asking the obvious question. "Where is he now?"

"He's in the hospital in Rabaul," said Mr. Race. Then after a suitable pause and with a studiously offhand inflection, "He'll be back home when they've fitted him with a wooden leg."

Later we looked over the farm area behind his house, on the backward slope of the hill. He had the poultry and duck runs on one side, and on the other, farther away from the house, the pig pens and the milking yard; and beyond these the main garden area for growing kau kau and other food crops to supply the hospital.

That night, up at the house on the hill, sitting at a table set with clean linen and dignified cutlery, on a spacious veranda overlooking the medical center with its background of moonlit sea, we ate frog's legs cooked in batter and garnished with coconut cream sauce, then poultry, followed by paw-paw and pineapple salad, and a home-made liqueur.

We were attended at table by two young Buka Island boys, jet black, wearing white lap-laps, monkey jackets, and red bow ties. Down in the hospital area somebody was playing a guitar and sing-ing sad songs.

"My father," said Bill, wiping his lips with a napkin, "was a coal miner."

Bill speaks with a noticeably broad north of England accent, and also has a sailing ship tattooed on his arm, so that when he says that his father was a coal miner one is not taken by surprise.

"He had eight children," added Bill, pouring me another glass of liqueur.

I did not wish to appear curious but he was clearly in the mood to talk, so I asked, tentatively, "How did you come to be interested in medicine?"

I had asked the right question, for he leaned back comfortably before answering. "If you live in a coal-mining community, or in some other place where people earn their living dangerously, a lot of young fellows take to learning first-aid as a kind of hobby, like other fellows take to pigeon racing or stamp collecting, and that is what I did."

He called the boys to clear the table and to bring coffee.

"I got my first certificate from the St. John's Ambulance Society when I was twelve years old," he said, "although it was not right to be having it before fourteen, though I were never found out.

"Then I got my second certificate at the age of thirteen, and my third certificate on my fourteenth birthday. And on that same day I went to work in the mines—straight to the coal-face."

After a moment's reflection he added, "What a bastard that were."

One needs only to be acquainted with Mr. Race for an hour or so to realize that a man of his genius could not remain for long satisfied with the emotional and intellectual outlets provided by a coal-mining career.

Before long he took up needlework and became adept at fancy embroidery. He also learned conjuring and ventriloquism and took up music, becoming proficient on the accordion. By the time he was twenty he had branched out as a part-time entertainer and was making a little extra money to supplement his pay as a coal miner.

Then England went to war with Germany.

Mr. Race, keeping pace with history, joined the Royal Navy.

"Father," he said, "didn't like it at all, and complained that I had shamed the family by leaving the pit to 'join the bloody Navy,' but I took the accordion and the St. John's Ambulance certificates and a bit of embroidery that I hadn't finished, and went off to be a sailor."

They posted him, on the evidence of the certificates, to an armed merchant cruiser as a sick bay attendant, but after two weeks of cruising in the Mediterranean they were sunk by a submarine. Then he went onto a destroyer and got sunk again. Then another cruiser, and finally an aircraft carrier that came to Australia, where he had a pleasant shore leave and the sight of new and wider horizons.

Back in England after the war he found that being a naval sick bay attendant in peacetime was not very satisfying, and offered little scope for the exercise of his multiplying capacities, so he went to London and served for sufficient time in a public hospital to become a fully qualified male nurse. With this professional status as a stock-in-trade he emigrated to Australia, thus shaming the family still further.

Father was speechless for some time, but finally explained the shame away by remarking to his friends in the pub that "Willy were always a bit queer, like."

But it was not in Australia that his particular genius was to reach its full flowering. Life in a Sydney hospital proved no more rewarding than hospital life in London, so he applied to the Australian Government for a job in the public health service of Papua and New Guinea, and in a little while found himself set down on the shores of Bougainville, the biggest of the Australian-administered Solomon Islands,[1] where the great Pacific swell con-

---

[1] The southern Solomons are administered by Britain.

tinuously pounds across coral reefs and, with its strength attenu-
ated, sighs smoothly up onto strips of black sand day after day.
And coconut palms lean over the water, their high heads waving
gracefully.

It was here that Mr. Race felt the Holy Ghost descend upon
him, bringing a deep peace and a sense of understanding and
knowing and certainty—for there are fifty-six thousand people on
Bougainville and its little sister island of Buka, and one Government
doctor to serve them, and the only other qualified medical practitioner an American nun on a mission station many miles from
Wakunai. It seemed to Mr. Race that Providence had placed him
there.

After coffee we moved to easy chairs on the edge of the veranda,
overlooking the medical center, and with a bottle of rum beside me
on a side table I was content. But Mr. Race seemed restless and
after a while went back into the house and fetched his accordion.
Then he sat on an upright chair, facing out over his little empire,
toward the moonlit sea, under a sky alive with a million stars; and
he began softly to play the old songs of England.

He had been playing for a half hour or more before I first heard
a faint stir and susurration in the darkness at the foot of the house
steps. And peering into the black shadows I saw scores of white
eyes staring up in love and wonder at Billy Race, Medical Assistant,
and knew them to be his orderlies and patients from the hospital,
and their families.

And for some reason I suddenly thought of Dr. Schweitzer in his
hospital in Africa, writing about Bach; and in the north of England
an elderly coal miner, sipping his beer and thinking about his son
who "were always a bit queer, like."

The pretty Chinese girl was lying limp and had her head hidden
in the hollow of the boy's shoulder as we scraped under heavy wet
clouds, and slipped between two hills to come within sight of
Rabaul. Her forehead was damp and she was past caring for the
creases in her dress; the young man looked sadly solicitous but
inadequate.

It had been an unpleasant two and a half hours of rough and
bumpy flying, especially for the last half hour as we battled through
a storm and groped our way down through clouds and sudden buf-

feting squalls. The Highland lad, sitting alone, had a cloth over his head most of the time, too terrified to allow himself to look.

The Chinese boy spoke softly to the girl and she opened her eyes a little and tried to smile. He was telling her that the journey was almost over—that we were coming out into the clear over Rabaul.

The whole family would be there to meet them, and all would be full of sympathy and concern for the girl. And as soon as her brothers had collected the baggage from the aircraft they would all go off in American cars and disappear into the back of one of the big wooden-frame buildings in Chinatown that are half home and half store, and where whole families of three or four generations live secret, clanlike lives, insulated almost entirely from the Australian and New Guinean communities. When she had rested they would talk about her trip, and tomorrow the flight would be forgotten.

We came in across the harbor, skirting the crater of Vulcan, which erupted and almost destroyed the town twenty-five years ago while the people scampered in panic out into the bush; then we circled the broken cone of Matupit, which has erupted several times since then and looks like a rotted tooth, hollow-cupped and discolored, with wisps of sulphurous smoke seeping through its fire-eroded sides.

The town lies in a strip along the waterfront, hemmed in tightly by an arc of these volcanic cones. They rise up behind it like the sides of a lush green amphitheater (except for naked Matupit at the far end, with its feet in hot and orange-colored mud); and the only land for an airstrip is on the narrow isthmus which links the town with the island village of Matupit, jutting out into the harbor.

The airstrip, lying crosswise on the isthmus, is too short for multi-engined aircraft and cannot be extended to take them. The Government would like to remake the strip, realigning it to gain more length so that main-line aircraft flying between Australia and New Guinea could come right through and terminate here at Rabaul.

But the land is village gardening land belonging to the Matupit people and they, good Methodists mainly, and many of them model Government servants, refuse to part with any of it for this purpose.

This is typical of the curious and many-sided relationship which exists between the Australian administration and the people of the New Guinea Trust Territory, a relationship quite unlike the attitude of firm paternalism that has become the tradition if not the rule in Papua. It illuminates the second of three distinct faces that the people of Papua and New Guinea present to the traveler, and it is in Rabaul that this second face is seen in a clearer and more revealing light than anywhere else.

These people of Matupit village who remain obdurate, and steadfastly refuse to discuss with the Government the issue of their land and the airstrip, are a clan of the Tolai people who occupy the eastern end of New Britain.[2] In an area that was characterized by a general addiction to savagery and cannibalism throughout the nineteenth century, the Matupit were outstandingly savage, feared by their neighbors to such an extent that when the missionary George Brown set out from his first camp to visit them, adjacent clans begged him to desist from so rash an enterprise.

But a little later some Matupit people came to visit the missionary. It was a Sunday, a little before Christmas, and he noted the visit in his diary. "The Matupit people were over today. They had been out murdering some poor wretches from Kininigunun, whom they caught going out to fish. They killed four who were in the canoe. Two of the bodies sank, but they took the other two to Matupit and ate them."

Today they are almost a suburban people, with their mature men holding moderately important positions in the Government service, and many of the young men schoolteachers, clerks, and technicians. They have their own pastors and local government councilors, and are represented on the Rabaul Town Advisory Council. But they will not give in about the airstrip.

Their home is a small island, and they say that with a constantly growing population they need every inch of their land for gardens. Furthermore, they complain that the Government doesn't play

[2] The name Tolai is commonly used to denote a common-language group that lives in the Gazelle Peninsula on the eastern end of New Britain. They number something over forty-five thousand and are generally regarded as being the most affluent and advanced of the New Guinea tribes. They are also, but less commonly, referred to as the Kuanua or Gunantuna language group, but these seem to be purely linguistic headings.

fair, but one day comes with cajolery to beg a little extra land for its airstrip, then comes again another day and asks for more; then it sends a Matupit man who is important in the Government service to suggest a new plan altogether. They say that a longer airstrip will not bring much advantage to Matupit but that the loss of their garden land would be a serious matter.

Compared with the great issues that divide the world today it is a trivial matter. Elsewhere it might be resolved by physical or financial pressures. But Australia hesitates to use these pressures. First of all because she feels that the New Guinea people should willingly contribute toward their own advancement, and secondly because any suggestion of coercion would bring well-instructed watchdogs baying at the bar of the UN.

It is across this rickety bridge of compromise that Australia is trying to lead a straggling cavalcade of mutually antagonistic and heterogeneous human beings into the twentieth century, out of an isolated and amorphous past, into a gregarious and unified future. It seems an impossible task.

Five

John Rollo Foldi, district commissioner for New Britain, met me at the airport. It is a courtesy he extends without any meriting on my part for I am not important to him. He smiled shyly when I congratulated him on having recently been honored by the Queen with a decoration acknowledging his work in New Britain. Then, in his office, we discussed developments that had taken place since my last visit.

He spoke enthusiastically about the new broadcasting station, the first to be established in the district, giving the northern New Guinea people their own local program with sessions in English, Pidgin, and Tolai. He talked of the problems of population increase and of new resettlement schemes being planned to meet them.

Then he begged to be excused, saying that he had to adjudicate and present prizes to the winning choirs at the annual choral contest organized by the churches. As he was leaving he asked, I thought wistfully, if I would care to go with him but I asked to be excused, having much writing to do and also remembering an occasion when I had endured "Swing Low, Sweet Chariot" sung fifteen times for a tape recording by the boys of the George Brown Methodist College, a few miles out of Rabaul.

The district commissioner said, "Ah well," adding that he had arranged for a vehicle to be made available if I wanted to go anywhere. Then he called for his own driver and went off to the choral contest.

The civilization introduced to New Britain by the German traders and missionary Brown, almost ninety years ago, has never penetrated deeply into the interior. All evidence of progress that has taken place in that time is tightly concentrated at the tip of the Gazelle Peninsula, in an area contained within the swing of an arc reaching no farther than twenty-five miles from Rabaul.

This encloses less than five hundred of the fourteen thousand square miles of New Britain, yet it sustains forty-five thousand Tolai people who, if they continue to multiply at the present rate, will soon represent half of the population of the island. In the remaining 95 percent of the island, even within thirty miles of Rabaul, "civilization" is limited to elementary law and order, and "progress" is denoted by nothing more spectacular than the usual missionary schools in the villages, and a few government patrol posts.

But there is no question about the remarkable development of the Tolai people. They live the self-satisfied, prosperous lives, of comfortably situated landowners. There is no poverty in their villages. As a group they provide a shining example of colonial achievement, and at the moment are the most self-conscious political unit in the country. At this point in New Guinea's history they are the tribal elite of the territory.

One of the most practical explanations for this highly concentrated development of a small group of people in so circumscribed an area is the fact that the early Germans built a network of roads on the peninsula to link their plantations and settlements to the port of Rabaul. And these roads, maintained and in places developed by the Australian administration, have made the material elements of Western civilization easily available to every Tolai village.

The Gazelle Peninsula road system is unique in New Guinea. It has brought even the most distant Tolai village within an hour's drive of the administrative and commercial center of the district, and has made it possible to organize efficient cash-crop farming and marketing.

The result, set against the general level of development in New Guinea with its multitude of back-breaking problems of contact and communication between government and governed, has been dramatic.

A car came to the hotel to pick me up, and the driver, Topuka, who knows me well enough to speak up when he has something to say, asked how far I would be going and at what time would we return to Rabaul. He would like, he said, if it was all the same to me, to be back by four o'clock, as he was scheduled for baseball practice in the park by four-fifteen.

I replied that I wanted to visit several places on the peninsula, but we should be back by four o'clock if the vehicle was in good order, so that it depended on him rather than on me. He thought this unfair but got in and drove off, and talked baseball all along Mango Avenue because it is the number one sport in Rabaul, and Topuka is a first-grade player. He said that the Tolai team, the Brown Bombers, was holding its own, but that the combined European-Tolai-Chinese team seemed likely to win the pennant this year.

We stopped for a moment at the new Central Methodist Church Administrative Center so that I could arrange a rendezvous later in the week with Saimon Gaius, a circuit superintendent, who was out in the bush somewhere attending a series of *vartabar*, which are the annual thank-offering ceremonies held by each of the 394 Methodist churches in the New Britain and New Ireland districts.

The Methodist Church still has Australian missionaries in New Guinea but the majority of its ordained ministers are New Guineans, and the government of the whole church is in the hands of local members. Ministers from Australia are not appointed to circuits without the approval of the village church elders.

We came to the end of Mango Avenue and its two rows of sun-exposed shops and offices, and turned along lush-green Malaguna Driveway to run under an overhang of great shade trees along the waterfront.

Passing the solid, stone-built Catholic cathedral I saw Father Franke, the parish priest, hovering anxiously while workmen raised a great stone crucifix in the grounds, facing the driveway.

The cathedral is the biggest building in New Britain and Father Franke's pride and joy. He has filled its great walls and spacious aisles with small-town murals and statuary from his native Bavaria, and when he looks at them he murmurs "so beautiful," and his eyes fill with tears of joy and sentiment.

A few years ago his parishioners gave him the money to go home to Germany for a thorough vacation. He was so affected by this unexpected gesture of affection that he could hardly speak for days.

The missionaries of the Sacred Heart came to New Britain soon after the Methodists had settled there, and in the early days most of them came from Germany. Today there are still many priests, nuns, and brothers of German birth and upbringing in the mission, including the Bishop, but in recent years most of the teaching and nursing work has been taken over by Australian religious.

The influence of the two churches is deeply rooted among the Tolai people. Their missionaries have remained continuously in the country through two wars, whereas there have been German, Australian, Japanese and, again, Australian administrations. And because the Tolai are, at present, the most advanced group in New Guinea, the missionaries possess a great deal of backroom power in local politics, even if they are careful to use it with the utmost discretion.

Until quite recently they ran between them the whole educational system in New Britain, and although the Government has lately established special schools of its own, the missionaries, with Government financial aid, still conduct the 525 village schools, as well as their colleges for training priests and pastors, teachers and technicians. Consequently every Tolai man, woman, and child who has been to school has grown up with an ingrained sense of allegiance to one of the two churches.

But the Government has always been represented mainly by census-takers, tax-gatherers, and magistrates, all accompanied on their rounds by policemen, so that, although there is a sense of respect for authority, and a general willingness on the part of the Tolai to co-operate in schemes devised for his advancement, he shows no basic feelings of loyalty or affection for the Government as an institution.

At the town limits we turned onto the coast road and skirted the grounds of the handsome technical school. It was built largely by the students, supervised by their instructors. Topuka, the driver, is a graduate of the school and always carries with him a certificate to show that he completed the motor mechanic's course.

Then, a little farther on, where the air is sickly sweet with the heavy scent of crushed copra, we passed the mill. A tanker from Europe, tied at the wharf, was piping coconut oil into her holds from the great silver-painted storage tanks that dominate the southern end of the waterfront.

Coconut products worth five million dollars were processed here for export last year, mostly in the form of commercial coconut oil for soap and pharmaceutical manufacturers, and copra cake for the makers of animal foods. This is about a third of the total coconut-product export of New Guinea as a whole.

A few miles out of town the road rises onto a plateau, but continues to keep along the coast, overlooking the huge and smooth expanse of Blanche Bay with its background of volcanic clusters. As the car climbs there is a succession of lovely views across the bay, framed with thick stands of giant bamboo, forty or fifty feet high, and foregrounds of steeply sloping gardens of volcanic loam planted with bananas and large-leafed taro.

And from the heights of Taliligap a few miles farther on, looking back across miles of sun-silvered sea, Rabaul looks like a toy town seen through the wrong end of a telescope, shown up only by roof-tops reflecting rain-washed tropic light, its outlines blurred by heat glare and haze. And always a wreath of wool-white cloud hanging on the brow of Mother Mountain.

This panorama is a fantasy of sheer size and color: the great silver stretch of sea, and the sky hanging down to meet it in blue sheets, and between them great multishaded geometric patterns of green vegetation ranging from jade to almost gray. I know of no seascape in the Pacific that is more majestic.

There is an agricultural extension center at Taliligap, and the men who staff it live on the rim of this enormous view. It is inevitable that one stops here to look across the bay and wonder at its loveliness, and almost certain that one will be invited to stay for a few minutes to look around, while the wife of the officer in charge makes a cup of tea.

I did that, and while Topuka magically disappeared to find a one-talk[1] to gossip with, I watched a group of men and lads being shown the simple but scientific way to lay out a new area of cocoa land.

Their instructors were New Guinean agricultural assistants, and instead of using costly shop-bought rope or chain measures, they had marked and measured lengths of bamboo and vine to work out, on the ground, the geometry of the planting, taking into account the area of the available land and its contour.

The officer in charge of the center, Bob Pulsford, found me, and

[1] One-talk: Pidgin English for a person from the same village as oneself.

having sent a message to his wife to make tea, stood with me watching the villagers under instruction. They were, he said, people who intended to plant up new areas of cocoa on land some distance from their village, that had been idle for many years, and they had come to the center to find out the best way to prepare this land and lay it out for planting, using only the simple materials available to them in the village.

Cocoa has been grown by settlers in New Britain since German times, but it is only in the last decade that villagers have been encouraged to plant it. Before then the feeling seemed to be that cocoa-growing, fermenting, and marketing were operations too complex and too technical for New Guineans, calling for too much capital and specialized agricultural training.

So, in 1951, a few advanced Tolai villagers produced only a doubtful ten tons of cocoa between them. But in 1961, having been stimulated by a new vitality in official thinking, there were almost three million cocoa trees planted on village lands; and a new element was added to the landscape, with thin and feathery shade-trees lining the roads row after row, and the cocoa trees below them sprouting hard-cased multicolored pods bright with violent mauves and orange-reds and yellows. And in those ten years production had climbed high to almost two thousand tons of dried beans from the villages.

Also, during those same years, scores of young New Guineans were trained as agricultural assistants; and now an agricultural college has been opened near Rabaul, so that it is possible for a student to gain a diploma in agricultural science without leaving the country.

Mrs. Pulsford called us from the veranda of the house and we went up and sat for a few minutes having tea, and looking at the view across the bay through a brilliant frame of gold and purple bougainvillea relieved with deep and creamy yellow hibiscus. In the room behind us the two Pulsford children sat frowning over lessons sent by a teacher at the correspondence school in Port Moresby.

The other two extension officers stationed here at Taliligap were away from the center. One of them was at a village nearby, helping to build a new copra drier. The other was on patrol for a week, inspecting village cocoa gardens to see that they were free of weeds

and disease, and thinning out trees where needed, because many of
the villagers tend to plant too thickly on the principle that the more
trees in production the bigger the crop.

It was pleasant sitting there with a cool breeze blowing up from
the sea, but Topuka came and sat ostentatiously in the driving seat
of the car to remind me that even if I had all day to waste gossiping, he hoped to be back in Rabaul in time for his baseball practice.
So I said goodbye and we drove away.

We left the coast and turned inland, still keeping to the high
ridges, and after a while passed the village of Nagananga, and
then Tapapipi with its rural health center, where Topuka seemed as
though he might like to stop for a moment, because he is friendly
with one of the infant welfare nurses. But the health team was out
on its rounds so we went on without stopping.

Away to the northwest, down in the wide valley of the Kerevat
River, the patterned patches of cultivation around the Government's agricultural experiment station stood out, and I remembered
a day spent there when Leon Bridgeland was the director.

He was, and is, a New Guinea enthusiast, for having resigned
from the Government service he remained in the Territory as a
private agricultural consultant, and still lives in Rabaul. It was he
who reminded me that the land is the only significant possession
of the primitive; that he has virtually no other permanent point of
focus around which to compose his life; that he owns nothing else
of any historical or lasting value. The primitive's house is made of
grass and may stand for three or four years before being pulled
down or abandoned to make way for a new one. He moves his food
garden every year or so to a new place, letting the old one grow
over and return to bush. He has no literature, no books, no works
of art or jewelry, no monuments. He has not even a nationality of
which he is conscious. The produce of the land is the measure of
his wealth, demonstrated by the splendor of the feasts that he is
able to give. His rituals are the rituals of planting and harvesting of
garden magic and fertility rites. In some places he beds his young
wife in her food garden.

Apart from the trivial wages earned by laborers and minor
Government employees, few New Guineans (except those who are
completely urbanized) have any source of wealth other than their
land and the sea that may bound it. Nor is there any way at pres-

ent by which an average New Guinean can raise his financial status, or share in the creation of a prosperous community, except by utilizing his land in ways that are often opposed to the traditional ways of the tribe.

For instance, leadership, under the old tradition, is based on a tribally acknowledged authority to allocate land to individuals within the clan, or to decide when and for what purposes land shall be used, or when it shall be planted or harvested or burned for hunting, or for making new gardens.

Traditional marriage customs, and the economics of interclan relationships, are inextricably entwined with the allocation and inheritance of land through lines of descent. Land is the symbol of prestige and the only source of wealth. A man without land is a "rubbish man," less than a "bush kanaka" who eats his dead. All of which means that to advance in any direction at all, the New Guinean may need to change the whole design of his life and not simply learn to speak English and add up.

This was Leon Bridgeland's reasoning and it seemed sound enough to me; but at the time, I think, he was railing against the government's two-million-pound budget for education, and less than half that amount for agriculture.

I had spent that day with Bridgeland at the Kerevat Experiment station, where he and other scientists were engrossed in researches into cocoa bean fermentation, and the development of disease-resisting strains of cocoa plants, and were producing tens of thousands of carefully bred plants for distribution to the villagers.

There was other interesting work going on, especially in the entomological field which, so the specialists say, is exciting in New Guinea from the purely academic point of view, there being so many strange insects to collect and study; and at the same time, there is much challenging practical work in dealing with expensive pests like the rhinoceros beetle that deflowers coconut trees, and the cacao tree borers that ruin cocoa crops.

It was approaching eleven o'clock as we pulled into the cocoa fermentary at Ngatur, one of the fifteen fermentaries on the peninsula owned and managed by Tolai local government councils.

Between them these fermentaries are pouring the approximate equivalent of half a million dollars into the villages of the peninsula, and this, together with the continuous if modest income from copra, and the high fertility production of garden food crops, give the Tolai people the best living standard in the country.

There was a crowd at the fermentary, two or three hundred men and women with baskets of wet cocoa beans, white and slimy. They came in family groups along the tracks between coconut groves and cocoa gardens, the women in most cases carrying the green-plaited palm-frond baskets full of beans. Some of the boy children had pet parrots either perched on their heads or sitting on long sticks carried over their shoulders. The men came to collect the money and talk and squirt betel nut juice around.

They all have a solid and well-fed look, men, women, and children; shiny skins and close-cropped curly hair, many of them hennaed yellow either for effect or for comfort, since the dye kills head lice.

The women wear lap-laps and loose smocks although they either take off the smocks or wear them as capes when working, to leave their arms free and allow the air to circulate around their bodies; and the men also wear lap-laps, adding a shirt only for formal occasions. Very few New Guinea men wear trousers, even when they become important in the new social and political order that is changing their lives in so many other ways, whereas among the Papuans of the south the wearing of Western dress has become a status symbol.

Mr. Gorringe, the Government-appointed supervisor of the Tolai cocoa project, was waiting to introduce me to the fermentary manager and his assistants, and explain the workings of the cocoa scheme; and after the introductions we looked at the fermenting boxes being filled and turned, then admired the costly new oil-burning hot-air rotary drier.

Outside, the women come to the weighing tables to hang their bean baskets on the spring scales. The tally clerk gave them each a weight slip which they took to the paying clerk, who gave them the cash at a standard base rate for each pound of wet beans. A balance of payment is made later when the season's crop is sold and the running costs of the fermentary have been deducted. This is a sore point with the villagers, and it creates a situation which illustrates the kind of problem that goes with political and economic adolescence.

The fermentaries are owned and operated by the native councils which are elected by the villagers, and are financed by a head tax, so that the village cocoa grower actually owns the fermentary. But the councils, with the backing of the Government, have built the fermentaries with money borrowed from private banks. And as this money has to be paid back, with interest, it is crystal clear to everybody but the villager that he is in debt to the bank and has an obligation to meet. So when he takes his wet beans to the fermentary he gets only a proportional payment on the spot and collects the rest of his money as a dividend based on the total fermentary profit for the year, after the bills have been paid and the bank interest met.

But if he takes his wet beans to a Chinese trader a little way down the road he will get a bigger immediate payment than he gets from the fermentary, and the deal is closed. He has the money in his hand. The fact that it is probably less than he would ultimately be paid by his own fermentary does not affect his thinking.

Some government men in Rabaul estimate that up to a third of the Tolai cocoa crop is marketed for this reason through Chinese traders instead of through the native-owned fermentaries, and that if the Government withdrew its support and supervisors, the Tolai cocoa project would collapse.

I sat talking with Mr. Gorringe on the edge of one of the long drying trays while elderly widowed women, employed by the council, turned the chocolate-purple, heavy-scented beans with wooden rakes.

Like many other Australians who devote almost their entire lives to the country (for Mr. Gorringe is unmarried and gives most of his time to the people), he worries about them and says that they seem to lack any real sense of purpose, and that they are not using this considerable new income to better themselves.

He thinks that they ought to set an example to the rest of the two million people of Papua and New Guinea and should take a leading part in the political advancement of the country; but, he says, shaking his head sadly, in ninety years they do not seem to have developed any capacity for sustained effort or initiative, and have shown no desire to change their basic way of life.

I think that he is perhaps a bit hard on them, even if in general terms he is right in his assessment, for in most communities there are a few who lead and the mass who follow, and it is too soon yet for national leaders to emerge from the fragmented and multi-tribal society of a country which is still struggling to escape from the chrysalis of primitivism and illiteracy.

Yet he has some grounds for his pessimism, for in spite of the enthusiasm for progress shown by the councils, most of the Tolai continue to live the old village life at the old tempo. A few enter-prising men may buy trucks and go into the carting business. A few others build themselves comfortable houses with modern materials, but many villagers are said to hoard the money earned by their cocoa just as they previously hoarded shell money, keeping it for display on ceremonial occasions and for reasons of prestige. Others, especially among the middle-aged men, squander it on drink and gambling. Only a few show any sense of adventure or seek new experiences beyond the village.

Tolai leaders who support the Government are afraid that if inde-pendence is thrust upon New Guinea the villagers will soon aban-don today's attempts to change their way of life. And the reason they give is that the villagers cannot see the personal goal toward which they are being partly driven and partly led, and are inter-ested only in those activities, traditional or newly introduced, which produce immediate and tangible satisfactions without too much disruption of the traditional ease of village life.

If this is the state reached by the most advanced people of New Guinea, what is to be expected of the backward mass for whom less can be done immediately, and who have no understanding whatever of the historical and geographic factors which have pro-duced the civilization that is being, inevitably, forced upon them?

I left Mr. Gorringe to his problems and drove to Tagitagi, where the headman is Councillor Tovilau, a young man. There was a malaria control unit there, unloading its buckets and spray pumps, but we did not stop, having in mind Topuka's anxiety to be back in Rabaul by four o'clock.

Most of the villages co-operate well in the antimalarial cam-paign, although the people probably find the repetitive spraying of their homes tedious after a while, and sometimes nullify the efforts of the teams with little tricks and evasions.

Each house in a village is sprayed six times at intervals of three months, and after each treatment the building is marked with a painted symbol to show the date and number of sprayings; and sometimes when a man builds a new house he cuts this symbol out of the wall of the old house and weaves it into the new one to mislead the spraying team.

But the control groups find allies among the women, most of whom show more concern for the health of their families than the men do, mainly because so many of them have lost a child, or two and even three, to the malarial mosquito, the biggest killer in the country.

After Tagitagi we climbed steeply into the hills and came to Paparatava, where a few years ago the people of eight villages, some Methodist and some Catholic, were brought together by a missionary and between them raised six thousand dollars, and then supplied the labor on a village roster system of sixty men a day to build a fine new community hospital and infant welfare center.

They cut off the top of a hill and made an artificial plateau with the rubble, because their land is steep and they have little level space to spare from gardening. Then they laid concrete foundations and built the hospital on this plateau, giving it an iron roof to catch the rain, and a system of tanks in which to store it.

There was a fine opening day, with the district commissioner performing the ceremony, and the Methodist and Catholic ministers beaming happily at each other. The village councilors wore their official white lap-laps and shirts, with brilliantly colored ties of Hong Kong silk bought at the Chinese trade stores, and big shiny councilor's badges, and looked somewhat confused by what they had achieved.

But it was the German missionary and the Australian Sisters who had organized the operation, collected the money, drawn the architectural plans, ordered the materials, and directed the work day by day, and who now take the responsibility for maintaining the center and training local girls in the hospital and clinic work.

I had lunch with the missionary and he told me about the building of the hospital. How the Bishop said that he would give the timber and supply wheelbarrows and picks and shovels, but the villagers would have to provide concrete and roofing iron and labor and such things, and pay the wages of the trained carpenters who came from another mission station. And the Government would help with equipment.

When the hospital was opened they still owed six thousand dollars to tradesmen in Rabaul, and there was not enough money for a lighting plant, but the first patient was already in bed when the opening ceremony took place, and within a year there had been seven hundred sick people taken in, and nearly a hundred babies born in the hospital, and five hundred children registered on the roll of the infant welfare clinic.

Before I left I went into the schoolroom in time to hear the children recite the midday Hail Mary which goes, in Pidgin, like this:

Alou Maria. Yu pulap long gratia.
(Hello Mary. You are full of Grace.)

Masta i stap long yu.
(The Master is with you.)

Yu nambavan belong ol meri,
(You are the first of all women,)

Na nambavan tru pikinini belong bel belong you, Jesus.
(and the true child of your womb is Jesus.)

Maria tokondo, mama belong Deo,
(Holy Mary, mother of God)

Yu raring belong mipela man belong pekato,
(You must pray for a sinner like me)

Nau, na long taim mipela i dai.
(Now, and when I die.)

Leaving Paparatava, and driving down a steep and waterworn track, we blew a tire, and Topuka swore coarsely in Pidgin.

It didn't surprise me that we had no jack and that he had to walk back up the hill to the mission to borrow one. He was gone for a half hour and came back in a temper, but by then a group of men had gathered and he was able to stand by and give instructions while they changed the wheel, for all New Guinea men love tinkering with cars and it made Topuka feel superior to be able to permit them this privilege. And when the job was done he brusquely instructed two small boys to take the jack back up the hill to the mission.

We drove on, heading now toward Rabaul along the high ridge road that runs across the center of the peninsula, so that on both sides of the tracks we could look out upon stupendous green landscapes, with the sea shimmering in the distance, both east and west, with such sky-reflected light that there was no horizon but only a merging of translucent silver air and water.

Then we passed through a high green cutting in the peak of a hill, and emerging, followed down a long curve in the ridge road until we came to a little plateau jutting out into the Kerevat Valley; and on the plateau, set in a neat lawn hedged with hibiscus bushes, a group of green and cream-painted buildings, and a signboard saying, "Vunadadir Local Government Training Centre."

When, in 1950, local government councils were first formed among the Motu people of Port Moresby and the Tolai of Rabaul, many high Government officials thought the move premature, while others thought it quite ridiculous.

The Government's intention was to provide a simple but practical form of political and governmental education for the most advanced people of the Territory, having in mind that one day in the unpredictable future the whole country would be ready for self-determination if not for self-government.

At that time there were substantial areas still unexplored, and it seemed reasonable to suppose that many years must pass before a network of these councils would cover the country. Yet such is the strength of the winds of change that blow all around the world today, and so forceful the pressures of international opinion, that local government councils are operating already in areas where, ten years ago, only armed patrols could move about with safety.

This is notable progress but it brings its own problems, chief of which is the education of the councilors, most of whom are illiterate, and of council clerks, so that these councils might be more than a mere statistical achievement.

Colin Liddle, a middle-sized, fine-faced young man who has fair hair and deep-set eyes (as well as a remarkably beautiful wife, five small sons, and two big dogs), is a pioneer local government officer and an idealist. As the car stopped I could hear his voice coming from the large meeting house, and guessed that he was lecturing freshly elected councilors from some newly created council area.

Ignoring Topuka's obvious impatience and irritation, I handed him a cigarette to show that there was no malice in my heart, then told him that we would be staying for a while as I wished to speak with Mr. Liddle. I walked across to the meeting house and stood outside, listening. He was speaking Pidgin and explaining to the councilors that they must no longer think of themselves as men of tradition but as innovators; that they must lead their people into new ways, expecting to be opposed by the old men.

He told them that to be an elected councilor was not an empty honor which permitted a man to strut about the village wearing a shiny badge, to shake hands with visiting officials and talk portentiously without doing anything. It was, he said, a responsibility and a challenge, and that they could no longer sit down and wait for the Government to do things for them, but must now lead their people into doing things for themselves.

Liddle is keen on his job. He feels that he is helping to shape the political future of the country because he is helping to form the minds of its future leaders. And he can point to practical things that exist because he put ideas into people's heads.

For instance, he and Council President Nason Tokiala of Vunadadir are mainly responsible for the rural health center at Tapapipi with its permanent district-visiting staff, because they encouraged the village people to build it, and induced the Government to appoint Dr. Moi, the two nursing sisters, a health inspector, and a malaria control officer to staff it.

Then there are the new school buildings that he suggested to one council, and a series of solidly constructed medical aid posts all over the peninsula. And the installation of the water reticulation system here at Vunadadir, to supply the training center. These are achievements of which he is proud.

I could hear him speaking to the newly fledged councilors as a prophet speaks to his people, and could see him through the open louvers standing before them. He was saying, "Your women have dents in their heads where the ropes of their baskets cut into their skin. Their backs are bent with loads of food and wood as they come from the gardens, even when they are heavy with child; and they die when they are young. But as councilors you can make the men cut roads, and build bridges across the streams, so that the produce of your gardens can be carried to market in carts and motor trucks, and the loads lifted from your women."

He went on speaking to them about the familiar things of their everyday life.

"When you were born the midwife made a fire and covered it with green leaves to make a thick smoke, and they passed you back and forth in the smoke to make you breathe and cry out. And of every three babies born in your villages, two died. But now you councilors can collect money from the people to build a hospital, and the Government will then give you nurses to look after your wives and babies."

He spoke of the land. Of how some villages are situated on steep and broken country that is no good for plantations, so that the people of those parts cannot progress. But the councils, he said, can change the old tribal laws and the taboos, and use hunting land for planting cocoa or coconuts instead of burning it off each year just to catch a few rodents and snakes.

Liddle knew what he was talking about because he had helped old Councillor Toguria and the young headman Tovilau of Tagitagi to write their letter to the Government, asking that unused land in the valley be leased to them so that they could resettle some of the young men made landless by the increase in population.

When he had finished speaking he came out, and we stood for a while by the car while he told me of his plans to start a course in elementary civics and social leadership for councilor's wives. Had it been anybody else but Liddle I might have smiled at the idea of Tolai men allowing their wives to waste time at school, but knowing him I could see it happening.

Topuka, sitting in the car, wound his watch and coughed.

A few minutes later we charged down the hill from Vunadadir toward Rabaul, and sent a peripatetic hen squawking all over the road in a demented attempt to gather her panic-stricken chickens. Topuka knew that I disapproved but pretended not to notice anything, so I made him stop for a few minutes at Navuneram village, where I spoke to the headman, Manoa, about filming a harvest dance. The last time I was in this village, an armed government patrol was camped here to restore order after an antitax riot, in which two villagers were killed.

Manoa is typical of many of the older Tolai leaders. A big man, beginning to run to fat, he is taciturn with strangers and authoritative Government officers. He is also arrogant at times, and stubborn about changes in the traditional structure of tribal authority. Yet he is generous and co-operative with people whose work does not bring them into conflict with his own concept of what is good for his people.

Such men are not easy to know. Some, like Manoa, remain aloof from most of the diverse activity of change that is going on around them. They refuse to take their place in the new forms of political organization introduced by the Government. Yet they continue to wield a local power that withstands pressures imposed both by the government and missions.

A Government officer who worked for many years in Rabaul told me not so long ago that many of the village headmen and clan leaders of the Tolai retain their traditional influence over the people because of their reputed powers as sorcerers. I have heard nothing of Manoa that would support this theory, but top Government officials hold in general that the almost universal dread of sorcerers in New Guinea is a barrier to progress among even the most enlightened tribal groups.

It was ten minutes to four as we drove back along Mango Avenue, and Topuka let me off at the New Guinea Club where I expected to meet Patrol Officer Grant, who was to take me in the morning out beyond the Tolai country, into the undeveloped part of the Gazelle Peninsula, no more than forty miles from Rabaul. It would take us two days to get there.

Six

It is a pleasure to go bush with Patrol Officer Grant, for although I am twenty-five years older he contrives to both father and mother me while yet preserving the illusion that I am perfectly competent to look after myself. He also maintains a childlike attitude of respect for my advanced years without deviating a single inch from his own inflexible purposes.

Some years ago we walked together for three months out beyond the far highlands of mainland New Guinea, into the no man's land of the Strickland Gorge where not even the most miserable primitive is able to live, so arid and desolate is the country. So Grant and I are well acquainted.

He makes friends with bush people easily and without dramatics. He is efficient at organizing carriers and all commissarial details of a patrol, and can bridge a swollen river without fuss or shouting while the passengers sit in the shade. And by New Guinea standards he is an Escoffier in the cookhouse.

He can also run uphill backwards, an achievement that goes back to the days when he was aiming to gain his university blue for boxing (which he did at Sydney), and to represent Australia at the Olympic Games, which he didn't, being defeated on points in a split decision in the final of the elimination contests.

He picked me up at eight o'clock in the morning in an ancient utility wagon wheedled out of an overworked transport department. It was already piled high with bedrolls, patrol boxes full of personal gear, cooking equipment and food, lamps and fuel, shovels, axes, bush knives, a theodolite and chain measure, two policemen named Gawi and Marengal, their rifles and personal gear, and Joe.

Joe is Patrol Officer Grant's cook. He comes from a Sepik River village where he is a man of importance who could, if he wished,

sit down all day and be waited upon by small boys. He hates walking and gets exceedingly morose when asked to prepare for a patrol,
but he has been with Grant for six years and shows no signs of
leaving him although he is always talking about it. On patrol, which
is often, he tails along glumly at the end of the line, carrying a
ancient shotgun over his shoulder in case he should see a bird of
paradise or a hornbill.

The chances of him ever hitting one of these elusive targets is
negligible but he dreams that one day he will go home to the
Sepik with a bundle of golden-red Raggiana bird of paradise
plumes, or even a skin or two of the Paradiseae Minor, which is an
even more beautiful bird in spite of its derogatory classification.

And when he opens them up the men of his village will immediately imagine themselves at the next sing-sing with a set of
these bright new plumes on their heads, catching the sunlight as
they shuffle and jump to the rhythm of the Kundu drums. And they
will covet them, and want to buy them.

And when he uncovers the hornbill's grotesque beak at the bottom of his box the old men's eyes will shine with admiration and
envy, and they will speculate as to whether Joe will wear it hanging from a cord between his shoulder blades as a sign of wealth
and the authority that wealth brings, or will sell it to a sorcerer to
be ground to powder, for the hornbill's beak makes powerful
magic.

I said "Hello" to Joe and tapped his slightly rounding stomach,
a familiarity permitted in acquainted age-mates, and said that
elderly gentlemen like us two (using the Pidgin word *lapun*) had no
business going on patrol but should stay at home and mind the
babies; at which he smiled wanly and grunted. And my patrol box
being stowed into the back of the truck by the policemen, Joe
slowly climbed on top of the load, settled, and lit his pipe.

The driver of the utility was a friend of Topuka's but not as
bright, having failed to pass the mechanic's course at the technical
school. We had our first flat tire within a half hour of leaving
Rabaul and not only did we have no jack, we had no spare wheel
or tire. Grant wrote a note to the transport officer in Rabaul asking
for two spare wheels and tires and some basic tools, and sent the
driver back into town by the first car that went past in that
direction.

It was pleasant sitting in the shade of a clump of bamboos looking out over the bay while Grant, with a map spread on the ground, showed me where we were going and explained what he hoped to achieve for the people in his care who live in the shabby villages of the lower Baining Mountains, just beyond the boundaries of the Tolai country.

There are no more than thirty-five hundred of these Baining people and they occupy an area of land about as big as that occupied by the forty-five thousand Tolai. They are a short-statured people, muscular, wide-eyed as though always surprised, good-natured, and very poor. Their women wear nothing but a small pad of grass no bigger than a hand, and a ridiculous tuft like the tail of a bantam cockerel.

Few of the children get to be three years old because the people are nomadic and move from the malarial coast to the cold inland heights each year, and the babies die like flies with the sudden change of climate, pneumonia being aggravated by malarial debility.

The Bainings' land, like that of the Tolai, forms a rough square raised in the middle, with two sides bounded by sea and two by rivers; the Kerevat, the Warangoi, and the Toriu.

Their immediate neighbors, the Tolai, live in a similar environment, and the two people are separated only by the barrier of disconnected rivers. The most remote Baining villages are no more than thirty miles farther from Rabaul than many Tolai villages. Yet the Tolai are rich sophisticates and the Bainings are poor primitives.

The difference is that the roads which link every Tolai village with the commercial outlet of Rabaul and the center of Government administration, stop suddenly at the rivers. No Government specialist, doctor, teacher, or agriculturalist can visit the inland Baining people except on foot. If they grow cocoa or hill coffee there is no way of getting it to the market. So they have no money and no progress. And until Patrol Officer Grant decided to adopt them they had little hope.

Joe produced a cup of tea.

In the old days, two or three generations ago, the Tolai used to raid the Bainings, and if they killed any of the people they sold the bodies for meat, but the captives they used as slaves. The early missionaries sometimes bought these Baining slaves from the Tolai to make converts of them.

Grant pointed out the Baining villages on his map: a few hamlets scattered along the two coasts, and some villages among the middle mountains; six or seven people to the square mile in a roadless area of some five hundred square miles. They pose, in microcosm, an administrative and governmental problem that is duplicated all over the Territory.

To link each village with its nearest commercial and administrative center is, more often than not, impracticable, especially when little population is scattered over big areas of land griddled with rivers and upheaved with mountains; and tropical rainfall brings landslides and continuously flooding rivers.

The answer to such problems, says Patrol Officer Grant, is to move the people. Put them where the world can get at them and they can get at the world: if not, just leave them alone and let them find their own way to civilization if they want it.

He has spent two hundred and fifty days out of a year walking around among the Baining people, talking to them, looking at their problems, figuring the possibilities of the land and the people, and coming to mean something to them as a representative of the Government and as someone, not a missionary, who is interested in their problems.

He has found that in the few places where missionaries have schools, however elementary, some of the young people have begun to feel conscious of their isolation and backwardness, and to wish for better things; and in villages where the people have access to mission or Government medical aid posts, and have been visited by a medical assistant on patrol from Rabaul, there are more children surviving.

The headman of one village, Simbadka of Ranaulit, has been to Kerevat to get cocoa plants, and Grant has taken some young men to Taliligap and left them with Bob Pulsford for agricultural training. He has also taken specialists from Rabaul, from other departments of the Government, to look at the problems of the Bainings; from Education, Health, Agriculture, Forestry, and Public Works, and a man from the Scientific and Industrial Research Organisation, who took soil samples.

When he had sorted out his own thoughts and the opinions of the experts he talked to the district commissioner, who called the District Economic Development Committee together to consider the problems of the thirty-five hundred Bainings, and Patrol Officer Grant's plans for their future.

Then there were the murderers. A group of Sepik laborers, working on a plantation on the Baining coast, had finished their two-year contract and were going home. To get to Wewak, which is the port of entry for the Sepik district, they would have to get the weekly plane from Rabaul; and to get to Rabaul they could either go by copra boat around the coast, or walk to the boundary between the Baining and the Tolai country, and from there ride by a council trucking service into Rabaul. They elected to walk.

It is a fairly easy walk, following the track used regularly by the Baining people as they move back and forth between the coast and the mountains. There seemed every prospect of it being a pleasant journey of three days, staying each night at a Baining village to rest and to gossip. It would be like a vacation after two years of labor on a copra and cocoa plantation.

The first night they stopped at Galivat and had a pleasant evening, talking and showing off the presents and possessions that they were taking home to their villages in the Sepik; each man having a tomahawk, a bright, orange-painted wooden suitcase, a new lap-lap and singlet for Sundays, a knife, spoon, plate, blanket, razor blades, mosquito net, and many other minor possessions, as well as money saved in two years or won at cards, perhaps ten or fifteen pounds. One man had an alarm clock.

The next day their start was delayed. Their generous hosts pressed food upon them and gave them meticulous directions as to the best route to follow. Some of the village men even went part of the way with them to make sure that they took the right track. It would have been pleasant to have stayed a little longer with these amiable if uncouth bushmen.

In the middle of the morning, following a narrow sunken pathway between tall trees, they were ambushed and killed with axes and knives, all except the first man who had been allowed to pass through unharmed. The dead laborers were stripped of the possessions they had so proudly displayed the night before, and the murderers went back to Galivat with the loot.

There was no motive but theft. No deep-seated animosity. No history of viciousness or of tribal antagonism. Just a hunger for possessions.

The district commissioner felt that Patrol Officer Grant might do some good among the Bainings if he could help and encourage them to acquire clean lap-laps and alarm clocks by less violent means than those used by the young men of Galivat who now languished in the jail at Rabaul. So, having considered Grant's scheme for resettling them into accessible communities, he gave it his blessing and instructed him to proceed with the attempt.

The driver came back with the spare wheels and tires and within fifteen minutes we were on our way again.

An hour later we got bogged in the Kerevat Valley, where the car tracks disappear at times beneath pools of stagnant rainwater (but it had been an exceptionally wet season, with fifteen inches of rain during the month), and being greatly overloaded we sank down to the hubcaps.

But it happened within a mile of the Forestry Department's logging camp and research center, so Grant and I took the opportunity to stretch our legs and visit, leaving the driver and the two policemen, with Joe's disinterested assistance, to dig the vehicle out.

The Forestry Department plays the key role in Grant's scheme, for it has been agreed that an area of the Bainings' land can be used for logging and reforestation, which means that a bridge must be built across the river and access roads put in at the expense of the Forestry Department.

We walked the mile, and finding the road engineer talked with him about the project. He would, he said, bring bulldozers into the proposed forestry area for road-making as soon as the bridge could be built to take them. The Baining people will find this exciting. Few of them have ever seen a bulldozer.

The truck caught up by midday and brought us to the river where eight pairs of carriers were waiting to take over our gear. The two policemen distributed the loads and the carriers set off at a trot, each pair carrying a load of up to seventy pounds weight suspended on a pole, slung between them on their shoulders.

They ran across the big log that spans the river, some twenty yards or more from bank to bank and a dozen feet above the swiftly flowing water. I shuffled over with one hand outstretched and resting on the shoulder of Gawi the policeman, for I am affected by heights and a little out of practice.

We walked into the hills for nearly five hours and came to the village of Ranaulit, and camped there in a bush hut. The next day we came to Malasite, a village of about a hundred people, occupying the whole of a small oval plateau, with hills all around and reaching back to a low horizon lost in gray-rainy cloud. Malasite is in the approximate center of the Baining country at an elevation of some two thousand feet, and it is in this area that Grant plans to resettle many of the people who are now scattered about the hills in isolated hamlets. Already one small group has come close and built its houses within sight, and on the side of the nearest valley others are making food gardens so that they, too, can move in; and columns of white smoke rise in the still air where men are burning off bush to clear the land.

On the way up, while we were walking, Grant had pointed out areas that seemed suitable for cocoa lands, and hillsides that might be cleared for cattle-grazing, as well as a patch where he had already put out some coffee bushes, and seedlings of hill coconut palm, to see how they would do.

It was toward evening when we walked into Malasite, and sad, dull-eyed, naked women with vacant faces were coming from their gardens bent under loads of food and firewood, with babies clinging to them on top of the loads, and little children following behind.

We walked about the village, and Grant pointed out that although there were many little children, there were none between the ages of five and ten, which seemed to coincide with a period of unrest among these hill-dwelling Bainings, during which time they migrated back and forth between the heights and the coast, losing their children to malaria and pneumonia year after year.

In the middle of the village a new house, not yet finished, stood out above the rest, not only because its timbers were clean, being freshly stripped of bark, but because of all the houses in the village it alone stood up on posts, with its floor raised above the ground; and it was bigger than the other houses, having two enclosed rooms and a veranda, whereas the other houses are simply single-roomed slab-sided timber kennels set on the bare ground.

"This," said Grant, standing before the unfinished house, "is the beginning of our new housing project." He turned and waved an arm around the village. "Look at those dog boxes: too small, no ventilation, the people live on the ground, cook, eat, sit, smoke, spit, and sleep in the same poky space, men, women, and children, uncles and aunts and grandparents."

He turned back to the new house.

"When this is finished I am going to pull down the headman's house and move him in here with his family, and when he can afford to buy blankets for them all I will put a window in the sleeping room; but without blankets it will be too cold to have a window. And I will have the women taught to weave mats to cover the floor so that they can sleep clean and not on the bare ground like they do now. And one by one, if I can't do it quicker, I will pull down every house in this village and build a new one to replace it."

Some men came up out of the valley where they had been hunting, one of them carrying six parrots perched on a stick, but tied to it by the feet so that they could not fly away. They are used by the hunters as decoys, tied to the branch of a tree in the bush while the hunter hides; and when the decoys' cries bring other birds, the hunter lets fly with a slingshot.

A plane passed overhead coming from Rabaul and going toward the coast, and after a while it returned, then came back again later. It seemed strange. There are no airfields in the area yet, and no aircraft would be flying the regular routes in and out of Rabaul so late in the day. But for some time afterwards we could hear the sound of aircraft in the distance, over toward the coast, and wondered what was happening.

More men came back into the village, and the last of the women from the gardens, and there were little scurries of sound and movement as children chased each other among the houses, and a slow procession of men strolling about, with a knot of them gathered around our camp talking to the policemen. And Joe had two small boys fetching and carrying wood for the cooking fire and vegetables from Grant's experimental garden plot.

There is a Methodist Church at Malasite but it is a sorry, tumbledown, bedraggled and very humble building, not much bigger than the village houses, and as bare. It is nothing like the sturdy and lovingly designed churches of the Tolai.

The New Guinean pastor Saimon Gaius comes when he can to

hold a service, and there is a mission schoolteacher stationed in the village, a young man trained at the George Brown College who does what he can to open the eyes and minds of the children.

He came and stood by me, looking over my shoulder at the rough map that Grant had drawn for me. I pointed to the name "Malasite" and said that it marked the spot where we were standing. He looked puzzled and was silent for a while. Then he said cautiously, "That is a map?"

I said, "Yes, it is a map, and here," pointing with my finger, "is Malasite."

He was again silent. Then he said, "I am the schoolteacher of Malasite."

I couldn't think of any answer.

Grant hopes that the Education Department will put two schools into the Bainings when he has concentrated the population, one in the hill country around Malasite and the other near the coast. He hopes also that the Health Department will send a medical assistant to start a hospital, although the population is perhaps too small to justify the luxury, and in any case there is a German priest, Father Hagen, stationed at the next village beyond Malasite and he is an experienced man and can deal with most medical problems.

The day's last light whitened the horizon and we saw, sharp against the narrow band of bright sky, another plane, one that neither of us could identify, swooping low over the ranges to the north, no more than two hours' walk away, somewhere in the vicinity of Kombi village on the track down to the coast. We watched it take one last low swoop, then climb and fly back toward Rabaul.

We turned away, and a moment later Joe clattered pots and plates, signaling dinner, though with little grace; but the meal was good and we sat afterwards in semidarkness yarning until it was time for the news from the new radio station at Rabaul.

Grant triggered his little transistor and there was movement outside in the darkness as the two policemen came to listen, and the schoolteacher, and a few of the village men who could understand Pidgin. Then, when everyone was settled, Joe sauntered over smoking his pipe, and stood beside Grant.

It was the first item that told us what we wanted to know and what we more than half-expected. There had been an air crash in

the Bainings, near Kombi village, and the aircraft we had seen over
the ranges had been searching for wreckage and for signs of survivors. We looked at each other but kept quiet, waiting to hear more,
especially about the strange plane swooping about at sundown.

It was, said the news reader, a helicopter that had crashed. Grant
and I raised our eyebrows. There are no helicopters in New Guinea;
and Joe, puzzled and irritated because he could not understand,
and hating to seem ignorant in front of two illiterate policemen
and the villagers, not to mention the schoolteacher, muttered, half
to himself and half to Grant, *"Wonem dispela helicopter?"*

Grant hushed him, and explained quickly that it was a special
kind of plane that we didn't have in New Guinea. But Joe looked
sulky and dissatisfied with the explanation.

The helicopter had been operating, said the news reader, from a
U. S. Navy survey ship off the coast of New Britain.

This explained the unidentified aircraft as being almost certainly
an American plane brought down from Guam to join in the search.

The helicopter, continued the news reader, had crashed while
landing technicians and equipment at the proposed site of a U. S.
Geodetic Survey installation high in the Baining Mountains, and
had burst into flames, being immediately and totally destroyed. It
crossed my mind that only a few months ago we had welcomed a
Russian survey ship into Port Moresby.

Fortunately, the pilot of the helicopter and his two passengers
were safe, though badly burned, and were at this moment being
carried down to the coast on stretchers by a party of Baining villagers organized by Cadet Patrol Officer Hart.

There was much more to the item, explaining that the U. S. Navy
was installing a network of signal stations in the Pacific as part of a
plan to meticulously map the whole of the earth's surface elec-
tronically. The Russians, I think, were mapping the floor of the
ocean.

It seemed strange to suddenly realize, sitting there in a grass
house in Malasite, preoccupied with finding ways and means to
bring these backward people of the Bainings expeditiously into our
civilization, that they had already become, without their knowledge
or ours, a minute cipher in the mammoth calculations taking part
in the Pentagon and the Kremlin.

They were now, already, standing out there in the darkness, a

part of the high mystery of this top-secret world of today that jug-
gles with survival and destruction; the world in which we all inescapably live whether in Malasite or Moscow or Manhattan; a
world that does not bear thinking about and cannot be mentioned
except in cabalistic doubletalk.

The news item went on to its conclusion and was then repeated
in English and in Kuanua, the Tolai tongue. The cost of the destroyed helicopter and the rescue operation, said the news reader
with awe and astonishment, might amount to a million dollars.

"Mother of God," said Grant, who is a pious man, "I could settle every family in the Bainings in air-conditioned villages for that
much, and have enough left over to educate a couple of doctors."

Later I spoke to Joe, asking him what he thought about it all. He
shrugged and looked down at the ground and replied with studied
disinterest.

*"Mi no savvy dispela samting . . . im i samting belong white
man, tasol."*[1]

[1] "I don't understand this—it's white man's business."

Seven

Grant was busy the next day, surveying, assisted by Constable Gawi, the headman of Malasite, and three boys. He was roughly measuring the amount of land available for food gardens and small plantations of coffee, estimating how many people might be resettled roundabout, and where a road could go to link these proposed settlements with each other, and with Rabaul.

I stayed in the rest house and worked on a rough script for a film on economic development among the people of the Gazelle Peninsula, and toward evening took a few photographs to illustrate locations; so we were both well occupied until dusk.

During dinner Constable Marengal came to the door of the rest house with a note which, he said, had just been brought by two men of the Methodist Church at Malabunga, a lowland village of the Bainings right on the edge of the Tolai country.

It came from Pastor Saimon Gaius, and said that the vartabar ceremony of thank-offering was to be held at Malabunga in two days' time, and that a fire dance would be performed afterwards, and would I care to come? It takes from six to eight hours to walk from Malasite to Malabunga, depending on weather and how much water is in the rivers.

I went outside to talk to the men. They were deacons of the church who had walked from Malabunga during the day to bring the invitation. We agreed to start back early in the morning because, being deacons, they would be much involved in the ceremonies and wished to be back as soon as possible.

We settled for six o'clock when there would be light enough to see the track and time enough for us to get over the highest hills before the sun got hot. So, in the morning, we beat the sun to the top of the high range out of Malasite and dropped down through forest toward the valley of the Kerevat River, so that the walk, though humid, was not hot.

There had been rain overnight and in steep places the track was slippery, and where it led into flat and shallow claypans it disappeared altogether under mud and water. And the leeches were particularly vicious.

But except at a few rocky outcrops, where the track was attentuated into six-inch footholds, we made good time and crossed the river no more than waist-high at the ford, reaching Malabunga soon after noon.

The Reverend Saimon Gaius, superintendent of the Bainings circuit of the Methodist mission, is a Tolai, big, serious, and solid. He was educated for the ministry first at the George Brown College at Rabaul and then at the Methodist Training College in Sydney. He is greatly respected by his colleagues and his congregations.

I went to the village rest house to let him know that I had arrived and to thank him for his invitation. He was busy with church affairs and had a group of village catechists and teachers around him, but left them for a few minutes to welcome me.

He seemed, in spite of a natural reserve and quiet dignity, to be happy in a deep-down, silent, and satisfied way, and when I asked him if he were pleased with his visit he said that it had so far been fruitful, for he had baptized eight babies at a special service that morning, and had interviewed two lads who wished to study to be teachers so that they could later work among their own people farther inland.

He said that the village people had tidied a corner of the new school building for me, and he called a lad and sent him with me to help set up a cot. So I left him to his business and went with my helper to the school and was busy for a while settling in.

Then I cooked myself a meal, wrote some notes, and went to bed, for it had been a fairly long day. And having read for a few minutes, I went to sleep to the sound of villagers rehearsing their hymns for tomorrow's services.

In the morning, soon after eight o'clock, people began to arrive from nearby villages, bringing food for their own casual needs during the day, and bigger quantities to contribute to the general feast that would be held later, when the formal religious ceremonies were finished.

As they arrived they found places for themselves in the shade of big trees on the rim of the village, or in temporary bush shelters built for this purpose by their hosts. They hung their own food in the trees in palm baskets or nets, and put their water gourds and a few young coconuts containing clear milk, in the shade at the foot of the trees. But the food for the feast they stored in the shelters out of the way. Later it would be put together in the middle of the village to form part of a great display of feasting food, after which it would be distributed in a traditional exchange of courtesies.

It is the custom for several villages that are within reasonable distance of each other to hold the annual vartabar in combination, each village taking its turn to be host to the others, and in this way the responsibility for organizing and preparing the essential framework for the ceremonies falls upon each village only once in five or six years.

This is very important, for on the level of traditional village economy it is no light undertaking to be host to the combined population of five or six other villages.

The New Guinea villager is not able to go to a store to buy food, firstly because he has no money for this kind of lavishness and secondly because there is nothing to buy in the stores but rice and tinned meat. So before a village can undertake the responsibility of inviting other villages to a feast it must first prepare a special food garden.

The selection of the land to the harvesting of the crop might well span a period of two years in a pattern of conference, invocation, ritualistic digging, working of magic, blessing of seed, consultation with sorcerers, waiting on the appearance of certain propitious stars or other phenomenal signs, the holding of minor feasts and dances associated with gardening cycles, as well as the practical work of burning off the ground, clearing, turning, planting, tending, and weeding.

And this is done with intense earnestness, for if the crop fails the village will lose its reputation for giving good feasts; then shame and dishonor will be shared by all, and the villagers will seek a scapegoat to blame and accuse of failing to perform the proper rituals or garden magic.

But this is not all. A village does not uphold the honor of its ancestors merely by providing a spectacular display of yams and taro and sweet potato: there must be pork to kill and distribute on an impressive scale, and it takes time to breed a supply of pigs surplus to normal needs.

Then the village itself should look well. Perhaps the church is in need of repair, or some of the houses are a disgrace, and the well needs cleaning out, and for these tasks the village must supply its own labor, and the material must be gathered from the bush.

And in the weeks before a vartabar or similar great occasion great stores of firewood must be gathered, not only for cooking but for illumination, and for feeding the ceremonial dancing fires; and there are masks and other dance decorations to be made, rest houses to be built for visitors, songs and dances to be taught to the young people and rehearsed by the others.

All of this places a considerable strain on village resources in terms of time, labor, land, seed, and breeding stock, a strain that is often far more personally demanding in a primitive or semiprimitive community than it is in our cash-culture society, where food and entertainment can be organized professionally and paid for with a signature.

But this is not the total picture. The people of Malabunga, and their neighbors, and their fellow countrymen all over New Guinea, live in two worlds, each making its demands, and this is demonstrated by the requirements of the vartabar: for the practical purpose of these mission-organized ceremonies is to raise funds to support the work of the church in New Guinea, and to meet this requirement the Baining villages must find cash money as well as provide the traditional evidences and symbols of faith and status in the form of food and the furniture of traditional rituals.

To find the cash for the support of their church the young men must go to work for white or Chinese people in Rabaul, or on plantations, or become casual laborers, working locally among their Tolai neighbors making copra or cleaning weeds from cocoa gardens (for the tradition of Baining man working for Tolai still lingers). And a man too old to work might sell a fowl or a few pounds of copra so that he can also make a contribution.

And women who are too old to work in the gardens or to carry firewood but have other skills, make mats and baskets and net bags

to sell in town or to Chinese traders. And the money earned by the
old people and the young men is shared out so that everybody in
the village can make a contribution to the cash offering to Christ.

So, in these ways, the whole community is actively involved over
a lengthy period in a project that not only occupies their time, but
is part of the breath of their being and the fabric of their existence,
both old and new. Many modern universities strive hard to inculcate
such an attitude in the educated young of this current civilization.

By nine o'clock the village was busy with people arriving, the
men meeting friends, the women finding places where they could
sit in comfort and hang their food and their babies, in nets, in the
shade. Among them a few church deacons, teachers, and elders
wore shirts or clean singlets with their best go-to-meeting lap-laps,
and some of the most advanced women wore cotton dresses or
Mother Hubbard blouses; but most of the people, men and women,
were bare-breasted in the manner of simple bush people, and the
small children ran naked.

A little later two elders of Malabunga came from the rest house
to set up tables and chairs near the village church, from which a
temporary shelter of bamboo had been extended to accommodate
the additional congregation, and this sign started a mass movement
so that in a few moments everybody had gathered together in an
expectant phalanx, sitting in village groups, facing the table.

Pastor Gaius came down the steps of the rest house and took his
place, standing behind the table. He waited for silence then spoke
quietly, saying that he would pray. Heads bent together, and after
a quiet pause his voice came over them like slow music being played
in the distance. The children sat silent and wide-eyed.

Saimon gave thanks that they were all gathered together in peace
and in the love of God, and when he finished stood aside while
the preacher of Malabunga announced a hymn, first declaiming it
verse by verse. Then someone from each village prayed, or led a
hymn or uttered words or praise.

When the church leaders of each village had led the congregation, Saimon Gaius spoke about the vartabar, going back in time to
Dr. Brown and the Fijian preachers and teachers, tracing again
the history of the mission and its impact on the people of New
Britain, telling a story, casting a spell, bringing to the people a

sense of belonging and purpose, and sudden inexplicable joy for being Christian.

When Saimon finished they sighed, and the sound was like wind in a field of wheat. Then they sang another hymn and were satisfied and sat back to wait for the practical things.

The preacher of Malabunga came forward first. He had nothing in his hands and his face was a caricature of misery, shame, and woe. The people watched him expectantly as he approached the table, and when he came to where Saimon sat he half-turned so that he could talk to the pastor and at the same time let the people see and hear him.

He told a sad story of how the people of Malabunga had worked and slaved to earn money for the church. How each person in the village (he named the oldest widow and the youngest man) had come to him with an offering to be added to the sum that he kept hidden in a bag under his sleeping mat.

And then, he said, a thief, a wild man out of the bush, had come while he was at the river washing himself. The people, spellbound, looked at each other in horror, and there was a sudden short hiss of whispering, while he waited, head bent, to continue.

The money was gone (he held out his empty hands). The people of Malabunga were ashamed. They had nothing to give to the vartabar. The preacher hung his head. Saimon tried to look sympathetic. There was an embarrassed, almost uncomfortable hiatus while the people waited.

Then the deacon's eyes opened wide and his chin fell and he pointed a shaking finger across the heads of the congregation. A shrill cry of excitement went up from the children, and several young men of Malabunga jumped to their feet, and all heads and eyes turned.

At the edge of the village stood a wild man, his head hidden in a bark mask, a girdle of leaves around his middle, and his body and legs plastered over with mud. In one hand he held a bouquet of croton leaves and in the other a bag of money.

The young men gave chase. For five minutes there was hysteria as the "thief" ran among the people with the young men after him, until they caught him near Saimon's table. The preacher of Malabunga retrieved the money and everybody sighed with relief, and then with pleasure and gratification as the coins were poured out onto the table and counted, and the amount written by Saimon on a blackboard that stood beside him.

He thanked the people of Malabunga and praised them for their generosity, and playfully scolded them for the fiction of the thief, and they loved it because they have a childlike joy in make-believe. Then Saimon prayed for Malabunga and its people. And a hymn was sung. After this each village in turn made its contribution of cash.

The chief deacon of one village came with a bunch of bananas, saying that the young men had found no work on the plantations and the women no buyers for their weaving, so that his village had nothing to give but this bunch of bananas which, perhaps, someone in the congregation might care to buy, seeing that they were good bananas, from his own garden.

Then there was a great and serious enactment of buying bananas one by one until a package wrapped in leaves was found in the center of the bunch, and being opened contained the village offering.

Another village, imaginative even if unintentionally sardonic, had rigged a wire stretching from a housetop to Saimon's table, and down this wire came a model plane carrying the village contribution in a little wooden crate.

So it went on, interspersed with hymn and prayer and ejacultory praise, until each village had performed its byplay and made its contribution to the mission, and had seen its name and the amount of its contribution written up. Then everyone was satisfied and dispersed to talk and to eat a little.

In the early afternoon most of the visitors rested, although some of the men had preparations to make for the preliminary dances that would start toward evening and lead to the main events of the night.

The women of Malabunga became busy fetching food from the special garden, while their children collected fagots of wood stored on the outskirts and stacked them near the center of the village. Men disappeared deeper into the bush to get ready for the ritual dance, which is hedged in with secrecy and considered traditionally sacred.

I spoke to Saimon, telling him that I would like, if it would not offend, to see something of the preparations for the ritual dances, and he called two men, one of them being of the two who had brought me down from Malasite, and when they agreed we went into the bush and followed a narrow track that brought us, in five or six minutes, into a small clearing.

There were five young lads in the clearing, three of whom were withdrawn into the darkest corner of a bush shelter where they stood peering out at us like young animals as we came upon them. They had been disturbed, no doubt, by the clumsiness of my approach, realizing that only a white man would make so much noise walking through the bush. But the men with me spoke to them and they came slowly out into the open.

The other two lads, though naked except for a narrow band of cloth drawn around the waist and pulled tightly between the legs, seemed less embarrassed. One was fitting a mask over the other's head, twisting it so that it came down to cover his neck and rest upon his shoulders.

These masks are made of tapa cloth or pandanaus leaves sewn together and stretched over a frame of thin cane, shaped into the semblance of strange, imaginary animals with big, discoid ears and flat, protruding lips.

Some of them look oddly like primitive caricatures of Mickey Mouse; others are shaped like great birds' heads but with long, pendulous tongues hanging from the lower bill, and a high, ornamental excrescence growing above the nostrils.

The masks are decorated with formal designs of big bull's-eye circles, and connected triangles, colored red, brown, and white, and are fringed all around the neck with long streamers of shredded leaves so that when worn they not only cover the head but hang down in a wild mane over the shoulders.

They are called *aios* or *miaus* (which Saimon later told me is the Baining word for a spirit), and the dances in which the masks are worn are called by the same name, and are known as spirit dances; and the men who wear the masks represent ancestral ghosts.

The red markings are made with the blood of the man who will wear the mask. He cuts his tongue with a leaf folded in two, and chews the cut to bring blood, and this he spits into a cup that is half a coconut shell or gourd. Then he paints the design onto his mask with a stick of cane chewed to make a brush; but sometimes

[10a, b, c, d, e] Pictures a, b, and c, taken toward evening, show a young man of the Bainings people dressed in readiness to take part in the traditional fire dance. The young men who participate in the dance spend several days in a secret place in the bush, observing certain rituals of purification, and making their masks and magumbets. They do not show themselves publicly until late at night.

Pictures d and e were taken during performance of the dance. At one time these dances accompanied orgies of feasting and sexual excitement. Today they are performed mostly in connection with important occasions in the calendar of the Methodist Church mission.

b

c

d

e

[11] Kondom Agaundo, leader of the Wandi people in the Chimbu Valley, and elected representative in the Legislative Council of Papua and New Guinea of six hundred thousand highlanders.

Kondom was a grown lad when men from the outside world first came into the highlands, and had taken part in tribal wars, fighting with a bow and arrows and a spear. Although uneducated and unable to read or write, Kondom is now president of the native local government council in his area, a successful coffee-planter, and has been responsible for building schools, medical aid posts, and community centers among his people. Two of his sons are schoolteachers. He has eight wives.

[11a] Villagers of the Asaro Valley district in the Eastern Highlands of New Guinea. When this picture was taken, in the middle of the morning, the women of the village were out in the gardens, leaving the men behind to look after the young boys and babies. In villages of this kind the people are in the middle stage of transition, having abandoned their traditional pastimes of warfare and tribal fighting and not yet become completely involved in more modern activities such as coffee-growing and planned social development through native local government councils.

[12] Father Nilles, priest and anthropologist, preaching to his Chimbu parishioners in the valley language during Sunday Mass at the Mingende mission church.
   Figures in the mural behind the altar represent men, women, and children of
the tribe, together with a white priest and a nun, and native catechists and novices.
Most of the educational work in the highlands is done by the missionaries.

[13] Nop Nop Tol, one of the most important leaders of the Minj people in the Wahgi Valley. Nop Nop has five wives and nine thousand coffee trees. Officially he is the Government interpreter for the district, president of the local government council, and was recently a candidate in the Legislative Council elections. Nop Nop is becoming rapidly Westernized, and on his visits to the district headquarters or to Port Moresby wears a white linen suit. He remembers, as a small boy, the coming of the first white men to the Wahgi Valley.

[14] Wahgi Valley men coming to a government station to take part in preliminary elections for the Legislative Council. Some groups come in mock-battle formation, wearing traditional dress and shouting war cries; others come in solemn procession wearing shirts and other Western clothes, and chanting mission hymns.

[15] At the declaration of the poll, following election of members to the Legislative Council of the Territory, Kondom Agaundo (also see Illustration 11), winner of the highland seat, is congratulated by a tribal voting representative. Nop Nop, on the left of the picture (also see Illustration 13), an official government interpreter and a powerful clan leader of the Wahgi Valley tribes, came second in the election. Both men are local government presidents and coffee-planters.

[16] Girls and young men gathered for the conventional courting play known as the *kanana*. As can be seen on the left of the picture, the young men sit facing the girls with their legs laid across the girls' thighs. As the chanting goes on the couples rub their faces together and go through other motion of sexual stimulation. After a while the young men move on to the next girl. If a couple is especially attracted to each other they move out of the hut and continue their courting privately in the bush, or in the girl's house. The kanana is a fundamental part of the courtship conventions of the people of the Central Highlands of New Guinea. This picture was taken at Nondugi, in the Wahgi Valley.

[17] A coffin of the type used generally in the Southern Highlands. When a person dies the body is first exposed on a platform for a period of public mourning and lamentation. Profesional morticians of the tribe then truss the body and wrap it in leaves before enclosing it in a coffin raised on stilts, with the head at the high end. Later the bones are interred and a mortuary feast is held. The skull is kept by the family as a memorial.

[18] The author with Hebi, a young man of good family in the Kopiagu area of the Duna country, at present being brought under government control.

Bad flying weather preventing the delivery of film stocks by airdrop, Hebi made an unaccompanied journey of four days each way, through hostile country, to the patrol base to fetch supplies. For this he was rewarded with a steel ax.

Patrol Officer Grant is in the background of the picture.

he just spits the blood straight onto the mask and smears it with his finger.

One of the young men who had been hiding in the corner of the shelter seemed still shy and secretive and kept his back turned to us, but one of his friends grinned and said that he was fixing his *magumbet* and was bashful. And after a while, when they had become more accustomed to my being there, I was able to see more of this and became so deeply interested that I forgot my own embarrassment (for at the beginning I had felt an interloper).

The magumbet is a cylinder of bark about a foot long, topped with a mushroom or butterfly cap, and worn as a decorated phallus. A long streamer of bark cloth about eight inches wide hangs from the lower end of the cylinder and is pulled down over the sex organs and drawn tightly between the legs to be fastened at the base of the spine by a slither of bamboo that is pinned through the flesh. And there it hangs like a tail. The phallus itself is bedded at the bottom of the stomach and stitched rigidly into the pubic hair, projecting forward, and stayed with a fiber string tied around the waist.

The man who had been my guide from Malasite explained these things to me with signs and faltering Pidgin English, and I understood that these young men were initiates who had not previously taken part in the sacred dances of the spirits.

They had, he said, been living in secret for several days, a period of purification, during which they had fasted except for water, and would not eat until the big feast which followed the dance. In that time they had seen no women, and no women would see them until the time of the feast, for all females are sent into their huts while the sacred dance is done.

In other parts of the bush young men from other villages were being decorated for their initiatory appearances, and again, elsewhere, the older men were congregated to make their own special preparations for the dance.

At four o'clock, or thereabouts, we heard the drums start, and my guides said that we must go back because it would be ill-mannered of them to miss dances being done by the visitors.

The village was alive when we arrived, with most of the people crowded around a small group of four dancing men, each of whom wore a high hat made of wickerwork trimmed with leaves and

bark, towering twelve feet or more above his head, each hat held
in place by three or four men holding long props attached to the
top of it.

They shuffled around in a small space hemmed in by villagers,
scuffling the dust and giving little hops while the prop-holders jug-
gled to keep the hats in place. There was no apparent pattern in
the dance and it seemed that the excitement derived from a form
of contest between the dancers trying to dislodge the hats, and the
prop-holders striving to keep them upright.

But there is this thing about the dances of New Guinea: in most
places the choreography is monotonous and uninspired and not of
much consequence, it being the dress and decoration and general
demeanor of the participants that is the important creative mani-
festation and achievement, so that the spectator is looking at a display of unique handicrafts presented dramatically, rather than
watching a dance.

The Malabunga people, being hosts, were busy with other things.
Men carrying great logs laid them in the center of the village to
form foundations for three fires that would be lit at sundown,
spaced as the points of a triangle; and women came in slow procession, one after the other, with bundles and baskets of food, laying
them out on a carpet of coconut fronds thirty or forty yards long
and six feet wide.

They came with sweet potato and yams, bunches of edible leaves,
sticks of sugar cane and bundles of big-leafed taro; with here and
there a small basket of tomatoes, cucumbers, melons, beans, and a
few cobs of corn, all of which have been lately introduced into village gardens in the Bainings.

Meanwhile there were more dances, some for men and others
for women, among them a spear dance with its wistful recollection
of the old days when war was normal. Then a sugar cane dance
with overtones of sex symbolism, the women carrying sticks of
sugar cane on their shoulders and, after they had danced provok-
ingly, presenting them to the men who were drumming for the
dance.

Then suddenly it was dark and the fires were lit.

Excited children dragged thick fagots of dry sticks across the
village and threw them clumsily onto the fires, sending up sprays
of sparks; and hot air rising swiftly stirred the overhanging fronds

of coconut palms making them click together, with firelight flashing on their undersides.

A voice, high-pitched and primitive, cut cleanly across the background of crackling fires and children's voices and the dull thud of drums, sending a jet of song high in the air, to be answered with a surge of sound as fifty men or more responded in a chorus out of the shadows.

They were standing in a group, not yet settled down but milling about quietly like musicians taking their places in an orchestra, and as they moved they sang, freely and uninhibited, answering the solo voice without hesitation.

It was evidently a prelude or introduction to the main part of the ceremonies that they were singing, for it lasted only a few minutes, as though they were seeking pitch or tuning or settling on a cadence. Then, apparently satisfied, they squatted down in a tight cluster, elbowing themselves into positions of comfort while keeping close together, but separated into rows by long logs of heavy wood laid on the ground between each line of men.

Every man held in his two hands, vertically, a bamboo tube, two inches in diameter but varying in length from three to six feet or thereabouts, and these they bounced firmly onto the logs to produce a resonant, percussive sound, each bamboo having a different pitch of sound according to its length.

For a while they appeared only to practice, singing short strophes and cadenzas of onomatopoeic song that seemed torn off, without beginning or ending, and tossed about haphazardly on sudden, short spurts of drumming. It seemed a period of hiatus in the ceremonies. A few stragglers seemed to dance without purpose, and men went about straightening the fires and fetching new logs, while the singers fidgeted, some changing places, others discarding one length of bamboo to try another.

Then, when there was almost nothing happening, and most of the people were sitting quietly talking under the trees or around the steps of the houses, and the night seemed to have missed its climax and become dull, the moon came up, full-blown and butter-yellow.

The orchestra stirred for a moment and then sat silent.

A man walked across the empty village and threw a great bundle of kindling sticks onto each fire so that great yellow and red flames shot up and brought life into the night.

The leading singer threw back his head, stretching his mouth wide open like a dog about to howl, and a long-drawn, eerie, frightened sound found its way out of his throat to be drowned in a wave of thunderous drumming.

All around the village men moved out of the shadows, coming closer into the light of the fires, and little boys stood up uncertainly, excited but in part afraid, not knowing quite what to do, wondering whether to run for protection to the women (now obediently inside the houses or watching discreetly from the shadows), or if to stay and prove themselves men.

The decision was a serious one because the rising moon, and the new song, and the fires brought to flame, were together a sign that the aios, the ancestor spirits, were standing now at the entrance to the village.

From infancy each boy of the Bainings has been taught to fear the wrath of his dead ancestors just as a Christian child is brought up to fear the fires of hell. He knows, this Bainings child, that when he is old enough to stay awake and watch the miaus dance he will meet his ancestors' ghosts face to face, and that if he has offended them during his short life by bad behavior, they will punish him there and then.

So, as they wait for the first of the spirit dancers to appear, the hearts of the little naked lads of Malabunga flutter, and they squat back in the shadows tightly hugging their knees, their mouths and eyes wide open with apprehension, watching.

He came slowly, emerging from the outside dark into the moonlit village, progressing by slow gyrations into the firelight until he reached the singers and stood before them, his great horned and duck-billed head nodding and rolling on his long-maned neck.

His body shone black, spread with soot and pig fat from neck to knees, broken below the thighs with wide bands of white, then gaiters of grass tied like sheaves around the lower part of his legs, and armlets of frayed grass hanging from his elbows. And a python was draped across his shoulders, thick as a forearm and ten feet long, which he held by head and tail, its body hanging in twin loops, one on either side.

The bamboos thundered a strong staccato while he stood displaying himself, then as he turned away the drumming died to a rumble and the voices rose above it, building up layer on layer of sound in a manner most astonishing; unmusical yet harmonic, barbarous but controlled and tightly disciplined so that a whole body of separate sounds soared and swooped and looped through tonal evolutions like a flock of starlings flying at twilight.

Then it stopped as suddenly as it had started, leaving only the grumbling rumble of the bamboo tubes knocking quietly on the logs; until within a minute the next dancer appeared.

They came, one after another in ritual procession, fifteen in all, each making a circuit of the village periphery, each wearing a mask, similar in style but of distinctive design; some swinging snakes as though they were skipping ropes, jumping through the loops as they swung, others carrying several snakes intertwined, and some without snakes but carrying slabs of bleeding pig meat.

And for each dancer the singing drummers made their marvelous sound—whether improvised, or formalized by generations of tradition, learned or created spontaneously, I have no way of knowing; but fantastic and fascinating.

The last dancer displayed himself and for a few minutes the fifteen stood together in a block, swinging and manipulating the snakes (already unfanged). Then the music stopped as though cut off with a chopper, and everybody relaxed.

The dancers disappeared again into the blackness beyond the village to rest a while, and other Malabunga men took the snakes and killed them to eat later.

The singers passed drinking water to each other in bamboos or bottles, and other men renewed the fires and brought more bundles of kindling sticks and leaned them against the trees.

And the huge yellow moon hung low over the heads of the coconut palms.

In a half hour, or a little more, the singers settled down, creating again an air of expectancy, and as before a single wild cry came from a wide-open throat, issuing an invitation, half-beseeching, half-afraid, to the spirits of Malabunga, asking them to come and show themselves once more among the people.

This time there was no drumming to announce the coming of the ghosts. After the solitary invocation the choir was silent, and out of the quiet night beyond the village there came a single droning note, a deep-voiced siren sound lower than a bass flute.

As it came closer a vague movement took definite shape, and a great framework, eight feet long and six feet high, draped with bark and palm leaves, was carried into the village.

The Kavat.

The holy image and sacred symbol of the source of things; a double framework of split cane covered with tapa cloth, with incised patterns and painted designs, made with two sides like a steep-pitched roof, and two men inside carrying it by straps of vine hung on their shoulders; and one of them blowing through a bamboo tube like a dijeridoo.

The Kavat made a circuit of the village clearing, then moved away to one end. The drumming began again, and the singing, soaring voices. Then the spirit men came pouring back into the firelight, together this time, with free hands and no formal movement, but chasing here and there, racing around the village seeking for small boys to frighten, grabbing at them, making them run, dumb with terror, to their fathers.

I saw a little lad caught, tucked under a dancer's arm, and carried, ashen-gray and face transfixed with fear, his small, round stomach convulsing, across the village, in and out of the fires, and then put down again on the other side to lie like dead, drained of every feeling but fear, unable to get up and run away.

A second Kavat came out of the bush and into the village, and they both jogged round and round and back and forth across the clearing, making a background for the dancers who came now, racing back from their chasings to jump through the fires and scuffle with their feet among the piled-up embers and hot woodcoals, sending up showers of sparks and ash and tongues of flame.

And all the time the singers, with heads thrown back and throats extended, forced out long, wreathing streamers of violent, barbarous sound, bashing and stamping down on the log drums with their bamboo tubes in an ecstasy of expression.

I watched the ghosts dancing through the fires and looked for the deacons and teachers among them. This morning they sang the hymns so gloomily.

Perhaps, by the Grace of God, and their own good sense, and with the help of the missionaries and Government officers, they will be able to retain the best of both worlds.

They cannot, at present anyway, escape civilization, and they have much to gain from it. But in these dances and under the stimulating influence of tradition, they achieve their only genuine creative artistry; the making of the masks and the Kavats, the amazing music, the action of the dance reflecting active faith and imagination. These primitive achievements may mean nothing to us, but we have not yet given the people of the Bainings, and other places, anything that can replace them.

I went to bed at midnight, in the schoolroom, while the dancing went on. But my head was full of the sound of people believing, and I did not sleep a great deal.

Eight

Next morning, the Reverend Saimon Gaius took me on the back of his motorcycle along the rough foot-track from Malabunga and up onto the Tolai road, dropping me at Vunadadir, where I got a lift in a Government truck going to Rabaul, and by midday was under the shower washing the dust of the fire dance out of my hair.

There was a note at the hotel from Albert Speer, regional administrative officer of the Health Department, asking me to dinner, and saying that Albert Mauri Kiki and his wife Elizabeth were passing through on their way from the Solomon Islands to Port Moresby, and would be there also. This was pleasant news.

Mauri is one of the most active and earnest of the new generation of Papuan leaders. Something over thirty years of age, solidly built but not yet fat, good-natured and a bit of a worrier, he speaks English and is quite clear about what is good and what is bad for his people.

Elizabeth, his wife, is one of the few Papuan women who makes it her business to keep up intellectually and socially with a new-world husband. She and I once worked together on a film about New Guinea women, and became good friends.

So I looked forward to seeing them both, and hoped that they would talk about their work in the Solomons where Mauri had been lately stationed as a Government welfare officer among the problem people of Buka Island.

And to see them with Albert Speer would be especially pleasant.

When I first met them together, Albert Mauri Kiki and Albert Speer, I wondered at the coincidence of the shared Christian name, until Kiki said of Speer, "This man is my friend and my father, who shaped me out and made me, and whose name I have taken."

He was, of course, speaking metaphorically. Speer is an Australian from the highland sheep-country of the Southern Alps of New South Wales, and Mauri was born in Orokolo, a village west of Kerema in the Gulf of Papua, son of Kiki the village constable.

It is a steamy country where he comes from, swampy and hot, where the hundreds of rivers which start in the high heart of middle New Guinea funnel out through huge estuaries and deltas of black and brown mud, alive with crocodiles and snakes.

Mauri's mother was an inland woman, by name E-au. When she married Kiki of Orokolo, the coast people and the inlanders had no liking for each other, but she was evidently a woman of character and determination, for soon after her marriage she arranged a formal exchange of visits and the two peoples became friendly.

She and Kiki between them raised ten children, although only Mauri and one girl were of their joint begetting. Of the others they each brought two from previous marriages and adopted four more, for they were both people of purpose, and passed this characteristic on to young Mauri.

When the boy felt big enough he followed the older children to the village mission school, and for seven years absorbed Bible stories, fragments of English kindergarten verse, the multiplication tables and most of the alphabet, and so exhausted the educational possibilities of Orokolo.

All that now remained was for the lad to complete his tribal education, acquire a wife, canoe, fishing gear, and a house, and settle down to life in the village, perhaps eventually to succeed his father as the village constable, although by then the office would have been abolished and that of local government councilor substituted.

However, being the son of Constable Kiki, it was not surprising that Mauri should be sent to relatives at Kerema where there was a Government station, and on account of his father's official status and high reputation it could be confidently expected that the lad would find a place there in the Government service.

So it fell out. Within a few days of his arrival at Kerema, Kiki's young son was appointed tea-boy to District Officer Ivan Champion, the man who had been first to walk across New Guinea eighteen years earlier.

But because young Kiki could speak the Papuan lingua franca,

Police Motu, which he had learned from his father, as well as his own Orokolo language and the inland talk of his mother, he soon graduated from tea-boy to interpreter, and accompanied patrol officers on their expeditions, and was said to be a helpful lad.

Yet even at that early age he was conscientious and a worrier, and it bothered him that his English was inadequate to convey true shades of meaning to the Government officers for whom he was interpreting, or even to understand precisely what they wanted him to say to the villagers.

He left his job and went back to the mission school but found no solution there, for the teacher had even less grasp of the finer points of English than he had himself, so he went back to the Government office at Kerema, only to find his old job filled by another ambitious lad. He could not even start back at the beginning again as tea-boy, because Mr. Champion had decided than an older man would be more reliable and less likely to have ambitions.

Writing later about this period of his life Mauri said, "I realised that I had made some mistake, and I was sorry. But it was too late. No use to cry over the poured milk!"

But also stationed at Kerema at the time was Albert Speer, in charge of the Government hospital, and he needed a clerk. Mauri got the job, and for two years Mr. Speer supervised his education. Then he arranged for him to go to the Government teacher training school not far from Port Moresby, where he studied for three years.

At the end of the course Mauri could speak good student English and also had two years' experience in medical field work; and at that time the Government was looking for young men to send to the British medical center in Fiji to train as assistant medical practitioners and public health officers; and Albert Speer was watching out for chances for his protégé.

So Mauri went to Fiji and after five years graduated as a laboratory pathologist, and for this achievement was rewarded by his patron with a vacation in Australia, during which time he stayed with the Speer family and discovered that all white men are not bosses, gods, masterminds, or even natural-born segregationists. Nor do they have all of the answers.

He came back to New Guinea to work in the hospital at Port Moresby, and married Elizabeth, who presently had twin girls, one of whom was named Agnes, for the Fijian wife of a medical school classmate, and the other Helen, after the American heroine Miss Keller.

Horizons had certainly widened for Mauri, son of Kiki the village constable of Orokolo. And, looking at his own people through different eyes, he saw that too many of them were drifting into the dead and empty area between two cultures.

He realized that they needed a more personal form of leadership to augment the activity and good intentions of the Australian Government and the missionaries, and that this new kind of leadership should be based upon a participatory understanding of the people and their problems.

Being the son of Kiki and of E-au, he did something about it.

First he started the Kerema Welfare Society to look after the hundreds of people from his home district who were coming to Port Moresby in search of civilization, but coming without means of support or prospects of work. Then he enlarged this society to take in immigrant people from other parts of western Papua, and also formed a women's welfare association with Elizabeth as president.

In the next year he called some like-minded friends together and they began the Papua and New Guinea Workers' Association, the first trade union in the Territory; then the Papuan Rugby Union Association, to organize sports facilities and fixtures parallel to those of the white people of Port Moresby. In each of these geneses he went to white men for technical advice and assistance, and had the wholehearted support of top Government officers.

Elizabeth had a son, and he was called Percy after Albert Speer's father in Australia. Mauri Kiki looked like a man who was beginning to bridge the gap between two worlds.

Then trouble broke out on Buka Island in the Solomons.

The Buka tax riots followed a familiar pattern, imported from New Britain just across the water. The Government had imposed a head-tax as a sign that the people had reached a stage where they could contribute to their own advancement. For two years the people paid the tax; then many of them rebelled against it, saying that they were getting nothing in return.

The rebels were led by young men who had been to school in Rabaul and were able to compare the high standard of Tolai living with the general backwardness of their own people. They accused the Government of neglecting Buka, and blamed the missionaries

for keeping the village people quiet with promises of a happy life
that never seemed to come. A group of them formed their own welfare society and collected the taxes that should have gone to the
Government.

A team of officials and a big contingent of police went up from
Port Moresby. They took a medical team in case there were casual-
ties in the field. Albert Mauri Kiki was in this team. He was not
long at Buka Island before he found himself with another worry.
He wasn't sure whose side he was on.

In spite of fundamental goodwill in both camps the dispute was
not settled until, on the recommendation of two New Guinea members of the Legislative Council, everybody concerned was arrested.

The local magistrate handed down 587 sentences ranging from
fines of one pound to jail sentences of six months. The Government
wasn't sure whether it felt relieved or vaguely guilty. The Chief
Justice resolved the doubt by revoking all of the sentences and
sending the prisoners back to their villages.

Peace was drawn over Buka Island like a sheet but no problems
were solved, and although the Treasury in Port Moresby announced
that it would provide fifty thousand pounds to spend immediately
on road-making on the island, the people of the villages remained
sullen and resentful. It seemed to Mauri Kiki that it was time for
him to act again.

He spoke to the rebel leader, John Teosin, finding him a quiet
and thoughtful man, and felt drawn toward him by threads of
brotherly understanding; and a strong urge came over him to help
the man and serve the Government at the same time.

He suggested that he should come to live for a while in Teosin's
village, and work day by day among the Buka people and get to
know them and their thoughts. In this way, he said, the people
might come to see that the Government was sincere in its desire to
help them and all the other people of New Guinea.

The quiet man agreed. He seemed to like Mauri and said that he
could talk more easily and frankly to a brown-skinned man, even if
he was a Papuan, than to white officials who, though well-disposed,
were rulers and not of the family. He said that he would be happy
if Mauri would come and live in his village.

The Government agreed and made Mauri a welfare officer on

Buka Island, hoping that some good might come of it. Elizabeth and the children joined him.

Now, less than a year later, they were on their way back to Port Moresby.

He told the story after dinner, sitting in Albert Speer's apartment, while Elizabeth sat watching him from across the room where Speer had settled her on a comfortable chair, for she was heavily pregnant and had visions of another set of twins.

There was concern in her face, for she understands her husband and his problems, and his almost desperate desire to do something for his country so that his father and mother and Mr. Speer can be proud of him, although Mr. Speer is the only one of them still alive to give him any advice.

And she knew, as we sat in the room, that Mauri was feeling the shock and bleak hurt of failure.

"This man, John Teosin, was my friend," he said, leaning forward on the settee. "He asked me to come to his village and bring my wife and children and live among them. He was excited. He said that I should come, and we would talk about the Buka people and the Government, and would be friends.

"I was happy. I felt that I was going to show that Papuans and New Guineans could solve many of their own problems. I was glad for the chance to show Mr. Speer that he had done a good thing when he helped me to be educated."

Mauri shook his head.

"But it is not easy. John Teosin is not the real leader of these people. He does what the old men tell him. He is confused because he had made trouble for himself, and for the village people, that he does not understand very well. He is trying to walk in too many ways at one time. I think I could have helped him to find one good way but he would not let me."

He glanced at Elizabeth, looking for her support, not entirely sure, even with Speer whom he worships, and me for whom he has respect because I am a friend of Speer, how much he should say. And she spoke for him.

"Mauri is tired. He trusted the people of Buka and they hid things from him, and told lies to him. And when the old men saw that he believes in the Government and would not follow them along their wrong paths, they made John Teosin send us away. And

Teosin was also glad to be rid of us, because we would not agree with many things that he is doing."

She stopped, not wishing to speak openly of the "things"; but Speer came across to fill my glass and interrupted for a moment to explain in his quiet, unemotional way. "John Teosin was educated by American priests and sisters of the Marist mission. He became a village schoolteacher. Then he was sent to Rabaul to the Government central school and learned to be a carpenter. If you go to the village of Hanahan on Buka Island you will see the church that he built there for the mission when he came back from Rabaul. It is very good.

"At present the villagers don't use it very much but they will go back to it sooner or later, when this trouble blows over.

"John Teosin doesn't go to church any more either. But he is one of the founders of a new and exclusive society that they have on Buka. It is called 'The Stable of Bethlehem' and the patron saint is Joseph, the carpenter of Nazareth.

"The 'stable' is a big house in the bush where the society keeps a number of selected young women who come from the rebel villages, about twenty of them, and these young women have babies that are born without sin. The idea is that they will grow up to lead their people into the Promised Land.

"Some of the Buka people call John Teosin The King, and his wife The Queen, and she has a crown made of tapa and palm leaves and a bit of ribbon. They've seen pictures of the Queen of England at the district office, and on store calendars, and get the idea from those.

"The Government appointed John a member of the District Advisory Council, but the Advisory Council advises against the Government working through John's welfare society until it gives up these cult activities.

"To be vulgar," said Speer with finality, looking down at me, "poor Johnny Teosin doesn't know whether he is Arthur or Martha."

He poured cool drinks for Elizabeth and Mauri, and when he had done this and gone back to his own chair, Mauri leaned forward again. "I thought I could deal with these things," he said, "they are not new.

"When I was a child in Orokolo, before I understood anything about the Government, I listened to my father speak about many foolish people in our district who had 'the madness,' as he called it. These people who lived in the villages round about where I was born used to think that a ship was coming to bring them cargo, and that their ancestors would be on the ship. And they thought, also, that these ancestors were white men.

"None of them went to the garden or did any work, so they began to get hungry and to starve, especially the children. And some of them watched all night, staring out over the sea into the dark, looking for a sail, and sometimes waking up all the other people, saying that the ship was coming. But it never did.

"My father was worried because he was the village constable and stood for the Government and wished the people to progress and learn properly. So he went to Kerema to tell the Government officer what was happening.

"The Government officer came and found the people very sick, falling onto the ground and calling out that Jesus was going through their heads. So he took them to Kerema and kept them there until they got better, and gave them plenty to eat. But that was more than forty years ago."

Albert Mauri Kiki looked almost angry as he faced us across the room. "He is a good man, this Teosin, but he is lost like many of our people." He looked at us both earnestly, as though asking us not to doubt him.

"We talked many times together about our country. I told him that we surely need Australia more than Australia needs us. I said that it is always wonderful to go to mother in time of need. The breast that has fed you when you were infant. The hard times she has suffered to bring you up to take your part in advancing the whole family.

"And John Teosin agreed with me," said Mauri. "He told me that he would like to go with the Government and perhaps represent his people in the Legislative Council. But the old men do not wish to lose their power. Also they are angry because, they say, the Government broke their heads at the time of the tax-collecting. They told my friend Teosin to send me away.

"'Go down to the beach,' he said to me, 'and take a canoe and sail it to Port Moresby where you belong, and take your wife and children and live there with your Government friends, and leave us alone to find an answer to our problems.'"

There was a faraway look in Mauri Kiki's eyes and he seemed to be speaking to himself, and Elizabeth watched him almost anxiously as he held out his hands, first palms up and then palms down, before speaking again.

"I am not a white man, I am a Papuan, with a brown skin like you." He was speaking to Teosin, not to Speer and me. "My flesh is your flesh and my blood is your blood, and if you will let me, I can sit down and live with you as a brother."

But John Teosin had turned away.

The missionaries have an explanation. They say that the Buka rebels want the best of two worlds. That they covet the ordered economic progress of the Tolai people that has come through cooperation with the Government, the cash results of planned agriculture, the community-owned health centers and schools but, say the missionaries, they also wish to keep the traditional forms of authority, the prestige of tribal elders, the rituals and ceremonies and involved economics of bride-price and pig-and-yam displays.

Other people think that the Government has left too much to the missionaries and, in its efforts to advance the people unhurriedly, has not kept pace with their growing needs and their readiness to accept responsibility. That there has been too much importance placed on education and not enough on common sense.

Two things seem certain. First, that the people and the Government and the missionaries are aiming at the same goal and hope to reach it together, as friends. And the second, that there is no painless way to salvation for anybody.

Albert Speer poured himself a drink, wondering how a man could tell when he was doing God's will.

Elizabeth was considering names for the twins, presuming them to be boys.

I thought of the plane leaving at six o'clock in the morning for Goroka. It seemed hardly worth going to bed.

PART 3

The Papuans of the south coast of New Guinea were delivered from historical obscurity by missionaries, and were reared almost exclusively in the decent, middle-class traditions of Victorian England.

The people of the north coast and adjacent islands had Prince Otto von Bismarck and the merchants of Hamburg for godparents. They, too, were treated kindly but firmly like children, for several generations.

But the highlanders of the great upland valleys of central New Guinea, who are almost half the total population of the Territory, have emerged straight from primitivism into the twentieth century, in the time of the coming of age of the colored races.

In this climate of changed attitudes a different kind of relationship is being developed between the newly discovered native and the white man. The future of Papua and New Guinea, and perhaps of Australia, may well depend on how sensibly this relationship can be developed and maintained.

One

Gold-seekers were first to find these upland valleys in the highlands.

Escorted by a Government officer, they picked their way along steep green ridges, heading upward to high passes that would let them through to look upon discoveries such as had not been made anywhere in the world for almost a century past.

They were followed at a respectful distance by hundreds of excited stone age men who cried out that the strangers were spirits come back from the dead. Each highland man carried an adz with a stone head, and some had digging sticks. Many led their favorite pigs by a vine string, believing that if the spirits would only touch them the animals would miraculously increase in vigor and fecundity.

This was in 1933.

The highland valley floors are thickly grassed, and patchworked with food gardens. They bottom at about five thousand feet and in places have a width of fifteen miles. The ranges rim them at nine or ten thousand feet, though peaks of fifteen thousand and more rise above the ruck. There is nothing like them, say geographers, in Asia or Indonesia (excluding West Irian, a U. N. Trust Territory administered by Indonesia).

They hold an estimated eight hundred thousand people, more than are in the whole of Papua, or in the New Guinea islands and coastal regions, or in West Irian across the border. Newspapers in many parts of the world reported the discovery of these valleys and their people. But world war came and nobody had time to worry with stone age people, who were insufficiently advanced to make even a menial contribution toward winning or losing it.

In 1953, the war being over eight years and civilian authority resumed in New Guinea as elsewhere, a small hotel was built in one of these highland valleys, at Goroka, where the Australian Government had established its main administrative center for the further exploration, penetration, and pacification of the newly opened areas.

Three of us sat on the shaded patio of this hotel having morning tea.

Myself, Jim Leahy, and John Akunai.

Jim Leahy, with his two brothers Mick and Dan, was one of the first to fly over this valley and the others farther to the west. He was among those mistaken in the early days of exploration for spirit men come back from the land of the dead. He now has a coffee plantation and a farm here, close to Goroka, and a coffee factory and various other interests in the town.

John Akunai, sitting beside him, is highland-born. His father was already dead when the white men came, killed in a tribal fight. John, then less than ten years old, lived with clan relatives in a village close to Goroka.

The Government set up a patrol post at Goroka. The pattern becomes familiar. John finished the mission school curriculum and while still a young teen-ager became a station interpreter at Goroka, and went on patrol with Government officers.

One of the patrol officers, Ian Downs, being transferred from Goroka to Rabaul, took the lad with him and put him to school, but the war came and the Japanese occupied New Britain, and Akunai's formal education was interrupted, although his knowledge of the outside world and its complexities had increased enormously.

With war ended he became a policeman for three years, and then was chosen to take a schoolteacher's course at Port Moresby. Having finished the course he went back to the highlands to teach a new generation of children.

John Akunai's patron, Patrol Officer Downs, had meanwhile become the district commissioner at Goroka, and by driving through a spectacular road-making program had opened up the highlands to settlers and to agricultural development.

Coffee-growing soon became the touchstone of progress and the hope of an economically integrated relationship between the many powerful highland tribes and the white people who had settled in the valleys.

John Akunai gave up schoolteaching to become a coffee planter and commercial farmer, giving the lead to thousands of his fellow highlanders.

District Commissioner Downs also resigned from the Government service to become a planter, and was elected president of the Highland Farmers and Settlers' Association, and a member of the Legislative Council of Papua and New Guinea, representing the white people of the highlands.

John Akunai and Jim Leahy are both vice-presidents of the Farmers and Settlers' Association, and members of the executive committee, and I was sitting with them on the veranda of the hotel at Goroka waiting for a group of visiting officials from the World Bank, who were due to arrive by plane from Port Moresby.

They were coming to make a brief study of the financial problems and potential of these highland valleys while I, at the request of the Minister of Territories, was gathering research material for a film on "The Economic Advancement of the People of Papua and New Guinea." To one who has been brought up in the old historical tempo of the last two thousand years it all seems a little unreal.

We heard the plane approach, then watched it come out of the cloud above the range and circle inside the mountain wall which seems, in some lights, to approach so close that it lips the airstrip. Then, when the gentlemen from the World Bank were decently installed at the hotel, we all went to look at John Akunai's plantation, two miles out of town. John gave me a lift in his Land-Rover.

His plantation land is his own, purchased through the Government from its original tribal owners. He has twenty acres under coffee which makes him wealthier than most Australians. In addition he grows a variety of vegetables for the coastal markets, and sweet potatoes for the Goroka hospital and other Government institutions. He also breeds poultry from imported stock.

Laborers were spreading fertilizer as we walked around, and two of them were spraying coffee trees. Half a dozen women worked over drying trays, picking out small and discolored beans. A carpenter, watched by a line of old men sitting in the shade, measured door frames for a new storage shed.

The eldest of his four children goes to the Government school near Goroka. When the boy is bigger he will go to school in Australia.

This brief biography of John Akunai is significant only if one keeps remembering that he was a stone age child, that he has jumped two thousand years in half his own lifetime, and that almost half the total of New Guinea's crop of coffee is grown by native highlanders who, like him, were born into a completely primitive society.

It points up differences of historical development between these highlanders and the rest of the New Guinea people, and throws doubts on the theory that it takes several generations to civilize primitive people.

The World Bank men seemed impressed with John Akunai's farm and plantation. When they had gone John drove me back to Goroka and left me at the district office. Then he went to see his accountant.

Each of the eight hundred thousand highlanders does not have John Akunai's capacities, nor has it been possible to give them all the same educational advantages in the same amount of time. His achievement is exceptional, although there are hundreds of highlanders in the same general category heading in the same general direction with less personal coaching.

Already there are more native members of the Highland Farmers and Settlers' Association than there are white members, and interracial business partnerships are becoming commonplace. Several coffee marketing and processing companies have both New Guinean and Australian directors. One such company has two thousand local shareholders.

But there are also tens of thousands of highlanders who have not yet been given any real opportunity to advance beyond their stone age state, because the Government is short of staff, short of money, and stretched to the limit of its resources at all points of the New Guinea compass.

The district officer was speaking of these problems, and what is being done locally to overcome them, when a barefoot sergeant of police came stumping along the passage in a hurry, to stand at the door of his room rigidly saluting, quivering with urgency and indignation.

"Law and order," said the district officer sententiously to me, ignoring the policeman who was a Sepik and wore the scars of the crocodile totem, "are pretty well established in these parts and we have little or no intertribal problem, mainly because of our local road system which not only brings most villages within easy access of a Government station or patrol post, but provides, as it were, an interarea corridor of communication guaranteed by a balance of power supplied by the Government."

He grinned. "You must forgive me but I have just finished writing the official district report and my English has become inhibited."

The policeman continued to vibrate, his lips trembling on the brink of speech, but the district officer went on. "I think it might be a good idea if you went up the road to Chimbu and then on to Minj. I'll work out an itinerary for you that will give you a pretty full picture of what we are doing in this district. It will be a change from flying, and the road should be in a passable condition as it hasn't rained much lately. I'll lend you a driver and a police-man to look after you."

The use of the word "policeman" reminded him that the sergeant was still waiting to speak. He looked up, raising his eyebrows in-terrogatively. A torrent of words fell out in a tumbling rush. It was difficult for me to catch them, for highland Pidgin is thick and guttural and, to me, unlovely. But it seemed that a murderer had escaped.

"Which one?" inquired the district officer amiably. "The chap from Lufi?"

The policeman was excited and words gushed out from him as he explained how it had happened, but the district officer cut him short.

"It's a pity you didn't think to bring in the witnesses with you when you picked this fellow up. He's sure to be heading back home to knock them off before they can be brought to give evi-dence against him."

The sergeant shuffled and said, "Yessir." If the man were not caught by nightfall he would lose face and his life in the police barracks would become unlivable.

The district officer continued. "Your friend will probably have cut through behind the hotel to hide in the gully at the end of the airstrip until nightfall. Then, if he is not caught, he will head back to Lufi by moonlight. Now you take four men and find him."

The sergeant saluted and went. And in a moment there was a gabble outside and the sound of a truck being started and jammed into gear, much shouting, dust, and voices calling to each other over a widening distance. Then quiet again.

The district officer winced.

"Now, where were we?"

Reminding him of his little speech on "Road Systems and the Preservation of Law and Order," I ventured a tentative question about the murder at Lufi, but immediately he looked disappointed in me as though I were a visiting journalist or tourist, inquisitive for sensation. So I apologized, and explained that having once camped in Lufi village I have a sentimental interest in anything that happens there.

So he forgave me and sat back to explain.

"In this part of the highlands we have completely eliminated tribal warfare and have given the people other community things to do such as road-making, bridge-building, coffee-planting, building schools, and so on. But domestic murder is another matter, and so long as pigs and women are used as articles of exchange the problem will continue."

He lit a cigarette.

"Now this chap from Lufi is not a wicked fellow, in fact he's a good churchgoer and a progressive citizen. But he's a young man and he wants to get married, and the only way he can get a wife is for his family or clan to exchange one of its females for a female of another family or clan.

"This is tremendously important to him and it becomes an obsession. Without a wife he is a rubbish man, with no one to grow his food, tend his pigs, give him sons to boast about or daughters to exchange for other women or pigs or ornaments. He might as well kill himself.

"So what happens? One of his girl cousins is promised to a young man of a neighboring village, and this means that by tribal custom our lad now may hope to acquire a wife from that village on the bride-exchange system.

"But three other men of his clan also have a claim to this girl. Two of them already have a wife apiece, and the other man is single like himself.

"The two married men, aiming to build up wealth with which to purchase other wives in due course, reason that it is better to forego the bride-exchange and to ask the neighboring village to pay for their girl cousin with pigs, shells, feathers, and perhaps money, to be split up between the four men and other of their various relatives. But the two single lads press for a bride-exchange in which one of them, at least, gets a wife.

"There is a discussion which becomes an argument. Blows are struck. Who starts it, nobody knows. One of the married men is cut across the neck with an ax and dies.

"In the old days this would have meant an exchange of compensation all around and there would be a widow available for remarriage, as well as the exchange bride, and both young bachelors might thus have acquired wives.

"But now we have one man dead, one widow without a man, one unhappy murderer mucking up my day by escaping, and two men in Lufi who are likely to be knocked on the head if we don't find him before nightfall, because their evidence has put him temporarily in jail.

"The public solicitor is almost certain to get him off on a plea of self-defense, so if he'll come back and relax we'll look after him, and keep him out of the way of vengeful relatives, and in due course send him back to Lufi to woo the young lady." He smiled benevolently. "May we now, please, get on with more immediate matters?"

I suggested that we have lunch.

Goroka is the metropolis of the eastern highlands.

It has a population of almost five hundred white people, including children, though many of these spend much of the year at school in Australia. It also serves about one hundred other whites, mostly settlers and missionaries who live farther out.

It is a pretty town. The landscape that contains it is majestic. The wall of mountains rising behind it is enormous. The climate at five thousand feet is warm by day and cool by night and lime-rich soil, constantly renewed by wash from the rock formations which ring the valley, make it possible to grow garden flowers of all kinds all the year round. Mountain streams keep everything green, and labor is plentiful enough to hold fast-growing gardens, paths, lawns, and hedges in check.

There is a race course, golf course, sports club and arena, swimming pool, tennis courts, football and cricket clubs. Teams fly to coastal towns to take part in tournaments and match games. The Rotary Club meets fortnightly at the hotel. There are movies, dances, and a drama club. The town has five churches, three general stores, and two banks.

From its beginnings Goroka has seemed to emanate and keep a sense of purpose and determination.

Its first Government official, Assistant District Officer Jim Taylor, who came with the Leahy brothers, sounded the keynote clearly when he wrote to his superiors in Port Moresby saying that the exploring party had found "a fine grass uplands region which may prove to be the most important part of New Guinea."

It is country in which white people are able to live comfortably, identifying themselves with land that can produce familiar things: flowers, vegetables, fodder for cattle, and consequently fresh milk and butter and other civilized foods.

It has a climate in which a man can sleep soundly at night under a blanket, and wake refreshed; not, as on the coast, living constantly in a sweat by day and lying all night restless on a wet sheet.

The highland people look you in the eye and smile openly, without doubt or guile or shyness. They have self-respect and are prepared to meet you halfway and to do things for themselves, not needing or wanting charity nor being forced by poverty to subservience or deceit. Nor are they physically and mentally undermined by malaria and malnutrition as so many of the lowland people are.

We were talking of these things later that night after dinner, for in New Guinea there is little conversation that does not concern local matters.

A lady anthropologist, who had been living for some months in a mountain village studying the domestic economy of a single highland family group, remarked that the people with whom she had been staying still seemed glad to co-operate with white men and women, believing that whatever curious activities they engaged in, such as counting the number of tubers in a family garden plot, such activities seemed designed to help the highlander.

She ventured to believe, though cautiously, being well-disciplined, that the highland people still have faith in the good intentions of the white people and are not yet disillusioned as are many Papuans, or doubtful of our purposes and motives as the Buka and Tolai people tend to be. But, she added, we should hurry if we are to keep their confidence and goodwill.

A barrister from the Department of Law, visiting Goroka in connection with the Lufi murder and other legal matters, suggested that the future of New Guinea might well be decided in the highlands rather than in the sophisticated centers of Port Moresby and Rabaul, and that the decision could come soon.

He reminded us that in 1964 the Legislative Council of the Territory would be dominated by native members and that the highlands would, on a population basis, have the strongest representation.

"And," he said, with the studied deliberateness of a lawyer giving an opinion without committing himself, "they have the least history of contact with white people and consequently the least reason to be equivocal about the relationship between them and us, whereas in places where the people have known us for eighty years, opinions may be fairly evenly divided as to whether we should be permitted to stay or not."

Of the two planters present one said that his views on the future could be summed up simply in that he had plans to plant another twenty-five acres of coffee this season.

But the other said, "It is neither the highlander nor the coastal sophisticates whom we whites need to worry about, or even the disgruntled and confused Buka of the Solomons or the arrogant Mekeos of Papua. It will be governments, including our own, following paths of political ambition or expediency, who will decide our future without reference to ourselves or to the people of New Guinea, or any kind of morality or justice, unless we ourselves do something soon."

He turned to his friend, the other planter, pouring him a drink as he spoke. "Faith in the future is a fine thing, but history is what happens. Look what they did to West New Guinea. Even semi-literate villagers in this country were shocked and dismayed when seven hundred thousand people of their race were given away in a political poker game played in the antechambers of the United Nations."

He looked indignant, yet a little embarrassed by his own vehemence.

"I am not denying that the Indonesians had a logical and historical claim to West Irian as it is now called, and I believe that the Dutch were foolish to try to hang on to it, but the manner of settling the problem could suggest that unless we quickly give the New Guinea people the opportunity to make their own decisions, their future and ours will be decided elsewhere, certainly not in our favor, and perhaps not in theirs."

I filled his glass and he took a sip of claret. Then, speaking more quietly, he added, "Many of us in the highlands accept this possibility as a fact of life, even if some face it reluctantly. But the truth is that we need the highlander more than he needs us, for he has not yet much to lose by any transfer of authority."

He looked thoughtful, and the barrister took advantage of his silence to tell us of a court case in which he had recently appeared at Kikori, in the gulf country of Papua.

There was, he said, the usual intervillage raid in which men were killed and women carried off; but an interesting feature of the case was that after the women had performed the usual ritual wailing for their dead husbands, and in one case had chopped off two fingers as a sign of deep devotion for the deceased, they joined in the eating of the bodies.

Furthermore, when the processes of law and justice had caught up with events, and the raiders had been committed to a corrective institution to have their manners mended, the court instructed that the women should be returned to the village from whence they had been abducted.

But the women themselves objected, saying that they had been captured in a perfectly conventional manner and had become the property of their captors and were, indeed, perfectly happy with their present situation except for the fear that their new husbands were, apparently, about to be removed from them by the Government.

"There is," said the barrister, "an element of classical Greek drama in the lives of these people."

The planter, unwilling to retreat entirely, remarked that this was simply another illustration of the realistic attitudes of all ordinary people when faced with the inevitabilities of history.

He pointed out that in all wars including the last, returning servicemen of all races brought back the women of hated enemies as their wives, and that the New Guinea highlander, like all other human beings from the beginning of time, was a simple realist concerned with present facts and not with theoretical futures, and that we should bind him to us with bonds of steel today while he still believed our friendship necessary to him, and not wait until tomorrow, by which time he might have changed his mind.

The lady anthropologist got up and said that she was going to bed. As she went she reminded me that we were sharing a vehicle in the morning and that I was to drop her along the way at a place called Watabung, where there is a Government rest house, and where she proposed to work for a few days.

When she had gone one of the planters remarked that the New Guinea highlands grow almost as many Ph.D.'s as it does coffee trees, and that the number of beautiful women who devote themselves to anthropological studies of the stone age male suggests that there is a fundamental discontent with the present civilization among women of the Western world.

We returned to the dregs of the claret, but the argument had tired us and we soon stood up, yawning, and said goodnight.

Two

Already Goroka has become two towns, the old and the new, separated by a river that runs fast, clear, and cold over stones and boulders, and is overhung with bamboo clumps, with an occasional casuarina tree feathering against the sky like part of a Chinese painting.

Women sit in the river washing lap-laps or bathing their babies, and bigger children splash about naked and shout at traffic rattling over the metal-matting bridge. These are the families of medical orderlies and other minor Government employees, who have their quarters close to the river.

The old town is green and gardened and suburban, bordered by the airstrip and golf course. Over the river the houses are newer and raw-built, and roads freshly graveled; the coffee factory is here and the transport yards, and a Chinatown is springing up.

The villagers walk in single file through the town, keeping to the footpaths or the edge of the road. The women, near-naked, with net bags hanging from their foreheads, children perched on top, hands clasped behind the neck to give support, walk with their eyes down. Sometimes they bring pawpaws and vegetables to sell at the stores, or from house to house, and sometimes firewood. The men bring small bags of coffee beans.

They pad about the streets or gather in clusters at the trade stores to spend money gained from selling their vegetables and coffee beans. They buy useful things: lamps, flashlights, axes, spades, but also face powder and beads for decoration, and sometimes rice and tinned meat.

Although both men and the young women wear spectacular decoration on special occasions, their ordinary dress meets only the limited requirements of modesty. Women in the streets wear nothing but long and narrow aprons of cords spun from shredded fibers of wild-fig plant, one apron hanging in front and one behind, and both swinging with provocative rhythm as they walk. All else they wear is decoration: a single crescent of shell pendant above bare breasts, or if the girl is young she may wear beads in long ropes around her throat, either of blue or red glass bought at a trade store, or of grass seeds gathered in the bush and threaded at home.

The women have their hair close-cropped to the skull, but many men wear it hanging shoulder-length and in thin, twisted strings shining with pig grease. Some of the men, especially those from ten or twenty miles out, wear headbands of opossum fur, or bark decorated with sewn shells, with sometimes a single quill through the nasal septum. And for modesty they wear an apron of bark or cords in front and a clump of green tanket leaves to cover the buttocks, the twig being stuck under the wide bark belt that all men wear, so that the leaves hang down.[1]

But highland men who work with white people soon cut their hair short, and so do the advanced villagers who are local government councilors or commercial coffee growers. And most of these wear khaki shirts and shorts when they come to town.

We called at one of the general stores in the old town to get frozen meat and bread, and while my passenger did her shopping I talked for a moment with an elderly traveling salesman from Sydney who said that his biggest business was with the native trade stores.

His main lines of merchandise seemed to be face powders and other toiletries (as he called them), including a specially developed brilliantine impregnated with the smell of pig fat. He said that his biggest difficulty was to get the exact shade of powder demanded by trade store customers, and that he and his company had devoted much time to this problem, especially to the reds, these being most in demand.

He thought the highlanders conservative buyers, sticking to

[1] The tanket bush (Taetsia fruticosa) is used throughout the highlands as a male buttock covering. Some white people refer to it as the "trouser tree." The leaves are also used as "passes" or messenger identification by the highlanders. The Pidgin expression "*mi selim tanket*" means "I have sent him (or her) an invitation."

colors that are familiar to them by association, and mentioned
Poinsettia Red, Sky Blue, and Kunai Grass Green as favorite shades.

He was, he added, interested in the idea of experimenting with
the production of plastic gold-lip shell, and looked a little put out
when I suggested that as gold-lip is an important form of New
Guinea currency he might be fringing upon forgery if he pursued
the notion.

Rain in the night had laid the road dust, and the air was fresh
and cool as we drove out of town, and the sun warm but not yet
hot. Driving in the highlands is exhilarating for the first hour or
two but becomes wearisome as the sun gets higher and dust rises,
and sky glare and the strain of watching the white, winding road,
and continuous bumping, wear down resistance.

Yet here, as in few other parts of New Guinea, the country comes
alive before the eyes as vista after vista unwinds with the road,
and no longer is one detached and remote as when flying high
above the land, but in touch, stopping in villages, resting where one
can look over the valleys, or wade into a river to wash away dust.

Ten years ago Goroka was not much more than another little
patrol post like those in the Goilala and Kukukuku country, Woitapi,
Aseki, and Kainteba, little pockets of civilization, almost pathetic
in their isolation, hardly more than token gestures of occupation.

District Commissioner Downs drove this road through the highlands and side roads into the centers of population, using his patrol
officers as civilizing shock-troop leaders. And in ten years they had
brought peace, a sense of unity, progress, and achievement.

Not the long inertia of Papua where practically nothing happened for eighty years. Not the intensive concentration on a handful of people in a limited area, as among the Tolai round about
Rabaul. Nor the despairing neglect of the people of the outer islands and the Sepik, and the gulf country, who were too difficult
to get at.

In the highlands they put through thirteen hundred miles of
roads in ten years without bulldozers, and with very little money,
using picks and shovels and digging sticks, cracking boulders by
lighting fires under them and letting the night change of temperature do the rest. Women carried stones up from the rivers in little
baskets to make the road surface. Children carried clods. Thousands
of men, women, and children, picking bit by bit into the mountain-

sides to make the road, like ants picking at the carcass of a pig that has died in the bush.

Now these same men, who still wear bones through their noses on Sundays, and wear paradise plumes on their heads at weddings, drive into Goroka for council meetings, and truck their coffee to the factory, or wait at the roadside to meet Jim Leahy's sons when they come around on coffee-buying trips, and collect their cash in the hand; because there is a road.

We stopped at the top of the pass, an hour out of Goroka, and could see a line of men a mile away where the road ran around a shoulder of the mountain. The sound of chanting came up to us like a shanty, long, steady surges followed by excited shouts, then silence for a while when they stopped for breath.

They were hauling huge logs to make main bearers for a new bridge and we could see a plume of dust running back and forth beside them along the line of their hauling, and hearing the putt-putt of a motorcycle, guessed it to be the patrol officer urging them on. And when we had rested a little we went down and came to where the work was going on.

There were two logs, enormous, sixty or seventy feet long and maybe four feet thick at the butt, and a hundred men or more hauling each one in two teams of fifty to each tree, pulling them along by long ropes of jungle vine.

As we came they stood panting and wiping the sweat out of their eyes, and some slipped off quickly to the side of the road to drink from little rills of running water flowing out of the hillsides. They drank out of funnels twisted swiftly from thick, green leaves, then hopped back onto the road to stand by ready to haul again.

They seemed keen and alive and eager, like men achieving, and anxious to get on again after their rest. A few police were in charge, they, too, stripped and pitching in, not just standing and shouting orders, but hanging onto the ropes, giving leadership and setting the pace.

At the back of each team were the chanting choirs, some twenty men decorated sketchily with little sprays of leaves stuck into their hair and armbands, and holding twigs like wands, some of them roughly painted on the face and forehead with clay.

They began to shout with short, sharp barking sounds until they got into a rhythm and the haulers took hold of the ropes and laid on weight. Then the chanting took form and phrasing, and as the logs began to move it rose up urgently, and the pullers laid forward and swayed from the waist, the muscles of their legs and arms and shoulders bunching and knotting with the strain.

They moved forward slowly, edging the logs into a calculated line of travel from the bend where they had stopped, to the next bend in the road, a distance of some fifty yards or so; and when momentum gathered they began to run until the weight of the logs took charge and the chanters broke into wild shouts of excitement, and the haulers raced away, scrambling to avoid being run down and crushed, while the policemen and some key men strained to guide and break the pace until it slackened of its own accord and weight. And again they rested.

It seemed wildly dangerous and exciting, but as they gained the fifty yards they all laughed and danced and slapped each other playfully, then ran to drink more water, or stood panting and chattering together.

We stopped for a few minutes and spoke to the patrol officer, a cadet almost fresh from school, who told us that he was camped a little along the road and would be there for a fortnight until the bridge was finished. He seemed a little disappointed that we wouldn't be staying nearby overnight, for he was still young enough to be keen for company; but the lady anthropologist said that she would be camped at Watabung for some days and would be happy if he could visit in the evening and share a meal, at which he seemed shy and uncertain but said yes, thank you, he would like to come. We left him, looking happy, but very, very, young.

We came over Daulo Pass at seven thousand feet, darkly overshadowed to the north by the high peak of Kerigonuma, and looked down into the twisting valley of the Mai River. Here the landscape is dominated by the sheer, flat-faced pinnacle of Mount Erimbari away to the west, rising thirteen thousand feet or more, a landmark for a hundred miles around when flying a cloudless sky.

The river bed is at three thousand feet, and the country slopes down steeply to reach it, so that there seems to be no level land anywhere in sight.

Villages sit astride narrow spurs or perch on hilltops, twenty or more houses in each; round, brown, slab-sided and with candle-snuffer roof cones, some decorated with spires of reeds reaching up six feet above the eaves, and topped with a tassle of cane or giant grass.

They are spaced like a necklet around the edge of an elongated oval or lozenge of brown earth, with sheer drops on all sides except where the foot track into the village connects back along a narrow ridge of land to the parent range, and the road.

In a generation, maybe, they will build in easier places, closer to crop or garden lands; but villages today are still placed strategically as alpine people of all times and places have sited their settlements, defensively, on spurs and hilltops and at ridge ends out of bow shot, and where they cannot be overlooked, nor approached except along one well-defended pathway.

Yet in spite of its steepness much of the landscape is marked out with food gardens, some of them covering several acres and all fenced with thick timber palings to keep the pigs out, and patterned with a checkerboard of little hillocks sown with sweet potatoes, interplanted with taro, maize, cucumber vines, and other vegetables introduced by white people.

Because of the steep pitch of the land in this district, the potato mounds are laid out in an overlapping fish-scale pattern and not in geometrically intersecting lines as in other parts of the country; in this way the fast flow of surface rainwater is stemmed and slowed down, and erosion prevented. On flat country, in the valley beds where water tends to settle, the potato hillocks are built higher and divided with deep drains to carry away rainwater that would otherwise lie on the crops.

So each part of the highlands has its own garden plan and pattern suited to soil and contour, devised by experience and tradition; but everywhere the same general routines are basic and unvarying, for the same foods are staples in each place.

The men choose the garden site, meeting together informally to decide where it will be. If they propose to plant a domestic garden they need ground enough only to grow food for a "line" of related people numbering perhaps twenty or so, the sons of one father with their wives and children, or other closely related family groupings depending upon the convenience of numbers.

When the men of the family have formally decided the where and when of the new garden, they consult with village or clan headmen who have the traditional authority to allocate tribal lands to

individuals and families; and then, approval being given and dates
set for starting, taking into account other village activities which
may require the prior participation of the men, the clearing of the
land begins.

This is men's work.

They grub out or cut the kunai grass and undergrowth, and burn
it to make fertilizing ash. The trees, mainly casuarina, are cut and
split for fence posts and rails, though a few tall trees, perhaps too
big for cutting into fence slabs, or needed for later activities, are
simply trimmed of all their branches and a single knot of leaves left
on top to keep them alive.

Then the fence is made, with posts crossed as trestles to hold
lateral logs in place, strong enough to keep pigs out and completely enclosing the garden. After that the enclosed land, ready
for planting, is divided into plots measured out with long poles or
lengths of vine.

In domestic gardens an area of about a twentieth part of an acre
seems to be the amount of land tended by one woman, although
she may have other plots coming into bearing at the same time, or
if there is a small family ceremonial of some kind to be catered
for she may have part of an extra strip of garden to look after.

But if a special garden is to be made, to provide food for a
ceremonial occasion involving the whole village or clan, a big area
of land will be needed to grow, perhaps, two or three tons of food.

The discussions are then more ritualistic and involved, and garden planning and planting become one detail of a comprehensive
plan to entertain a thousand or more guests from other villages,
and perhaps to kill and distribute the meat of a hundred pigs in
honor of clan ancestors.

In this case the clearing and fencing of land involves every man,
and family plans take second place, for the primitive heathen is
a community man to a far greater extent than the Western demo-
crat, and the well-being and general pleasure, status, and dignity
of the clan is thoroughly understood and accepted as being of more
importance than personal gratification.

Clan ceremonials may well take place within intervals of two
years, for there are many of them of varying degrees of importance,
and together they form a continuing ritual and liturgy of the tribal
religion in which ancestors are worshiped, invoked, and appeased

in ceremonies which revolve around the main episodes and incidents of clan history.

The death of a "big" man calls for a series of feasts to ensure the safe conduct of his spirit to the land of the dead, to do him honor, and to win his goodwill and assistance in clan matters that depend on supernatural intervention for their successful undertaking; and there are feasts to accompany seasonal rituals performed to promote the fertility of clan lands, people, and animals, and other feasts held at the initiation of boys, or the betrothal of girls.

From the time of clearing land for a garden, until the day when the pigs are finally let in to scavenge and clean up the inferior tubers left in the ground, is about eighteen months, perhaps less. Then the area is left untouched for many years, until the timber has grown on it to a size that will make new fencing posts.

So the location of family and clan gardens is continually changing, and garden-making takes a great part of each man's days, while planting, tending, and crop-gathering, either for family or clan purposes, occupies a woman's time from her marriage until she dies or becomes too old for work.

Even the planting of the gardens has much detailed relationship to other aspects of clan and family life. When the women have made their sweet potato beds and have taken cuttings from old vines to plant in them, and have put out taro tops, and scattered maize and cucumber seed about their individual plots, the men come and plant banana suckers and sugar cane where they can be most easily reached by themselves without trespassing too far into the women's garden.

They plant yams, a male crop with implicit fertility symbolism, close to the trees left standing in the garden, or where they can put in sticks for the yam runners to climb on. Then casuarina seedlings, which will be left after the garden is abandoned, to grow up to become the fencing trees next time this ground is used. Sometimes a man will plant these tree seedlings at the birth of a son, with the intention that the boy will make use of them to fence his first garden when he marries fifteen or sixteen years later.

And to mark the boundaries of the family garden the men plant tanket bushes which make clear markers, and also provide a family supply of "trousers" for the men, these being the leaves used for buttock coverings.

This traditional gardening is now not all. Many of the men, especially those who live within reasonable distance of Government or mission stations, today grow coffee as a cash crop, and peanuts both for market and for family eating, and gradually the pattern of garden activity may change to make the burden lighter for both men and women.

There will, perhaps, be a breakdown of the complex traditional system of ownership and invested authority. Some land must become set apart for commercial and permanent tree crops like coffee, and the rights to its use be organized on individual or co-operative lines. These matters are beginning to concern the advanced highlanders already, along with a knowledge of new gardening tools and agricultural methods, fertilizers, seed selection, and the seemingly endless effects of commercial farming and cash income on village life and traditions.

These things we discussed as we drove down the long winding stony road from Daulo Pass, the anthropologist and I, with the policeman and the driver supplying detailed lore and information, until we came to Watabung rest house, by the river, overhung with huge, weeping casuarina trees.

There was a crowd around the rest house, about a thousand people, perhaps more. And to one side, where tall trees made a great patch of shade, the white ambulance of the infant welfare sisters stood sharp against the wide green background. And Sister Purcell, in white uniform and veil, with a crowd of women around her.

All the rest was grass, big groups of brown people, and the blue sky, making great slabs and blobs of color without detail. Or so it seemed. But coming closer one could see vivid green-backed beetles set in headbands of bark that some of the girls wear, and parrot feathers stuck in men's hair, and a few dressed ceremonially with face paint and decoration, though for what reason it was not clear.

Watabung, where three streams meet, is a Government post not permanently manned, but maintained as a medical aid center and general meeting place for a number of villages round about. The patrol officers stop at the rest house when they come to hold petty courts and deal with disputes, or make public announcements, or hold meetings to discuss projects. Medical patrols use it too when they stay in the area for a few days, and agricultural officers, road engineers, surveyors, and such-like.

And anthropologists.

The policeman and I helped unload her gear from the Land-Rover, for the driver, as usual, had found a friend and could not be seen. We moved her into the rest house and the policeman set up a bed, sliding thick sticks through a canvas sleeve to make a stretcher, then wedging it over crossed poles at head and foot.

She piled her food onto a rough bench, hanging the frozen meat in a wet sack between window and door where a draft would keep it fresh for two days. I hung a pressure lamp for her, and a canvas shower bucket, and a boy brought two buckets of water.

She would be comfortable enough and quite safe, and needing help could find it a few hundred yards along the road at the aid post where the medical orderly lives and works. And later the young patrol officer would come chugging down on his motorcycle from Daulo Pass to see that she had everything; for although anthropologists are thought of as odd by some and even as unnecessary by the ignorant, New Guinea men, brown and white, view almost any "missus"[2] as a treasure to be guarded, unless she is excessively unpleasant.

My anthropologist told me that in the village where she lives and does her main research, in an area that ten years ago was out of bounds to everybody but experienced Government men and missionaries, and they all armed for self-defense, the headman himself sleeps within call, and her finicky cook-boy will not let her enter her house (a grass one) until she removes her muddy boots.

When we had settled her I went across to Sister Purcell, who is a Canberra girl, and saw her arguing strongly with a big highlander who leaned on a long stick, regarding her with a mixture of awe, curiosity, and astonishment. It was not possible that he could understand her mutilated Pidgin, he speaking nothing but his local language, but he clearly saw that she was angry with him or whoever was responsible for the condition of the sickly child who lay whimpering in the dish of her baby-weighing scales.

She stood in a circle of some two hundred highland women, a few men among them because of some special interest in one or

[2] Missus: Pidgin word for white woman.

other of the children. She had a table set up with the scales on it, and a side table with medicines and ointments and hypodermics, attended by a New Guinea nurse in a green uniform. And another New Guinea girl stood at the tailboard of the ambulance where she had set out a card index and record books, and was making notes of complaints and treatment, besides filling in weight cards and general comment.

She, too, regarded Sister Purcell with wonder, for it is not normal for a New Guinea woman to speak harshly to a man she does not know, especially if he seems to be a "big" man as might be judged by the tufts of fur drawn through the lobes of his ears. And Sister Purcell is minute.

When her anger was spent, and the weakening child had been given an injection, and its mother presented with some vitamin concentrates to administer during the two weeks that would elapse before Sister came again to Watabung, I called and smiled and raised my hand, seeking an audience.

She nodded and I pushed my way through, and without interrupting her work she spoke, still bad-tempered.

"The woman is a fool and her husband should be put in jail."

These seemed strong words and I waited for explanations.

"That child is dying from malnutrition because the mother is still feeding a two-year-old boy at the breast and hasn't enough milk for both of them. And the new one is a girl so it doesn't matter very much to them if she dies."

I said, "Oh," not having much knowledge of these things.

She motioned her assistant to put the next baby on the scales, and smiled a motherly smile, for it was a fat and happy infant, and she beamed approval at the mother and looked into the baby's eyes and examined its skin and patted its round stomach, then noted the weight and gave the mother back the card.

Like an entertainer quickly changing faces, she again looked severe and continued to expel her anger. "Some of them are so stupid and their habits so uncivilized that I sometimes wonder why we bother with them." Another healthy child was placed on the scales. "Yet some of them are lovely, like this one."

She poked it, and the baby grinned toothlessly, while the mother made clucking noises; and the two of them, one in starched white and the other near-naked, looked at each other understandingly, admiring the miraculous capacity of women to create life and nourish it.

She gave instructions to the nurses to carry on, then rested a while to talk to me, wiping a wisp of wet hair from her forehead, for it was warm now, even in the shade, and she was pressed in on all sides by hot, naked bodies, and the scent of pig fat.

"Some of these women would rather feed pigs than children," she said, referring to a highland custom by which, it is said, women sometimes breast-feed piglets. It is a custom more spoken of than witnessed in my experience, for although I have seen many highland women fondling piglets and carrying them in their arms as though nursing them, and tickling their stomachs and sex organs, I have never seen a woman suckling a piglet, although the practice is referred to often by missionaries and Government officers.

It is certainly true that New Guinea women have a special relationship with their pigs, regarding them with an affection only second to that held for their children. They will sit with a sick pig for hours, stroking it and pouring water over it if it is hot, picking lice from its skin, and making presents to the sorcerer on its behalf to aid its recovery.

At the time of ceremonials, when pigs are killed, a woman may become emotionally upset and make a violent scene when her husband comes to collect the pig for slaughtering, nor will she eat any of its meat because she feels for it as for a personal friend.

They lead a favorite pig by a string attached to its leg, bringing it to the best pastures or feeding it with domestic food from their garden. And at night the pigs and the women and children sleep in one house together, while the men either sleep alone or in men's club houses.

One of the New Guinea nurses called to Sister Purcell and she got up again quickly and rejoined them, and I saw her take a needle to inject penicillin into a baby that was ugly with deep, slimy yaw pits in its back.

Many of the nurses who specialize in this work spend more than half their time on the road, sometimes making a circuit that keeps them out for the best part of a week. During this time they stop at three or four meeting places each day, usually where there is a Government rest house, or a mission station or aid post. If, on the outward journey, they see children who are seriously ill, they arrange with the parents that the child and a guardian will be picked up on the way back and taken to a hospital.

I left the sister and went looking for my policeman and driver, having yet four or five hours farther to go before stopping for the night. They were both listening to a dispute being waged with great rhetorical flourishes and much drama between a man wearing full ceremonial regalia, and a small, almost insignificant *luluai*[3] who wore a khaki shirt and shorts and no more decoration than a wilted pink hibiscus behind his ear.

There were several such disputes going on, and the policeman, who seemed deeply interested, said that this was now a regular feature of life here since the road had been put through and the rest house and aid post built.

He said that the people regarded the spot as a neutral meeting place where they could gather each fortnight when the infant welfare sister came, the women and children attending the clinic, and the men holding informal courts and airing grievances before an impartial audience. If there were arguments or accusations that could not be resolved at these gatherings they would be held over until the patrol officer came.

We moved off again, it being now well past midday, and crossing the river began once more to wind and climb. After an hour we passed the patrol post at Chuave, and came at last, as the sun began to yellow[4] in the west, to the bridge across the Chimbu River. We crossed it, and proceeded along the end of an airstrip which ends in a precipice.

There is a Government station here at the Chimbu River and the people are hospitable, but I thought it better to go on while the weather remained fine and the road dry, and had it in mind to spend the night among the Wandi people, who live a little farther along the road, and with whom I am moderately well acquainted.

---

[3] "Luluai" is the title given to a man appointed by the Government to be the official intermediary between the people of a single village and the various Government officers in the district. He is given a hat and a badge of office. He may not necessarily be a man of traditional importance in the village but may owe his appointment to the fact that he can speak Pidgin, or shows some special enthusiasm for cultural and economic advancement.

[4] It yellowed instead of reddened, perhaps because of the intense blue haze which acts as a filter.

There are no villages in these parts, as there are from Watabung right back to the coast. The people here live in family hamlets scattered about clan lands, with a central meeting place on a hilltop where they gather together to discuss clan matters. But now that they have local government the meeting place is occupied by a new council house built at the side of the highland road.

It was still light when we passed the first hamlets, and women coming from the gardens stopped to watch as we turned in from the road between two whitewashed stones, and halted at the council house steps.

The building would not excite interest in an urban area, not even in New Guinea where most towns are drab; but in the Chimbu Valley it has lineaments of magnificence, both as a building, and as a historic monument marking the end of one era and the beginning of another.

It is carpenter-built, standing on concrete piles and roofed with iron. It has a wide veranda for coolness, and the sides, under the eaves, are louvered with glass. The floor is machine-planed pine. Inside is a long table and a dozen chairs and a tinted picture of the Queen of England. At the back is a kitchen with a gasoline stove.

Yet the women outside, watching us arrive, wear only their cord aprons fore and aft, hung over a narrow belt so low on the loins that their bellies droop over, even the young ones. Net bags full of tubers. Sticks of sugar cane parceled in pandanus leaves and held on their heads. Babies. And some wearing holy medals because there is a Catholic mission in the valley.

They giggle behind their hands and call out to the few men standing around and about the council house, some of whom carry bows and arrows and have feathers in their hair, for they have been visiting.

I recognized two of the men in spite of the bones hung in their noses, and they grinned sheepishly, remembering that I last saw them wearing shirts and white lap-laps at a council meeting.

Then Kondom Agaundo, the president, came up from his house and looked pleased to find me, because we had been speaking together in Port Moresby only a few weeks ago and I had told him that I would be coming through.

He looked comfortable once more, in bare feet, and able to eat good solid food prepared by his wives and brought to him in his house, instead of picking at the fancy scraps served in the dining room of the hotel in Port Moresby, and cooked anonymously.

He sent a lad to tell somebody to kill a chicken and cook it for me, then told the carpenter to fix a cot in the council house. And later he and some of the councilors, all wearing their badges, came courteously to watch me eat, one of them bringing a handful of tomatoes from his garden, and another a pineapple. They sat at the long table, smiling, and watching me and making an occasional quiet comment while I asked Kondom about local affairs.

He complained about an upsurge of domestic murders in the valley, saying that young men liked to go to jail because it gave them a good start in life. He and the Catholic missionary and the members of his council all thought that the Government should hang a few of the young men who murdered without good traditional reasons.

All of the councilors around the table nodded and murmured together in agreement.

I could name some of them—Bomai, Kileng, Mondo, Malia—for I was here when they went to the Government station to nominate Kondom as a candidate for election to the Legislative Council, and had gone with them.

They had been seven, and all signed the paper with a thumbprint, including Kondom.

It had been a tight squeeze in the local Government officer's tiny room. Seven Chimbus standing around the table, the Government man and his Tolai assistant sitting, and me watching at the door because later we were to make a film about these elections and I needed to know the procedure that had been followed.

Kondom and the councilors had seemed nervous and uncertain, not understanding the purpose of the nomination paper that was being filled in for them, and wondering with the primitive parts of their minds what dangers they were exposing themselves to by imprinting their thumbs upon it.

And when the local Government officer put the paper in his safe the matter seemed incomplete and they felt that there should have been some ritual or spoken formula or dramatic action of some kind.

They left the office slowly, still mystified. But they trusted the

Government officer and were not really worried about the thumb-prints and the magic that might be worked against them if the paper fell into the hands of some sorcerer.

I finished my meal and we all stood up, shook hands, and said goodnight. Then Kondom looked to see that my bed was ready and told the council house caretaker to sleep outside. Then he, too, went away.

There was much laughter and loud talk down at the school-teacher's house, and the sound of a guitar, and I recognized the voice of my driver and knew that he and the policeman had found friends, sophisticates like themselves, all feeling civilized and some-what superior among these Chumbu peasants.

Kondom came again in the morning, shepherding two small sons who carried a tin pot of hot coffee, and little grass baskets with eggs and bread and fruit in them. When I had thanked the boys Kondom spoke and they went scampering off to school.

Almost all adult highlanders are illiterate, yet their leaders have an almost passionate determination that the children shall be edu-cated. Continuously they petition the Government to give them teachers, and whenever a senior official or politician visits them they make the same request.

A few years ago the district education officer came and explained to them that before a teacher could be sent they must have a school and a house for the teacher to live in, and that there were other parts of New Guinea where the people had been waiting much longer for schools, and that these must be served first. He said, also, that an area like the Chimbu required the kind of school where children could stay, and this meant dormitories and other domestic buildings.

The leaders listened courteously, making no argument, and he went away feeling relieved and rather pleased with himself for having given his department breathing space and possible relief from the continuous pestering.

But only a month passed before another message came from the Chimbu asking him to visit the valley again, for the school was now built, and only needed a teacher.

The Director of Education came himself to make the inspection, and walked silent and amazed in and out and around a block of

thirty buildings, all erected in a single month by the Chimbu people, without cost to the Government.

Four thousand men had worked on the project, some bringing
timber from the mountains, some leveling the ground, and others
building. All of them, with their women and children, stood watching to see if he would accept their gift and give them, in return,
their teacher.

The director was not an emotional man but he said that he had
now seen a miracle. And he sent them two teachers.

The reason for this unique sense of urgency and striving for ac-
complishment in the highlands seems, on the surface, clear, even
having regard to the fact that nothing which involves human beings
is as simple and straightforward as theorists would make it appear.
The comfortable climate of the highlands and the fact that there is
food enough for general well-being, and the absence of malaria, are
all good and contributory reasons why the highlander is more alert
and actively ambitious than the coastal Papuan, or the Buka, or the
outback Sepik villager.

But gradually an overriding factor looms larger and larger until
it becomes inescapably persistent, and that is, the image and example of the highland white man.

The Government officers, missionaries, and settlers who live and
work among the highlanders are twentieth-century pioneers, building according to the concepts of today, and not of Victoria's England or Bismarck's Germany.

The intelligent Government officer working in the highlands, and
they are many, does not view the New Guinean as a savage to be
tamed and turned into a docile and obedient colonial, but as a
human being who can be taught the dignities and practical ways of
modern man. The missionary, though still jealous for his particular
God, no longer seeks anxiously to save and salvage and remake a
pagan soul in the image of a European Christian, but tries to ensure
that the emerging leaders and their people will have decent princi-
ples with which to ballast their new ambitions. And the highland
settler knows that no army from overseas can keep him on his farm
or plantation, or in his store today, but that he must earn the respect
and goodwill if not the affection of the New Guinea man, so that
he will be asked to stay and labor alongside him to their mutual
gain.

And the highlander has come clean to this relationship. There is no long tradition of inferiority to overcome, no inherited resentments, no history of colonialism or continuous exploitation to embitter him; and no background of generations of neglect under a poverty-stricken administration, too poor to provide anything more than patriotic flags and the poles to fly them on.

The highlander has emerged into this new age under the protection of a United Nations in which numbers favor the non-white races. Everybody, almost, is theoretically on his side.

Yet he still feels inadequate. He realizes that he lacks the assurance and sophistication that comes with twentieth-century education and experience. His perception in this regard is astounding to one who has been brought up to believe that primitives are utterly dull and ignorant.

Many powerful men like Kondom Agaundo, rich in traditional wealth and authority, envy the young Papuan and Tolai schoolmasters, underpaid, and without land or family, who are able to teach their children the alphabet, and simple addition, and the rivers of Europe.

They resent and even distrust men like John Akunai, who have grown up with white men and speak English, and can read and write. They fear that if self-government comes too soon they will be outmaneuvered by these educated and politically adept men who are leaders of much lesser groups than their own.

Kondom was smiling and making simple noises of affection and pleasure as we walked together to the Land-Rover, but looking back as we drove away, I could see the puzzled furrows settling back again on his brow.

Three

The road from Wandi runs on westward, leaving the timbered ridges of the Chimbu watershed to drop down gently into the wide valley of the Wahgi River.

The country opens out now and slopes away in a long foreground of grass and garden land that stretches for miles to the river's edge. And beyond the river the ranges rise again, fold after fold, with white cloud lying in the crevices, and the sky a thin, rain-washed, whitish-blue.

It is a peaceful country of quiet and gentle contour in contrast to the violent and antagonistic uplands farther back, all pinnacle and crag and unresponsive, unaccommodating, giving nothing.

It was a relief to ride straight and swiftly, the driver not crouched or wrenching at the steering wheel every twenty yards or so, but able to sit back and sing, though he had no voice and the song was sad and tuneless.

We had not gone a half hour when a procession, spread across the road and coming toward us, made us stop. There were fifty or sixty people of all ages, ancient to adolescent, chanting, and carrying a display of wealth and decoration.

We stopped the car, and as they passed by, ignoring us, our policeman interpreted their chanting, and said that they were carrying bride-price to present to the people of another family farther down the road. So we left the Land-Rover and followed them on foot.

As they walked their headman and the older women kept up a recitative in canon form, one voice following another, enumerating (so the policeman said) the gifts they bore, saying who they were and where they were going, and for what reason.

The decorated men carried a heart-shaped frame of cane, four or five feet high at its widest diameter and three feet across, the whole supported on two poles and carried above the heads of the people like a banner.

Cluster after cluster of overlapping paradise plumes made a red-gold corona around the rim of this frame, set off and segmented with satin-black streamers of tail feathers. And along the top of the arc, inside the feathered edge, eight great baler shells with lips a hand's-span long, the bowls butter-yellow darkening through amber to the color of nicotine. Then inside, covering the face of the frame, overlapping leaves of gold-lip kina shell, twenty or more, each ten inches wide and five or six inches deep.

Three other men, undecorated, carried sides of freshly slaughtered pork across their shoulders. Two lads marched proudly on the outskirts holding new tomahawks erect. An old woman with a cowrie-shell headband in her hand chanted in a tuneless dry voice as she skipped along. Two men carried a stick between them with a beadbelt and two single pound notes hung on it.

We went with them until they turned in from the road along a narrow track that brought us, after fifty yards, into a small clearing with three houses in it, with two cooking fires outside, the whole fenced around with a thicket of bamboo.

A crowd as big as the one we followed stood waiting in this clearing to receive the visitors, some of the men highly decorated and holding three-pronged ceremonial spears and wearing plumes on their heads. They had slithers of mother-of-pearl through their noses, or long, frail tail feathers that stuck out eighteen inches beyond their cheeks, and their mouths were partly hidden by shell discs suspended from the septum of the nose.

These men wore headbands, some stitched with shells and others vividly red with raw ocher, and so deep that the plumes on their heads seemed to be growing out of pots. And each man wore woven armbands and anklets, and a collar of beads and kina shell; and belts a foot deep around their stomachs from which their frontal aprons hung; and behind, great bunches of clean tanket leaves like bustles.

The gift-carriers stood their frame of feathers and shell against the thicket, and the other men and women and the two boys put their presents on a covering of banana leaves laid on the ground, in the clearing between the three houses.

Then the hum of men and women murmuring together, and the short, quick cries of excited children, died suddenly, and old people who were standing together gently touching each other with affection and friendship, being relatives but separated by marriage into different villages, stood apart again to listen to the speeches.

One of the men stood forward, leader of the visitors who had come in procession, the oldest brother of the bridegroom or headman of his clan, and he began to speak, rhetorically and in a high-pitched voice like a man reading from a book.

One by one he enumerated the gifts that his people had brought for the bride's family, noting each one separately and naming the person from whom it had come, praising its quality, extolling the fine feelings and status and magnanimity of each contributing member of the bridegroom's clan. As he mentioned each item he pointed to it with his ax, indicating those for which equivalent articles were expected in exchange.

There were cries and ejaculations of approval from the bridegroom's clan but silence from the bride's party, until the headman made a speech in reply. Then others spoke, and some interjected, and there were sudden little flurries of cross-argument and laughter, until at last an old woman went into one of the three grass houses, stooping to enter through a low door, and in a little while came out with the bride and her companion.

She looked very lovely, but a little dull of expression, almost resentful, though she might have simply been shy. Her breasts were full and tight and glistening with pig grease. An enormous and dazzling headdress proliferated in tiers from her headbands, with first a crimson circlet of parrot quills, then black feathers above them, spreading out corolla-like over her naked, shiny, copper-colored shoulders. And fanning out above her head, spray after spray of massive golden plumes finishing in a foam of yellow.

And she no more than a child, fifteen or sixteen at the most. Her cheeks painted red, with lines of blue and yellow across her forehead and down to the edges of her mouth. Thin arcs of nacre through her nose and tufts of opossum fur hanging from her ears, and side blinds of flat shell framing her face.

Ropes of beads, blue, red, and yellow around her throat, and the bushy golden tail of a tree-climbing kangaroo pendant between her breasts. A waistband of patterned bark, and below it a bead belt with the words "Port Moresby" worked into it. Loops of cane around her diaphragm, and a new apron, and more shells at her waist.

The finery was all borrowed, all belonging to male relatives, and some of it part of the clan wealth kept for these occasions, treasures for brides to wear on their wedding day.

Within a year, with her first child, she would be indistinguishable from other Chimbu women, naked except for her apron, and it dirty with continuous wear and soiled from sitting on the dusty floor of her hut, or in her garden weeding. No more feathers or paint. Skin dusty, unoiled, and cracked. Breasts distended and grotesque, or hanging flat and ugly.

We had not time to stop longer and watch the procession of the bride to her husband's village, but went on our way again. But in the evening, at the mission station where we stayed the night, the priest, who is also an anthropologist, spoke of the courting and marriage customs of the highland tribes.

It is, he said, a strangely circumscribed life cycle that these highland women live from infancy to old age. A life that seems to fall quite clearly into three parts, each separate and distinct and utterly different, with only local variations, and perhaps the rare exception when a woman of outstanding character and capacity rises above the ruck.

From birth to puberty a girl child stays close to her mother, sleeping beside her for warmth, feeding at her breast until another child is born, perhaps until she is two years old. Each day she goes with her mother to the garden, even as a newborn babe, carried in the net bag. Then, when she is big enough to play, her mother gives her a little digging stick so that she learns from the beginning to weed and gather tubers, and to carry them home in a bag hung from her forehead.

Then, with her first menses she flowers, and for three years or more lives a life of almost complete liberty and leisure, enjoying her femininity and exploiting it for every pleasure and advantage that it can bring her.

She goes visiting with her friends to take part in courting games with boys from other villages, and spends nights with them in club houses where the young people are able to be private, and the adults undisturbed by the chanting and chattering and sex-play that goes on all through the night.

In these first years of womanhood she finds herself, becomes a person, achieves an adult personality. She explores the limits of her mind and body and discovers what she can do with them. She experiments with sex, learns about men, and looks for a husband.

She spends much time decorating herself, and borrows finery from her family and relations, wearing different plumes and shells and necklaces as often as she can, to impress the young men and their relatives with the wealth that her father owns and the richness of the gifts that may be expected at her betrothal and marriage.

There is, indeed, little difference in the behavior pattern of these girls of a primitive tribe and the teen-agers of the Western world except, perhaps, that the highland girls are encouraged to experiment sexually with a variety of young men during the period between puberty and enforced marriage.

But this butterfly-brief span of freedom, of gaiety and achievement and the tasting of all the delights of physical life, ends abruptly when the adults of her family decide that she has experimented far enough, and that the time has come for her formal betrothal and marriage to a man chosen for her by the clan. And the marvelous suddenly becomes the mundane.

For a while she fights against this fate, rebels, says she is yet too young for marriage. She seeks to escape back into the playtime from which she has been abruptly taken by the tribe, intent in her marriage with its own preservation. She may, if she is bold by nature, go headlong into an outbreak of wanton promiscuity, claiming that she is not yet ready to live with one man or to go each day to the garden to work. And in the early days of marriage she may run away as often as she can, though closely guarded by the women of her husband's family who keep her like a prisoner, and never leave her alone for a moment while he is away working or hunting with the other men.

And he, the husband, is desperately brutal, striving to get her pregnant quickly so that no other man will want her. And such is the emotional confusion of this period that some girls attempt to commit suicide. So, within a few months, the highland bride who on her marriage day is as beautiful as almost any maid, becomes a slattern, a dusty, unadorned drudge, a sullen stranger in an alien village, with nothing to look forward to but old age and the dour, uncertain pleasures of matriarchal authority and pride.

When she has gone from her own people her uncle or elder brother makes a *gerua* or spirit board to remember her by, carving it from a piece of wood and painting upon it the clan design and family totem. And he keeps this board in his own house to signify the girl's abiding presence within the family even though she may be lost to it physically. And her spirit board becomes the center of the clan ceremonies when she eventually dies.

So we talked well into the night.

The missionary, looking over his glasses, said that he thought it might be many years before traditional customs of courtship and marriage died out entirely, but it was clear that social and economic changes introduced by the Government and missions were already having an effect.

Intertribal fighting is finished and it is no longer necessary for "big" families to forge tribal and clan alliances by exchanging brides, a practice that has been abandoned in Europe only in this present century.

Nor does a man need any more to have many wives in order to acquire wealth and prestige and power, all of which are now more simply obtained and kept by planting coffee, or owning a truck or tractor.

In any case, the Government's policy of encouraging Christianity as a nationally unifying factor, and the introduction of a common legal code covering everybody regardless of color or tribe, must soon put an end to polygamy and make marriage customs and divorce laws uniform.

He said that the girl whose bride-price payment we had witnessed during the morning was most likely a Catholic, and that she and her young man would come to the mission within a few days and ask to be married according to the Church.

She would, he said, wear a cleanly washed blouse, and the young man a shirt, and there would be no feathers or shells or face paint, although if any relations came they might, perhaps, wear traditional dress and would afterwards escort them back to the village playing kundu drums.

We stayed overnight, and next morning, it being Sunday, saw two thousand people come to Mass in the great, barnlike church with its twin pyramid towers of wood. There were too many people to fit in at one time so a thousand stayed outside while the first Mass was said, waiting in small groups, sitting and standing about, some old and puckered up and wearing practically nothing, others with all their feathers and shells, a few in Western clothes, but not many.

Old women with heavy crucifixes banging on their hollow chests, young women with fat breasts feeding babies, four nearly naked laughing girls arm in arm, and a policeman's wife sitting under a sunshade smoking a pipe, her big bare feet stuck straight out.

Two lads, brothers, one with painted face and the other wearing a white shirt, shorts, and shoes. A file of nuns in white habits passing quickly through the crowd, smiling. Scores of dogs and babies. And a short missionary with a black beard and round stomach, beaming.

Inside the Church, sitting on the ground or on rows of low battens, the congregation facing the altar in four blocks, the men and women separated by the central aisle. Small boys on the left, then men. Then on the other side of the aisle, the women and little girls. At the back of the Church a row of headmen with thick beards, arms folded, great sprays of tail feathers sprouting out of their headdresses. Their eyes are alive with wonder as they watch the priest move slowly about the altar. Their lips whisper, responding to versicles spoken by the catechists who stand at the sanctuary steps.

There is a great, crude, and beautiful mural behind the altar. The Holy Family surrounded by men and women and children of New Guinea, with a missionary priest standing among them, and written above it, *"Gloria Tibi Trinitas."*

On the women's side a pattern of bent heads and backs draped with net bags. Babies at the breast. Young children, able to toddle but not yet big enough to sit with the older ones, play quietly in the aisles.

A little boy runs down toward the altar, then turns to laugh at his mother who is hissing at him to come back. He goes farther and looks around again, teasing her, then sits down and makes a little stream of water, and standing up again looks backwards between his legs and laughs, but is suddenly caught unawares by a man who snatches him up and carries him back to his mother.

They recite the rosary, catechists leading and the congregation answering with great waves of sound. The surge and sweep of men's voices, organ-deep, and the women answering, high, shrill, and passionate.

The priest came down and spoke to them of the love of God, and they watched, motionless, mothers hushing their babies, and little children staring with wide, white eyes. Over the altar the Holy Ghost looked down in the form of a dove.

Afterwards we had coffee and an omelette and went on our way to Minj, the main Government station in the Wahgi Valley.

The Wahgi tribesmen are big men of fine physique, made to look even bigger by the wearing of high head feathers and the tall spears they carry, and long frontal aprons which hang down almost to their feet.

A flamboyant people, given to great sweeping gestures and rhetoric and exhibitionism. Feminine in their love of color and display, brutal and barbarous and extravagantly savage at the big religious festivals in which hundreds of pigs are clubbed to death in one day, and blood is spattered about like red mud all over the ceremonial ground. They live, as the Chimbu and other highlanders of the western valleys do, in family homesteads or small hamlets of closely related families, the men and women in separate houses. But here and there are big villages built especially for clan gatherings, and used only at the time of major feasts or ceremonies.

In these villages the buildings form the boundaries of an oblong space used for dancing and pig-killing, and in this space, during the spirit festivals, they build a small circular house on stilts, and this is hung about with the jawbones of pigs killed at earlier feasts in honor of ancestors and the tribal spirit-gods. And there is usually an image of a god inside, carved in wood or made of woven fibers, and colored red and black.

Some of the men's club houses in these special festival villages are a hundred feet long, and more, for there may be a thousand people of one clan gathered together for the occasion. And the women also have a community house, long and low-built, just high enough for a short person to stand up in.

Each man also builds separate houses for himself and his wives, and perhaps a storehouse for the food they bring with them, but these ordinary little huts are not used much once the feast begins. During the nights of the pig-killings there is much dancing and uninhibited sex-play and mass courting in the long houses, and not much sleeping.

The ceremonies go on for several days until everybody is tired out and the food is finished, and men and women must go back to their homes to work or rest; but when they are recovered in strength and have gathered more food, they come back again to the festival village and go on with the dancing in honor of the great spirit-gods of the tribe, and the ghosts of ancestors.

Having built the special village and reared a sufficient number of pigs to make a feast possible (and this may take several years), the tendency is to keep it going as long as enthusiasm and food supplies can be maintained. And sometimes an impetus is given to the feast by introducing smaller ceremonies to honor individual relatives and leaders who have died within recent years.

Government officers and missioneries often complain that a clan has been feasting intermittently for two years, that food gardens are neglected and children allowed to get sick and die, and that the whole clan has become obsessed and hypnotized by a repetitive mixture of uninhibited sex and dancing.

They complain that this undisciplined attitude toward time makes it impossible for them to help the people progress in modern ways. Coffee-planting stops and growing trees are neglected. The roads deteriorate for want of maintenance, and women stay away from the infant welfare clinics.

The cycle of Christian feasts and Church ceremonies is forgotten. Houses get shabby and gardens overgrown with weeds while the whole active and creative capacity of a clan is dissipated in a pro-longed orgy of primitive sensuality and lechery.

Worst of all, they say, children stay away from school, and taking part in the feasts get steeped again in the most evil aspects of the old primitive way of life.

I wondered, once, if this were true, but one day saw a copy of a mission school news sheet written by the boys. Among the simple little stories and items of interest contributed by students was one which read:

A Murder.
On July 31st, the natives in the Eastern Highlands had a big feast. They wanted to dance and they went to one village. And a man went to the toilet but one woman came and saw him and she said, "This toilet is for women not for men." The man was very angry

with her and then he got a knife and he cut her throat and she died. They wanted to bury her. The man they took to the Government Station. He is in jail.

A second item said:

In the month of May, Senglap's tribe began their sing-sing for killing their pigs. They had beautiful feathers and they got their drums and tied cuscus skins on them with strings, and danced. In the holidays we heard the sound of the drums. There are six or seven clans in Senglap's tribe. They have a lot of pigs. Very many men have about thirty pigs each. They don't dance on Mondays or when the Government man comes and calls them to work. Sometimes they dance and sing right through the week.

In the late column of news it says:

Our Chimbu boys are beginning to come back to school after the pig feasts.

Some people say that traditional customs should be preserved. Others say that they stand in the way of progress. The United Nations complains that advancement is not being made fast enough. The Government says that enlightenment will only come with education and that education is a slow process. The district commissioner and his subordinates do the best they can with little definite guidance.

We drove steadily for two hours between hedges of variegated crotons and scarlet and orange canna flowers, and over little bridges with thatched roofs, and came to Minj. The Wahgi River is wide at this point and is crossed by a long suspension bridge, and having crossed the bridge, the road winds around the end of the airstrip, past the Government office and the assistant district commissioner's house, the hospital and the malaria research center, and ends abruptly at the entrance to the golf club.

There are over eight hundred thousand tribesmen in these central highlands, and a little over two thousand white people. And of these whites, less than two hundred are coffee planters, the rest being Government men, missionaries, traders, people engaged in commerce of some kind, wives and children.

This handful of planters occupies fifty thousand of the ten and a half million acres of ground in the highlands. Few of them have been here longer than ten years, many of them less, but in that time they have developed a coffee industry out of the bare ground, without machinery or skilled labor. By their example, and the creation of a transport and marketing system, they have helped to lift the highland tribesmen onto the threshold of the twentieth century in a single step.

Most of them are in debt to banks or trading companies but are beginning to see financial daylight now that their coffee trees are bearing; and Government action over tariffs has assured them of a reasonable part of the Australian market.

Some of them have moved out of the grass houses in which they lived for the first few years of their pioneering, and have built themselves decent homes.

If the coffee market remains stable most of them could be out of debt and making reasonable money in five years, but there is a feeling gaining ground among them that they might not have five years. That a new wave of history is about to sweep over New Guinea and wash them out of these valleys, and destroy what they have been trying to build.

There were a score of people in the club house, mostly young planters and Government officers and their wives, some with little children. A small group stood at the bar, among them a woman with a loud, clear voice. She was speaking of a recent visit to Sydney, and although there was music coming from a record player on the bar, her voice rode over it.

She was saying, "Down there in Australia they don't seem to know anything about New Guinea—they don't know that we exist." Her husband, a little man, standing at the end of the bar drinking beer, grinned at her affectionately. She looked around, trying to draw everybody into the orbit of her anger.

"It's all very well for the politicians to say that Australia is in New Guinea to stay, but what are they doing to see that we don't get thrown out?"

Nobody answered her because she was saying what many of them think but do not want to believe.

A truck pulled up outside, and the Local Government officer came in. He saw me standing alone and came, holding out his hand. "Just the man I was looking for, come and have a drink."

We went over to the bar and talked about the council elections to be held during the coming week, the first in the Wahgi Valley.

I said that a team would come in during the week to film the elections, and I asked him who he thought would win. He said Nopnop Tol, without doubt. It seemed a safe bet. Nopnop has five wives and consequent status among the Wahgi clans and the old traditionalists. He has nine thousand coffee trees and a motor car, and these put him well ahead with the progressive element. He is the official interpreter for the station, which means that he is the recognized channel of communication between the Government and the tribes.

He is a big man and looks impressive in traditional shell and feathers. Also he has a gold wristlet watch and wears white man's clothes to Government functions. He has been to Port Moresby as an observer for the Wahgi people at meetings of the Legislative Council, and has given one of the biggest pig feasts in the history of the Wahgi tribes. He would almost certainly be elected president of the first Local Government Council in the valley.

In the late afternoon, after the rain, we went for a short drive.

The Wahgi is one of the loveliest places in the world, and toward evening when the sun is nearly down, and black clouds lie golden-edged on the mountains, great silver bayonets thrust through gaps in the sky to make patches of washed light on the darkening land.

And the valley becomes a vast reservoir of tranquillity.

The people have gone to their homes, and thin spirals of smoke rise from huts and hamlets. Old men sit and gossip and chew sugar cane or areca nut. Women chatter and scold unmeaningly as they poke at sweet potatoes baking in the fire.

We stopped and watched from the valley side while a thin, pure, creeping sound came up from the station, swelling until it was clearly a trumpet calling the close of day. We could hear the notes feeling out across the valley and rebounding and sounding along its walls, and echoing out of gullies miles away.

The police guard would be saluting as the Australian flag came down from the flagpole for the night, their rifles held out rigidly before them, living symbols of the Pax Australiana.

How long will there be peace in these valleys for the tribes, for the planters, the missionaries, and the Government officers?

"What are they doing to see that we don't get thrown out?" That's what the girl had said.

Four

Minj is one of two air-traffic junctions in the Wahgi Valley
from which aircraft operate into the adjacent mountain areas where
landing strips are not big enough to accommodate the cargo aircraft which operate from the coast.

The little single-engined aircraft used for these feeder services
run on no regular schedules but come and go as required, or as the
weather will allow, so that on fine days the pilots work furi-
ously from first light until almost dark, shuttling continuously back
and forth between the mountain outposts and their base at Minj.
When the weather is bad, and the peaks and passes cloud in for
days on end, they cannot leave the valley at all.

Passengers who use the feeder services "sit on the strip" and wait
for an aircraft that can take them where they want to go. It is a
recognized New Guinea convention. In time one becomes accustomed to it and can tell by weather signs, and by picking up bits
of gossip around the station, just which pilot in what plane is likely
to be going where, and at approximately what time.

So when a Norseman aircraft came thundering in from Goroka
before eight o'clock in the morning, and the sky was clear to the
southwest, and a heap of cargo marked for Mendi was laid out on
the edge of the strip, I was standing beside it with my bag, ready to
go.

I was the only passenger and sat beside the pilot in the cockpit.
In the back we had a load of cement, sheets of roofing iron, cases
of nails, and other building hardware.

We bumped out of the loading bay, over the rough ground, and
took off without waste of time, heading westward down the valley,
and flew along its south wall, almost touching the treetops on the
foothills. The pilot sat steadying the control stick with an elbow

while he filled in the logbook. His dog sat behind him panting over
his shoulder and snuffling, pausing only for a moment to lick my
neck.

These central highlands are divided for administrative purposes
into three districts. Two are on the New Guinea side of the great
mountain divide and have their headquarters at Goroka and Mount
Hagen. These are known as the Eastern and the Western Highlands. The third district, called the Southern Highlands, is on the
Papuan side and its headquarters station is Mendi.

Mendi lies in a mountain mass that blocks the end of a long, fun-
nel-like land rise which begins a hundred miles away in the Gulf
of Papua and ends at the top of the great divide. Year round it
catches and collects the wet clouds blown in by trade winds from
the Pacific and Indian Oceans.

Most days the way into Mendi is open for no more than the two
or three hours of midmorning, between the rise and fall of an almost permanent cloud cover. Sometimes it is not possible to get in
or out of the Southern Highlands for two weeks at a time, so that
pilots will not willingly fly in at all unless it seems reasonably
clear from weather trends that they will be able to get out again
immediately.

We flew west for ten minutes, then turned south out of the valley,
aiming upward toward a high pass in the divide, and crossing it
came into Papua. Now, going against the grain of the country, we
were unable to fly low along the valleys but for safety stayed above
the cloud layer, navigating by line of sight between high peaks.

Behind us, to the north, Mount Wilhelm, 15,400 feet, named for
a kaiser. Kubor to the south, 14,300. On our right Giluwe at 15,600,
providing the western landmark, its pyramid head thrusting upward through a little field of cloud.

In between the highest peaks is a crisscross and confusion of
lesser mountains in which the rivers of the Gulf of Papua rise; in the
bottoms are a network of steep ravines through which they run to
the sea. Everywhere patches of cloud tacked loosely together, and
flashes of sunlit river far below. And away to the south the silver
mirror of Lake Kutubu, halfway to the coast.

Ivan Champion and Karius came this way though a little westward, in 1927, on their epic walk from coast to coast, but the two

men were explorers filling in blank spaces on the map, not pioneers looking for possibilities of settlement. They were impressed mainly by the warlike manner of the Mendi people and the misery of much cold and wet weather.

There were other exploration patrols in the area afterwards, but it was not until 1950, when the confusion of World War II had abated in the Pacific, that a patrol set out from Lake Kutubu and climbed again into these central highlands from the Papuan side, this time to find a place for a Government station. The leaders of the patrol chose Mendi because it seemed to be the center of a great concentration of people.

Since then substations have been set up, and patrol officers have taken a census as well as they are able, estimating an approximate 170,000 people in the sixty-four hundred square miles of the Papuan part of the central highlands, with roughly half this population in the Mendi area, though there are clans yet to be formally discovered.

They soon found, also, that this southern part of the central highlands holds much less promise of advancement than do the eastern and western parts, which lie on the New Guinea side of the divide.

The southern part has no wide and fertile valleys to compare with the Asaro and Bena at Goroka, or the Chimbu and Wahgi valleys. The wet and cloudy weather continuously funneled up from the Gulf of Papua makes it climatically unpleasant most of the year, and there does not seem to be suitable soil or enough sunshine for commercial agriculture.

The contour is badly broken and disordered, closed in on the north by the high and jagged spine of the main range, and blocked on the southern fall by a maze of rivers that run into coastal swamp, making roadways to the outside world almost impossible to build economically; so that even if agriculture could be developed there is as yet no practical way of getting the produce out.

The station at Mendi was established at about the time when the stations at Goroka and Mount Hagen were made district headquarters for the Eastern and Western Highlands. Then the people of the three districts were all, for the most part, living a stone age life, more or less at the same stage of primitivism.

They had no metals, used no tools other than the stone adz and digging stock, produced fire by making friction between two pieces of cane, went to war with bows and arrows and stone clubs, had not discovered the wheel, made gods of their ancestors, and divided their leisure time between the twin excitements of feasting and fighting.

They were all of a kind. Differences were only those of language and of domestic custom influenced by environment. Details of dress and decoration were dependent entirely upon local supplies of bird plumage and the proximity to trade routes through which shell and other wealth found its way from the coast. For these reasons the Wahgi and Chimbu people were the most colorful. Other than that, there seemed not much to choose between them and the Mendi as human material from which to fashion modern men.

But the difference in district development and progress since 1950 is remarkable.

There are, for instance, scores of men around Goroka, born during the last decade of their own tribes' stone age, who are now fellow members with white men in the Highland Farmers and Settlers' Association. A young Wahgi woman who passed through all the courting and marriage ceremonies of her clan is a laboratory assistant in the malaria research establishment at Minj, able to dissect a mosquito and to mount it on a slide for microscopic examination. Several headmen of the Mount Hagen clans own tractors and trucks, and operate trade stores and coffee-buying depots. A Chimbu man represents the highland people in the Legislative Council of the Territory.

But the highlanders on the Papuan side of the divide still live and think as primitives, and although in official statistics most of their tribal area is classified as being "fully under control" the people are continuously engaged in warfare, so that little progressive activity can be carried out either by the Government or the missionaries.

Recently, with good intentions, a native Local Government Council was formed in the Upper Mendi Valley, and after the elections a great feast was held, at which 350 pigs were slaughtered. But arguments broke out about the voting, and this first attempt at unifying the Mendi tribes ended with a fight. It seems a little too soon to expect these people to plunge headfirst into our civilization.

At present the Mendi people are divided into about one hundred clans, some with several thousand members and others, decimated by disastrous feuds and continuous guerrilla warfare, reduced to a few hundred fugitive survivors.

They are a lively and active people, and in spite of climate and dietary deficiencies seem fairly robust, the men being thickly built though short of stature, averaging in height little over five feet, but broad of shoulder and well muscled. They have a Semitic cast of feature, with large, strong noses, thick lips, and heavy eyebrows. Many of them wear black, spade-shaped beards like ancient Assyrians.

They have not the extrovert flamboyance of the Wahgi or Chimbu people, and do not as a rule wear colorful decoration, but reserve what finery they have for only the most formal of occasions. They seem, rather, to be an introverted people, quick to take offense, stubborn and slow to see the other man's point of view, more willing to fight than to make friends.

Such clothing as they have is useful and conventional rather than decorative. The men wear a tight-fitting beret of bark cloth to keep their thick hair dry, for hardly a day passes when they are not caught in a cold mist or drizzle of rain.

They have the wide bark belt or cane loops common to almost all highland tribes, with the string apron draped over the front and a bunch of leaves tucked in at the back. This duster of leaves is removed when a man enters his own sleeping house at night, and left in a dry spot under the eaves, just as a man might leave his muddy boots outside the house in an industrial country when coming home from work.

The men also wear armlet and leg bands of woven grass, and a kina shell on the chest, while women wear little else than a grass skirt, necklets of beads, and the net carrying bag worn as a head covering.

When Mendi girls marry they are covered from head to foot with a shiny black coating of tree oil mixed with the soot from wood fires, and their skin is polished until they shine like stoves. The oil is purchased from an isolated tribe that lives to the southwest in rain forest country, and is fetched in tubes of bamboo which measure from six to eight feet long, on journeys that may take many days.

This oil is one of the principal items of trade between the Mendi people and their neighbors, and payment is made with kina shell. Generally, of course, the oil is used by the men for decoration at high feasting times, and a woman wears it only at the time of her betrothal and marriage.

At this time she wears also a jet-black net bag especially and finely woven for the occasion, gathered into a topknot on her head and hanging down her back to below her buttocks. Around her waist she has six or seven loops of polished brown cane from which a new frontal apron is hung. It reaches to her knees, and is open at the sides so that her thighs are fully exposed. She wears tight armlets, two inches deep, on both arms just above the elbow, and around her neck a few strands of red beads and, as a rule, two overlapping gold-lip shells resting above her breasts. This, and a little red ochre around her eyes, is her wedding dress.

The only other occasion upon which the women decorate themselves to any extent is during periods of mourning. Then they anoint themselves afresh each day with a coating of blue-gray clay that completely covers their skin from forehead to ankles, and is relieved only by smears of a red juice around eyes and lips and chin. They continue to wear a head net, but an old and frayed one, and a tattered skirt that is little more than a few strips of shredded reed; but the distinctive feature of their widow's weeds are scores of strings of gray bush berries threaded like beads,[1] worn only at mourning times and in such bulk that they frequently cover the woman's shoulders and the whole of her torso to the waist. The women of a dead man's family will wear these, and anoint themselves with clay every day for several months, until the final mortuary rites are concluded with the cleaning and burial of his bones.

If the dead man has been a brave warrior, and especially if he has been killed in battle, his spirit will go straight up into the sky to join other good spirits who watch benevolently over those left below. But if he has been an evil man, or has met his death through the machinations of wicked spirits, his own soul will remain on earth to plague mankind.

---

[1] *Coix Lacryma Jobi*—commonly called Job's Tears.

The men of Mendi continue to engage in tribal fighting as though they had little else to do. Indeed, just as pig feasts and sex-play are to the Wahgi people the prime and most exciting delights in life, so is fighting to the Southern Highlander.

An arrow tied to a sapling beside a bush track points to a battleground, inviting the passer-by to either join in or stay clear, according to his disposition. Such signs are found with frequency when food gardens are at their flush of production, and no major clan projects are at hand to keep the young men occupied.

At these times fighting may be undertaken with the same innocent enthusiasm as college football, as played by lads of other lands, and may prove no more vicious or lethal. But if men are killed in these minor affrays new feuds spring into being and the ashes of old hatreds are fanned. The fighting proliferates and broadens to the burning down of hamlets and the killing of women. Gardens are destroyed and pigs stolen, and another long period of widespread warfare begins.

One reason why these Mendi people have been left so far behind by the people on the New Guinea side is that they have no road to link them to the outside world.

Their way to the south coast is barred by scores of rivers, unbridgeable within the ordinary limits of Government finance. The way to the north coast, out through the Wahgi and Goroka valleys and down to Lae, must cross the high ranges over which we were then flying, and these have so far proved too much for bulldozing or any other road-making machinery.

Even so, where the clouds are torn and drifting thinly, one can glimpse strips of a raw and unfinished roadway struggling upward over passes ten thousand feet high, always misted in, the viscous, ochrous clay too slippery to walk on, and not likely to bear the weight of wheels for many a year yet.

This road has been ten years in the making, with men working at both ends, from Mendi and from Hagen. And a variety of Government officers, determined and courageous, have bent themselves to finishing it, beginning again each year in the dry season when the tribes can be gathered together to work on it. Then abandoned again when the rains come and wash it out, or the tribes get tired of this white man's foolishness and slip away to work on their garden lands, or to fight.

If ever it gets done it will be little more than a monument to great intentions, the matter for an epic of determination, unless great amounts of money are available to seal it and keep it open. And the distance, in a straight line, is little more than fifty miles. That much between the stone age and civilization.

But that is not all. So difficult is Mendi of access, and so broken of contour, there has not yet been found, though searched for continuously since 1950, a suitable place for an airstrip long enough to allow a sizable aircraft to land.

This means that nothing much bigger than a wheelbarrow can be brought in over the mountains, except on men's backs. And this, in fact, happens. For there are a few vehicles at Mendi and they have been carried in piece by piece and assembled there for use around the station.

We were flying at nine thousand feet and judging by our landmarks were somewhere above the station. We cast about like a hunting dog in a field, looking for holes in the cloud through which we could let down into the Mendi Valley and find its inadequate airstrip.

The station stands on a narrow plateau. On one side of it the Mendi River runs over stones at the foot of the huge wall of limestone. On the other, the short, switchbacked strip occupies the valley flat.

A worried district commissioner is waiting at the airstrip. His wife stands beside him with a traveling bag. She is pregnant.

The pilot is scheduled to go on to Tari, a half hour away, to pick up another medical emergency, a Papuan woman in much the same state but with complications. There are anxious but brief discussions. Sharp orders to the cargo boys to get the aircraft unloaded quickly.

The woman goes aboard, smiling a calm, Mona Lisa smile. A quick, embarrassed kiss from her husband. The door is slammed shut and the aircraft engine thunders into life again. The pilot is to take the woman on to Tari, pick up the other patient, and fly them both straight back to Goroka, where there is a regional hospital.

We all stand and watch as he takes off, and wave at the aircraft flashing past, and look after it as it lifts into the air. The district commissioner standing beside me licks his lips nervously. Then he suddenly turns and holds out his hand and says, "Sorry to be a bit preoccupied, but the wife is not too well. Come up to the house and I'll make some coffee." And as we moved away, "I suppose you know that we've got the old sing-sing ground at last, and we're making the payoff this afternoon?"

Five

It had long been the contention of Government officers working in the Mendi area that if a bigger airstrip could be laid down it would be possible to fly in the component parts of a bulldozer and other earth-moving machinery, and so arm the station for an all-out attempt to push a road across the mountains into the Wahgi Valley to link up with the road that runs through the Chimbu and Goroka and so on down to the coast.

This, more than anything else, would let the twentieth century into the Southern Highlands and open the gates of the new world to those of the Mendi who wished to be part of it. It would bring them level with the John Akunais of Goroka and the Nopnops of Minj, and give the Government officers some heart and hope. It might even encourage settlers to come in and give the local people a lead.

But there appeared to be no flat land in the Mendi area. Even the valley floor is a series of hills and ridges, and until now it had seemed almost impossible to find a place for a proper district airstrip.

Nevertheless the Department of Aviation had kept a surveying team working out from the station systematically, and one day the surveyor, breaking through the bush into a clearing to look upon a new landscape, felt a sudden warm surge inside himself and a lifting up of the heart such as comes to a man who sees the first faint glimmer of success after long, discouraging, and pessimistic drudgery.

It was an isolated ridge with a clear approach at one end, and although narrow it would be possible, he thought, with special effort on the part of the Mendi people, to widen it simply by cutting a thick slice from the top of the ridge and using the spoil to fill in a gully on one side. He felt quite excited, and began to work quickly, thinking that he would walk back to the station later in the afternoon and tell the district commissioner about his find.

There was a ceremonial sing-sing ground at one end of the ridge where it jutted into the valley, the Mendi equivalent of the special pig-feasting grounds kept by the Wahgi people. But there were no individual family huts all around the ceremonial area, only a number of very long and low slab-sided houses, with a door at every twenty paces. There were five such houses on the ridge, the longest of which stretched unbroken for more than a hundred yards.

This was the men's house. The others were for women and visitors, and one for young boys being prepared for initiation. These long houses were in two rows with a wide promenade area between them. Then farther along the ridge, where the housing finished, a well-grassed circular space, about fifty yards in diameter, entirely surrounded by tall and closely planted casuarinas, and in the center of this circle, two mounds, from each of which grew a single tree. The whole area, outside the circle of casuarinas, was planted with a protective thicket of bamboos.

Each Mendi clan has a similar sing-sing ground where its special feasts are celebrated and its ceremonies held, and these grounds are sacred, as cathedrals, mosques, and synagogues are sacred to people of other cultures. But the surveyor did not realize this and thought only of his good luck in finding such a place, although it crossed his mind that it was an unusually pretty spot.

He set up his tripod and theodolite and sent his assistants along the ridge with the staff so that he could measure levels. He took bearings and made notes, and because his mind was full of estimates and possibilities he did not pay much attention to the yodeling.

For that matter he would not have given it much thought, even had his mind been free to speculate on what it might be about, for yodeling (or more accurately, shouting) is the commonplace mode of communication all over the highlands.

Had he thought about it he would perhaps have realized that something out of the ordinary was afoot, for as a rule the highlanders conduct these shouted conversations from ridge to ridge and across the valleys early in the morning or toward sundown, when they are either making plans for the day's activities or exchanging news of yesterday's happenings. And here it was not much after midday and voices calling and answering for miles around, and almost without pause for the best part of an hour.

They heard it at the station, and the district commissioner called to one of his officers. They got into his Land-Rover, and with a few police set out to look around. Before long it became evident that trouble was in the making, for small groups of men were padding through the bush carrying bows and arrows, all of them heading toward the sing-sing ground.

The district commissioner frowned, and muttered to himself, "Dammit, here they go, fighting again, and right on my doorstep." He could almost hear the tongue-clicking disapproval in Port Moresby.

For a half hour the Land-Rover bucked and thumped and clattered over the uneven track. It was nearly three o'clock.

The surveyor closed his notebook and told an assistant to mark some trees which he had used as fixes in his calculations. The assistant picked up an ax and walked toward the casuarinas.

There were yells and screams from behind the thicket of bamboo, and a shower of arrows fell into the clearing, and when the surveyor and his men looked up they saw a crowd of warriors break out of the bush and come toward them, angry and shouting, shuffling and skipping with short, hopping steps, plucking at their bows, and yelling, approaching with steady determination though cautiously, because the surveyor and his party were Government men and Government men working in these parts usually carry rifles for protection.

But for all their caution there was no mistaking their intent, and the surveyor and his men backed away, afraid, knowing that they could not easily escape, being trapped on the narrow ridge.

"We just made it," the district commissioner said to me, pouring coffee. Then he looked up and smiled widely. "Another few minutes and the Aviation Department would have been short of one surveying team."

I took the cup from him and added sugar. He went on.

"It was touch and go for a little while and I thought that we might have to fire a shot or two over their heads to frighten them off, but this would have added to their resentment and I was relieved when they quieted down and listened to me, although they kept muttering, and one nasty little chap at the back was jumping up and down, twanging his bow and urging them to finish off the lot of us.

"I assured them that it was all a mistake, that the surveyor had no intention of cutting their trees down, and that the Government would never desecrate their sing-sing ground unless they themselves agreed that it was to their own advantage."

He shook his head reminiscently.

"That was two years ago. Since then I have been working on them consistently, trying to get them to see that we can't do anything for them if they won't make sacrifices themselves. That if they want coffee plantations and schools and local councils we must have a decent airstrip, and if they won't let us have the land then we can't help them.

"Eventually they agreed, and today we are paying them compensation for the land and signing the transfer documents. But its been a struggle."

It had, I knew well, been a long and difficult maneuver, but when pieced together it made an interesting story in which the key figure is Village Constable Tinbol, youngest son of Sark, the headman of the Tend clan of Mendi, owners of the sing-sing ground.

The story goes back to 1950 when the Government patrol came through from Lake Kutubu, looking for a place to establish a station among these Papuan highlanders. It camped for a few days here in the Mendi Valley.

Needing local guides to take them on farther, the patrol picked on Tinbol, it being politic in all first contacts to do this so as to establish a personal link between the Government and the traditional leaders of the clan or tribe.

Tinbol signed on as a carrier and interpreter, staying with the patrol until it reached Mount Hagen on the other side of the range, where he was paid off at the rate of a shilling a day, plus an ax, blanket, and warm flannel shirt, and such other personal effects as he had been able to acquire on the journey. This was the first time that anybody from Mendi had seen the outside world.

Tinbol stayed at Mount Hagen, became an orderly at the Government hospital, and learned to speak Pidgin. Then after two years he went home, and by agreement between his father and the district commissioner was appointed village constable, which made him official liaison officer and interpreter for the Tend clan.

During his stay at Mount Hagen Tinbol had seen the Dakotas flying in and out each day bringing great loads of building materials and tools. He had seen trucks, bulldozers, and agricultural machinery come along the road from the coast for the Government and the missionaries and settlers.

He saw powerful Hagen leaders, men with his father's status, acquire new wealth and prestige and, washing their bodies and wearing clean clothes, take on a new dignity. He saw that their sons were chosen to be trained for Government work or sent to regional schools where they learned that New Guinea is a big country with hundreds of tribes, and that a man can move freely from one end of the land to the other, except among a few backward groups like the Kukukuku and the Mendi.

Now, back home among his own people, he seemed a lonely figure, uncertain, wondering in what direction his future lay, unable to decide whether his own inclinations and loyalties were to his father or to the district commissioner. To the past or to the future.

It was some time after he had been appointed village constable and interpreter that the surveyor's party was attacked on the sing-sing ground, and it seemed clear to him then that he must make up his mind where he stood in relation to the opposing forces of tradition and progress.

And it was also about this time that I first met Tinbol and his father, Sark, for I had occasion to visit Mendi and was taken by the district commissioner to see the sing-sing ground. Tinbol came with us in case there should be need for interpretation between the district commissioner and any of the local people met with along the way.

When we reached the sing-sing ground there were a number of men there, apparently discussing the recent excitement, for among them was Sark, and Sark's brother Nonga, and a younger but quite important man named Kisap, together with the heads of other families.

Though wearing as little as the other men, and just as grimy, and his skin wrinkled and dirty with age, and spittle in his gray, straggling beard, Sark nevertheless had the air of a leader about him, a kind of detached assurance, emanating authority.

He leaned on a long stick like a shepherd leaning on a crook, while Nonga looked up into the high casuarinas, speaking unceasingly in a low monotone as though invoking some invisible being. And the younger man stood beside them, respectfully silent.

We exchanged quiet greetings but did not stay to engage in conversation. Instead we walked the length of the sing-sing ground and stood at the far end of the long houses while the district commissioner explained to me the possible layout of the proposed airstrip.

Some women passed, carrying firewood piled on their backs in neat stacks, hung by cords suspended from their foreheads; little girls walked with them.

Then Sark and his brother and Kisap came toward us, and a few other men with their small sons. But these other men stopped a little distance away and let the headmen come to us on their own. It made a strangely dramatic picture. A backdrop of bush-covered mountains against a leaden and lifeless sky. The narrow long houses stretching away from us to terminate in the circlet of dark green towering casuarinas.

In the foreground, three men of Mendi, so natural a part of this landscape that they seemed one with the trees and shrubs and kunai grass, and the flock of screaming parakeets that darted across the scene. Facing them but separated by several yards, the district commissioner, taller by a foot or more than the Mendi. White trousers, shirt, and tie. Clean-shaven and neat. Wearing spectacles.

And between them, Tinbol, wearing a blue serge work shirt and lap-lap edged with red and yellow, signifying his rank of station interpreter. Less than his father, less than his master the district commissioner. But neither could speak to the other except through him. And it was for his future, and the future of the others of his generation, that his father and the white men were contending.

Sark looked up at the district commissioner and spoke, and as he spoke he pivoted slowly, and with a long, articulated movement of his thin and flaccid arm took in the whole of the sing-sing ground. Then he turned again and stood waiting for his son to translate for him in the language of the white man.

Tinbol spoke unemotionally, flatly, sounding almost resentful as he repeated his father's words.

"It is too big a thing that you ask of us, that we give up our sing-sing ground to make a place for your planes to sit down. For this has been our dancing ground for a long time, and our ancestors will be angry."

Tinbol stopped and looked again at the old man, and Sark spoke again, saying. "My brother Nonga and I were children when we came here with our father and helped him plant the trees that shade this ground, and if we let you take this land away from us his spirit will be angry, and the spirits of all our ancestors will be against us."

The district commissioner listened, then he spoke back. "For a long time you have complained that the Government does not help you. You come to me with stories that you hear about the men of the Wahgi Valley, of Hagen and Goroka and Minj. How they become rich and have white man's goods, and schools for their children.

"But the Government cannot give you these things if you will not provide the place where the big planes can sit down. And the time will come when your children will spit on this ground and curse your memory because they have nothing, while the other men of New Guinea can stand up as equals among the tribes of the whole world."

Then Sark grew angry and frothed at the mouth and shouted, and banged the ground with his stick and cried out that his ancestors would never forgive him if he gave away their dancing ground, that sorcerers would work magic against him and put insects in his belly, and an evil spirit called Temor would get inside him and eat his entrails.

No use then, said Sark, for the magic-men of the tribe to rub his body with nettles, or for his sons to kill many pigs. Nothing could save a man who so gravely offended the ancestral spirits of his clan.

He tore off his bark cap and threw it to the ground, exposing his ancient head, bald except for a tattered fringe above the ears. Then he lay down as though dead, stretching himself out stiffly with his mouth open, while Nonga stood watching, muttering to himself, and Kisap folded his hands across his breast and looked up into the sky and began to lament. Tinbol looked down, frowning and uncertain.

Then the district commissioner, being experienced in these things, and knowing that there is a limit to which insults will gain an objective, took a more conciliatory turn, and commended Sark for his devotion to his ancestors and said that it was clear that he and Nonga were zealous for the welfare of their people but that other, evil men, were giving them bad council.

He mentioned, also, that if they thought the matter over and finally decided to give up the dancing ground, the Government would be pleased and would give them many hundreds of gold-lip shells as compensation. Then he nodded his head to me as a sign that we should go, and we walked off, leaving Sark still stretched upon the ground and Kisap lamenting, and Nonga beating his forehead with his fist.

Tinbol hesitated for a moment, looking at his father, then followed us.

I left Mendi a few days later and heard no more about the affair of the airstrip until some months later, at Madang, on the coast, I ran into one of the Mendi patrol officers staying at the hotel. He was, he said, on escort duty, having brought six young men from Mendi out to the coast to see the sights of civilization. I must have looked surprised because he then said that this was part of the district commissioner's plan to undermine the resolution of Sark and the other Mendi leaders.

I smiled to myself and wondered if it would work. He had in mind, of course, that the old men would resent this attention paid to the younger men, feeling that if the Government wished to make gestures of goodwill to the Mendi clans they should be made to the recognized leaders and not to insignificant youngsters. And this was how it turned out as I heard later in a letter from the district commissioner.

He wrote to say that the ruse had been successful, for the young men had come back to Mendi full of the wonders of the outside world.

First, they had ridden in the plane from Mendi to Madang and were thus the first clansmen to fly. They had flown out beyond the edge of the world where a river stretched so wide that no man could see across it. And the airstrip at Madang was so long that if a man stood at one end and fired an arrow it would not reach a quarter of the way, whereas many a man could fire an arrow at least half the length of the Mendi strip.

They had seen houses as high as trees, and stores that were full of white man's treasure. There were trees that grew nuts as big as a man's head, and a strange box that spoke and sang (they had seen a record player in a store).

The old men were indignant. They came to the office of the district commissioner and spoke first in sorrow, then in anger. They said that they had always tried to meet him halfway in any reasonable request; that they had ceased fighting and were always prepared to supply labor for local work; they sent many children to the mission school, and supplied bush timber and other materials when he wished to build sheds or houses for the Government.

It was not that they wished to dictate, but he must surely know that by ignoring them and sending these young men of no account out to the coast, he was undermining traditional authority, and had brought shame upon them. As one leader to another, said Sark, he could only express astonishment and regret.

And Nonga was furious. He pulled out tufts of hair from his head and spat on the floor of the Kiap's[1] office, and said that he had never been so ill-used. In the old days, said Nonga, there would have been no alternative but to go to war over such an insult.

The district commissioner looked surprised, then pained. How could they think him so insensitive as to purposely bring shame upon them? Of course not. But it was clear since the disgraceful attack on the Government's surveyor that there was no hope of progress for this present generation. He therefore felt it his duty to begin to educate the younger men who would take over the leadership when Sark and Nonga went to join their ancestors. He looked sad when he said this, and put his hand on their shoulders, and shook his head sympathetically.

On the other hand, he said, the young men were only taken to Madang, which is but a village. There were other places, like Port Moresby, where the biggest white chiefs lived, and men like Sark and Nonga, if they went anywhere, should be taken there. But of course they were not interested in the white man's ways, and he would not therefore trouble them with the suggestion.

Four of the old men went to Moresby a few months later. I met

[1] "Kiap" is Pidgin for Captain—a title applied indiscriminately to Government officers but principally to the senior officer in an area.

them there with their escort and now, after almost two years since the attack on the surveyor, the day had come for the payoff.

After lunch I went down to the office with the district commissioner to see the counting of the gold-lip shell, and to watch the signing of the deeds formally transferring the sing-sing ground to the Government.

There was a crowd of several thousands, all members of the Tend clan, or relations by marriage, or trading partners and men to whom the Tend people owed money, and others who came only to look. For there were more than five hundred uncut gold-lip mother-of-pearl shells laid out on the grass in front of the district office, the equivalent perhaps, by Mendi standards, of a public display of a rich man's fortune.

The important men sit together, about two hundred of them, with Sark standing like a Moses among them, explaining once again the issues and the decisions: casting momentary doubts once more upon the wisdom of giving in to the Government, invoking the understanding and acquiescence of ancestors, spreading the blame around among the other leaders, setting himself up as a man of great enlightenment and humility, as one prepared to jeopardize his own happiness in eternity for the sake of his descendants.

Men of minor status sitting farther back strain to hear what he says and pass it back in whispers among the general mass of tribesmen, young men, and visitors. Women and little children sit on the outskirts of the crowd, keeping silent while the men speak.

When Sark stops speaking Nonga gets up and says flatly that this is none of his doing, that not only are they selling out their sing-sing ground but the land adjacent, and this good garden land. He warns them. They will be sorry for this day's work.

He plucks at the hair on his stomach and says that nothing is sacred any more, one might as well give one's manhood away. But let them never blame him, Nonga, for the mistake that is being made. Let them stop talking and go now and collect their money from the Government.

There is silence. Then a sigh. Sark shakes his head and moves away slowly.

Then everybody gets up. All around, brown bodies rising from the ground. They stand and shake themselves, straighten their buttock coverings, settle axes more comfortably in their cane belts, and begin to move slowly toward the open space in front of the district office where the gold-lip shell is laid out in three long rows like dinner plates, a foot between each shell, five hundred of them all told.

A small wooden table with papers on it. An office chair. A stone to hold the papers down, and an ink pad beside it.

The young chief, Kisap, and another young clan leader whose name is Binowe,[2] a surly fellow, walk slowly along the rows of shells inspecting them, rejecting any that are too small or chipped or flawed. Binowe demands an extra shell for himself and is given one for the sake of peace.

Sark and Nonga and a Government officer stand at the table while Tinbol interprets between them the meaning of the paper and the terms of their agreement. The Government officer signs. Sark puts his thumb on the ink pad, presses it with care and deliberation onto the paper, then stands and stares at what he has done.

I am reminded for the moment of Kondom, the Chimbu leader, who also signed a Government paper with his thumb; but he was accepting nomination as a candidate for election to the Legislative Council of Papua and New Guinea and is today known as Mr. Agaundo, M.L.C., although a stone age contemporary of Sark, headman of the Tend clan and keeper of the sing-sing ground.

Nonga stands beside Sark, watching him sign. He has his hands crossed and thrust down inside his waistband like a bishop. There is a look of pain on his face, as though he can hear the rend and tear of the tall casuarinas crashing down between the long houses.

It occurs to me that I have never seen a New Guinean weep.

The payoff took an hour or more to complete, for when the clan and subclan leaders had received the bulk of shell there was still the detailed division and distribution to be made to the head of each lineal group or family. And the people waiting to have old debts settled.

In Binowe's subclan group there was a dispute which led to shouts and screams and a shaking of axes; and one man, dissatisfied with his allocation, surreptitiously changed his shell for that belonging to another man.

[2] Pronounced Bin-*oh*-wee.

A fight started and for a moment I was diverted by the sight of a Government officer laying about him with a stick like a school-master, and policemen cuffing rioters like irate parents restoring order among children, and the timid running away.

But order was restored in a few minutes and the distribution continued, with Binowe looking even more ill-tempered and inadequate than before.

It was getting toward dusk when the last gold-lip shell was allocated, and every member of the Tend clan had involved himself in the abandonment of the sing-sing ground.

We showed films that night, in the open air, outside the district office.

For some time I have been experimenting with the production of films designed to impart elementary information and ideas to illiterate and primitive tribesmen, and with a big crowd of Mendi assembled, and the station projector available, the opportunity for a test run seemed ready-made.

Very few of the Mendi have seen films. The two groups of men taken to Madang and Port Moresby had visited movies, but regarded the pictures they had seen there as something directly connected with those places, not understanding the mechanism of the phenomenon, nor realizing that it was transportable.

Consequently, of the three or four thousand people congregated at the station for the payoff of the shell, no more than a dozen had ever seen a film, and indeed, apart from some school children, few were familiar with books or printed illustrations of any kind.

They sat patiently until the sun's reflection had left the sky, watching the screen and the projection apparatus being erected and whispering speculatively among themselves until the operator, testing the equipment, spoke into the microphone.

Then, as the coarse, distorted voice broke in noisily from nowhere, every man in the audience leapt to his feet, hand on ax, crouched low to the ground, knees bent, startled and afraid and ready to fight, eyes darting all around, seeking an unknown, invisible enemy.

The amplifiers crackled and some men drew back uncertainly, looking all around. Women picked up children and began to run clumsily. A few men followed them but police and station workers called out that there was nothing to be afraid about, that it was the white man's machine that was calling out.

The crowd settled down again, slowly and suspiciously, some grinning and joking but all uncertain and uneasy. A few families quietly moved away and disappeared into the bush along the narrow tracks leading to their hamlets.

First we showed a simple film about African animals, silent and slow-moving, designed for small children. They watched in silence, amazed more by the fact of the images appearing than by the images themselves, which seemed to them in any case incomprehensible.

Giraffes strode with ungainly grace across the screen in utter silence until one man whispered, "dog," but immediately his neighbors turned and struck at him angrily, and those around hissed him into silence.

A lion yawned and there was no response. Antelopes bounded out of the darkness and onto the screen, then disappeared again into the night, or so it seemed, and everybody remained still. Not until a hippopotamus lumbered out of the bush and stood looking at them reflectively was there a stir and a swift intake of breath, and all through the crowd a sudden, excited whispering.

Tinbol, standing close to me, said, "They say it is the spirit of a pig." When monkeys cavorted they whispered together again, saying, "man." Then they were silent again until the film ran out, and they all sighed at once.

Then we showed the key film. But first Tinbol spoke into the microphone, explaining in bald and halting phrases that they would now see people of different New Guinea tribes who lived beyond the mountains, and others who lived at the edge of the great water.

He said that those men who had been to Madang or to Port Moresby might recognize many of the things that they were going to see, and could tell the others that they were true. We did not ask him to say that the film included shots taken around Mendi and that they would see Sark and Nonga and other men whom they might recognize. When Tinbol had finished they settled down again to watch.

To me, in the vast quiet of the night, the persistent tick-tock of the portable projector motor sounded intolerably distracting, but the audience seemed not to hear it and sat immobile, staring at the screen.

I could see them in outline, intermittently illuminated by lifeless white light as the beginning of the film unwound. Men huddled together and holding each other, seeking assurance and security. Women, themselves hypnotized, hiding their children's faces against their thighs, afraid that this magic might damage the children's eyes or minds.

A fine drizzle of rain hung in the air but nobody moved.

The film ran for twenty minutes, and except for the noise of the motor and the voice of the narrator speaking in Pidgin, there was no other sound. Men sat with their mouths open but nothing came out, not even when Sark appeared speaking to the district commissioner on the screen, with Nonga standing beside him.

When the film finished nobody stirred or spoke, and I said to Tinbol, "What do the people think?"

He said, "They are afraid to speak or to move."

I said, "We must explain that this is a simple thing that will not harm them. That later, if they wish, we will bring other pictures to help them understand that they belong to a bigger tribe than the Mendi, that the men over the mountains and those who live by the big water are their brothers.

"Tell them," I said, "that we will come again and show them how to grow coffee and other things that will help them. That with the machine that makes pictures, and the box with one eye, we can help them to catch up with the people of Hagen and Minj and Goroka."

I wasn't quite sure what it was that we were promising, but it has always, in this work, been necessary for me to believe that we come with salvation in our hands and goodwill in our hearts; and faith is the only armor against doubt.

Tinbol picked up the microphone and spoke, telling them what I had said. And suddenly there was a tremendous shout from the thousands of throats, an acceptance of this mystery, a release from fear, a reaching out in trust.

Only once, when the plane landed at Woitapi, have I heard anything similar, the unconditional, ultimate cry of primitive men saying the unsayable. The sound that in civilization is the roar of the crowd at a football game or prize fight, or the almost unbearably great music of the temple or concert hall. The primeval cry from the human heart.

And all this for a very crude movie.

We showed the film again, and this time the men began to nudge each other and to say what they saw, and to point things out. Even the women whispered together but still keep the eyes of their children covered.

We showed it once more because they called out for it. And this time there was a babble of comment, and the men who had been to Madang or Port Moresby began to boast and air their knowledge. And when Sark and Nonga and the district commissioner appeared there were gasps and swift intakes of breath, and some small boys laughed happily. But they were quickly stopped by their elders.

Then everybody began to clap hands in rhythm, to show that they recognized the three men and some of the others who appeared in the background of the picture. They kept this up until the Mendi sequence ended. But after that they clapped for anything that they could recognize or identify.

How quickly they learn, and how little distance we ourselves have come since we were like them.

Six

The Norseman came back in the morning and we learned that the two women were in the hospital at Goroka, and comfortable.

The pilot, looking at the sky, said that the weather was closing in quickly and that we must hurry if I hoped to get to Tari, fifty miles farther west.

I said my goodbyes quickly.

The pilot climbed up into the cockpit, whistled to his dog, and it jumped in after him and settled itself under his seat. We took off and flew low between two featureless seas, a flat ceiling of cloud above us and the monotonous striation of drab-green hills and ridges below, lacking light and shade, though fretted with little tributary rivers.

A half hour later, and ten miles from Tari, we came to the twin peaks of Doma and Kerua, both over twelve thousand feet, and the clouds beginning to pile up around their feet so that in an hour they would be covered, and the way in and out of Tari closed.

We passed between them and in five minutes were down on the airstrip at Tari station.

There is mail, some deep-freeze foods, and a few parcels for the station people. Mrs. Burchett, the medical assistant's wife, who is also the postmistress, picks them over and complains that the stores she ordered three weeks ago from Goroka have not arrived, and are doubtless lying on some airstrip. She sighs and says that it's enough to break a woman's heart.

Then she invites the pilot to come in and have a cup of tea, but he points toward Doma and Kerua and shakes his head regretfully, gets back into the cockpit, and takes off again.

He spirals upwards over the station to gain height because now he must cross back over the main range to get into the Wahgi Valley and so make his way back to Minj or Goroka. We watch him soaring above us, climbing toward a patch of light like a lark ascending. Then he disappears.

But the station transceiver is switched on in the office and we can hear him speaking to the air control officers at Madang and Goroka, warning them that the southern valleys are already closed in with clouds and unsafe for further flying this day, that he is climbing at fourteen thousand feet, and is still not in the clear.

Then a few minutes later he calls again to say that he has topped the cloud layer and is on course for Goroka.

Assistant District Officer Crellin, standing beside me, rubbed an itch on the side of his nose with the back of his hand and said, "Well now, what can we do for you?"

His hands were black with engine oil and when I glanced at them he said, "I'm working on the Land-Rover. It should be ready for a road test tomorrow. Maybe you'll see some fun."

The Tari Land-Rover had been in the news for some months. It had been brought in over the mountains by carriers, piece by piece, and was being assembled on the station by Crellin. When mobile it would be the first motor vehicle to be seen by the Tari people.

I said, "I am making my way over to Mount Hagen to make a television film of the agricultural show, and it seemed an opportunity to do the rounds of the highland stations. I've nothing special in mind. Just keeping up-to-date. I hope it's not inconvenient for you?"

He looked noncommittal. "You're no problem. The Burchetts are expecting you to stay with them, and when you're settled in we have a few things to show you."

We moved off together, walking toward the subdistrict office.

"We've acquired a cow since you were here last. Bob Gibbes brought it in the Norseman. We had to give it a stiff dose of tranquilizers before his boys could load it into the aircraft, but it settled down nicely. It's an experiment to see how cattle will do up here.

"The new bridge over the Tagari is about finished and if the Land-Rover is serviceable tomorrow I'll take you down to see it. Father Barard has done a marvelous job of design and construction.

"There's some fighting going on over the other side of the range among the Huri tribes, and a patrol officer has gone out to stop it.

"Jim Sinclair, the assistant district officer from Koroba, has come in with Pugarapa, the headman. You'll see him this evening. There's a party at the Burchett's."

As we approached the station buildings Mrs. Burchett called from the steps of the post office, telling me to go over to the house and settle in. She would, she said, be over as soon as she had sorted the mail.

I had stayed with the Burchetts before and knew where to go. I had their little guest cottage to myself, twenty yards or so from their own bush house. It was built of grass, native-style, on the edge of a gully with a pleasant view across to the opposite hillside. A footpath, leading to a small hamlet, ran past it.

Women going to and from their gardens walked past the windows, morning and evening, whispering and giggling, and sometimes offering a few pieces of maize for sale. And an occasional man, going off to a meeting place, or returning home for a meal, would stop and watch visitors who used the guest house, curious and friendly.

Tari is on the edge of uncontrolled country.

Its people, and those who live still farther westward toward the border of Indonesia's West Irian, are among the last in Papua to be brought into touch with today's civilization. It is not necessary to go far beyond Tari to see stone adzes and axes still in domestic use, though most of the men around the station now carry steel axes. Otherwise tools and domestic articles are as primitive today as they have been for the past thousand years.

The station takes its name from the river which rises close by in the ranges of the great divide, and runs south through the valley in which the station stands. Government officers who operate from here are more immediately concerned with exploration, and with putting a stop to tribal fighting, than they are with the activities of social and economic advancement.

The language of the district is Huri, and some twenty-five thousand people call themselves by this name. Like most other New Guinea language groups they have lived for unknown generations in tribal isolation and exclusiveness, and until they were discovered a few years ago by Australian explorers there were no outside influences to affect their traditional way of life and its peculiar characteristics.

Consequently, the Huri, like the Mendi, Minj, Chimbu, and Goroka tribes have developed their own social and domestic customs, and a distinctive style of dress and decoration.

From Tari westward, and northward across the divide into New Guinea, men wear wigs as part of their normal daily dress, and among the Huri people wig-making and decorating is the high point of artistic expression.

It is by no means unusual to see a warrior, armed with bow and arrow and with a pig tusk through his nose, crouch down into the grass outside his hut and gaze into a half gourd filled with clear rainwater, using it as a mirror to titivate the floral arrangement in his hair before going off to take part in a pitched battle.

As I walked past the subdistrict office there were a dozen men standing outside, all wearing wigs of similar shape and size but each quite distinctive in decoration.

Most of them were Tari men, including Punga the station interpreter, and toothless old Ivahi, who seems senile and weak-minded but is always consulted by the clan leaders. But with them were three strangers: one I knew to be Pugarapa, the headman from Koroba, most westerly of all the highland stations in Papua, and two other men who, because they carried stone adzes, I took to be Duna tribesmen also.

Pugarapa is a "big man" among the Duna people, who are neighbors to the Huri but of a different language group and consequently enemies. He and his friends would never have come the twenty miles from Koroba to Tari had they not come under the protection of a Government officer.

Pugarapa has been a friend of the Government from the beginning. Under his protection the first patrol post was established at Koroba in the Duna country, and when patrol officers needed carriers to go with them on journeys of exploration still farther westward, it was Pugarapa who shamed the young men into volunteering, although they were afraid.

I have seen him, pacing up and down before a line of young warriors, pouring scorn upon them because they hesitated to step forward and shed their wigs and decorations, and take up a load of food or tentage and follow a patrol into the unknown.

"Are you women," he would ask, "that you must stay at home and mind the fire, or children that you are afraid of ghosts? Will you bring shame upon your ancestors in the eyes of this white man who is young, like you, and is not afraid of the spirits who live on the mountain?"

But the young men were afraid, and reasonably so, for they had been brought up since babyhood to believe that the high passes in the mountains that hemmed in their valleys were guarded by evil demons, and that the land which lay beyond was the limbo in which the dead roamed and devils dwelt.

But they went with the Government patrol officer and came back heroes, and Pugarapa went part of the way with them, and met them again coming back. Yet it must have been after much thought that he agreed to come the twenty miles to Tari, into the stronghold of the traditional enemies of his tribe.

He is a man past middle age, perhaps between forty and fifty, but still slender and straight and tall, with a fine medieval face, a thin beak of a nose, long isosceles chin, and high cheekbones. He is light of skin, almost honey-colored, though dusted with gray dirt like all of his tribe. And like most Huri and Duna men, he wears a thin beard but keeps his cheeks and top lip plucked.

His wig frames his face as far down as the cheekbones, a tightly matted mass of hair shaped like a Roman bridge, three to four inches thick at its bases and thinning to an inch or so on top of the head. The two flat panels that frame the face are studded with a meticulously intricate design picked out with small daisy-like flowers, yellow and mauve, interlaced with fine threads of pale green moss.

The foundation of the wig is a skullcap of finely beaten bark with a snakeskin headband holding it tightly above the eyebrows. On the flat of his head, above the brow, Pugarapa wears a large diamond of mottled tree bark, and at the back, like a rooster's tail, a long, single plume.

He has a thin smear of red ochre spread across his forehead, shading away to the temples, and a small patch on each cheekbone and at the side of the nostrils. From one ear hangs a short cord to which is attached a mother-of-pearl chip and three red beans. Through the septum of his nose is a ten-inch pencil of thin cane.

He wears a few tight strings of black seed beads around his

throat and a gold-lip shell high on his breast. Thin cords hang around his hips and thighs, and three loops of cane around his waist make a belt for ax and bone dagger. He has a short apron of painted bark and a sporran of pigs' tails. A small net satchel hangs over one shoulder, containing a bamboo smoking pipe, fire lighter, a pad of green-leaf tobacco, and some lucky charms.

Every man wears and carries similar things with only minor variations of detail, and it is only in the decoration of the wig that each man expresses his individual creativity.

Some smother the flat face of the wig with yellow flowers and use only a fine piping of mauve to trim it. Others use diamond or triangular designs of mixed color, or a facing of moss picked out with small clusters of flowers. Others crown their designs with an arrangement of leaves pinned into place with fine splinters of wood. Among the Huri and Duna people the wig is a sign of adult manhood.

As a child each boy has his hair clipped short, except for a little fencelike ridge that runs across the top of his skull from ear to ear. Wild, untidy hair is a sign of neglect, and if a boy is unclipped the chances are that he is an orphan, or that his parents are good-for-nothing, feckless, or feeble-minded folk; for it is part of tribal tradition and parental duty for a father to trim his son's hair and for the mother to store it, together with hair clipped from the family womenfolk, and to fashion a wig for the boy which he will wear when he becomes a man.

It is given to him when he has been initiated and accepted into adult membership of the tribe, and afterwards he is seldom seen without it, and spends much of his time decorating it. In some places a man sleeps with his neck on a wooden block so as not to crush or disturb the set of the wig during the night. In other places men take off their wigs at night and hang them on a wooden peg. One of the habitual activities of men in their clubhouses in the evenings is the delousing of their heads and wigs.

I spoke briefly to Pugarapa, asking after his small son, which pleased him. He said that he had come in with Mr. Sinclair and would be going back with the next patrol, and that his people were happy with the Government and wanted a school.

Then I went to Burchett's.

There was an additional visitor for lunch, an American linguist, studying New Guinea languages. He was, he said, camped two miles from the station, near the Methodist mission, beyond which it was not permissible to move without armed protection.

We went out to the mission together during the afternoon, an easy walk along the valley floor, and as we went he talked about the people who live between Tari and Mendi, not as an expert, for not much anthropological study has yet been done among these people, but in a fragmentary way about many things.

He said, for instance, that when these people marry they take a long honeymoon of several months during which time they walk about together dressed in all their wedding finery. They do no work and are fed by relatives whom they visit. During this time they have no sexual experience together so that the honeymoon is really no more than an extension of the rituals of courtship.

These people share a belief, held in different degrees by other civilizations, that the act of copulation is dangerous for the male, milking him of essential elements of body and soul, and exposing him to spiritual and physical dangers. It is considered a shameful thing, and a man never takes a woman within doors, but only in some hidden place in the bush where nobody is likely to pass or enter and where any evidences of the act will be quickly obliterated by rain, or overgrown by nature.

Before the young husband takes his bride he first learns the sex secrets and taboos from his father or an uncle, and at the cost of a pig or an ax or some similar valuable, purchases lucky charms that will protect him from the evil consequences of copulation. These charms take the form of sprays of leaves or plaited grasses over which spells have been spoken by the father or some other elderly male relative.

When the exchange of charms and payment has been made the mentor sets a date for the first copulation, and when this has been accomplished the honeymoon is over. Husband and wife now remove their wedding finery and settle down to the routines of ordinary domestic life, the woman to her gardening and child-bearing, the young man to hunting, building, and fighting.

This belief in the inherently physiological evil of the female is impressed upon a boy from the time he is able to even vaguely understand sexual differences, and it is unlikely that any lad older than five or six years will be found sleeping in his mother's house for fear of contact with a menstruating relative.

For it is believed by these people that any touch of menstrual blood, direct or indirect, on purpose or by accident, will cause a man to wither up inside, dehydrate and die. So a wife in her menses must not cook for her husband, nor touch him, walk over his legs, handle his personal belongings, or enter into his sleeping hut.

The menstrual flow is a potent poison, used in sorcery and magic. Applied secretly to the skin, or to food eaten by a victim, it will bring certain and speedy death. Men go in fear that their wives, or other women who might have cause to be offended with them, will kill them by this means.

Women are said to believe very much in this power with which they are equipped, and to regard it as some kind of compensation for the general lowliness of their social and domestic status, their physical indefensibility, and the dullness of their married lives.

The American told me that he had it from a missionary that women try to obtain some kind of lifelong power over men by contaminating them when they are small boys, but, he said, although stubborn in this belief, the missionary seemed embarrassed and not prepared to go into details, and he had no other evidence that it was true.

We stepped across a slit trench some two feet wide and six feet deep, a common feature in the Tari Valley where such trenches are used as fighting ditches in which warriors move quickly from one strategic position to another without being seen; and our talk turned to tribal warfare.

When a man of these parts is killed in battle, said my friend, his body is placed on an elevated platform of sticks for viewing by relatives and friends, as is done ordinarily in the case of death. And for some days the women of his family keep up a ritual wailing, and the widow and other close female relatives plaster themselves with mud. Then the body is trussed and enclosed in a coffin-like box on stilts standing in his garden.

This displaying and burying of the body is done by chosen fellow tribesmen who are specialists in these rituals, and who each receives a pig for his services.

When the flesh has left the bones, the skull of the man who has been killed in battle, or murdered, is removed from the coffin and hung in the mens' clubhouse, where it remains until he has been avenged by the killing of a man of the tribe that brought about his death.

Sometimes the leg and arm bones of the dead man are used to tip arrows that will be fired against this enemy tribe, for it is believed that the bone of the dead man will seek out the man who slew him, and will direct the arrow to its proper target.

Then, when the score has been evened, the skull is taken down and given to the man's family, or is left in a particular spot in the bush set aside as a resting place for the clan skulls.

We passed a coffin on stilts and my friend pointed out the knotted vine cord that passed through a hole in the top of the coffin. It was, he said, fastened to the skull and jawbone of the corpse, and when it was judged that the body had sufficiently decomposed, the lid would be taken off and the skull lifted out intact on the end of the cord. But we did not stay long looking at this thing because the stink was sickening.

He left me as we came to the mission station and I went alone for half a mile or so, and coming closer to the mission buildings could hear distant shouting and war whoops across the river. It would be, I thought, some young bucks engaged in throwing spears at one another.

A few children in a roughly constructed schoolhut looked up as I passed and I heard their teacher, a young man from the George Brown College in Rabaul, speak sharply to them and point again at the blackboard with a ruler. And the children began to recite with sing-song voices a verse about a Kookaburra sitting in a gum tree, watching a snake chase a rabbit.

I came to the hospital and found Sister Walker, motherly, and a rock of domesticated Australian common sense. She was standing at the steps of the house which she shares with another mission nurse, a German girl in charge of lepers. They were looking down toward the river which ran in a gully a few hundred yards away, and when I stopped before them and followed their gaze Sister Walker said, "They are a nuisance and I wish they'd go away. We have a lovely bathing place down there in the river and these wretched young men have been fighting along the bank for the past two days so that we have not been able to swim."

She looked thoughtful for a moment and then added, "I've a good mind to go down and shoo them off." Then she said, "You look hot. Come in and have a nice cup of tea."

We talked about her work. She was, she said, beginning to have a little success with the Tari women. Not much, but promising signs that they were beginning to accept her as somebody who could help them, although it had been difficult to get any of them to stay in her little hospital because they are shy and secret people, and afraid of strange places.

"But," she added triumphantly, "we've got one woman in at this moment and she's very precious, a wife of one of the local big-men." Then, with the slightest suspicion of grim disapproval, "He's got four."

She told me the story while the German sister made tea. "The infant mortality rate here is wicked. Probably three of every four babies die within the first few weeks of birth, but it's hard to get any kind of reliable information because the whole business of child-birth is so secret and hedged about with taboos and superstitions.

"The women here go off into the bush by themselves, with not even an old midwife in attendance until the child is born and the mother on her feet again. They go away and hide like animals, except that the woman takes a sharp slither of bamboo with her to cut the umbilical cord. But she doesn't tie it and heaven only knows how many babies become infected by the cord dragging in the dirt."

She looked affronted.

"But I managed to get one woman to come and have her baby right here on the station, in a hut that we built especially, some distance apart from any other building or any footpath. And I had to promise that I would not touch the woman while she gave birth, but would only sit and watch. It was then that I found that they don't tie the cord.

"Afterwards I told every woman I could see that this was one way in which they might save their babies, but I could see that they didn't believe me.

"Then I tackled this big-man, who has four wives and no chil-dren, and I told him that if he would let me take charge of the next delivery he might have a live baby instead of a dead one.

"He took a lot of persuading, but when I told him that he would otherwise die an old man with no children to sacrifice pigs to pay his way to heaven, he eventually gave in. I can tell you, I was a worried woman until that baby was born, but it's now three months old and very much alive."

I thought to myself that these Tari women are going to be civilized by Sister Walker whether they like it or not, and the young men will have to find another fighting ground, for she will not have her patients or herself put to inconvenience for much longer.

She put down her tea cup and jerked her head in the direction of somewhere outside.

"I have the big-man's number-two wife in there at the moment, and she will have her baby any time now. And if this one lives he has agreed to build me a separate maternity ward a little way in the bush, and will tell all of the women to have their babies my way."

After this I walked back alone, skirting the Government station, then going on farther to visit the Catholic mission as a matter of courtesy, for in a station as isolated as Tari the coming of an official visitor, however lowly, is an event hedged with protocol, and it would be a mistake to visit one mission without calling also on the other.

Father Paul had been to collect his mail and had a parcel of new discs on the table, a present from his family in Pittsburgh. He said that he was taking them to the Burchetts later in the evening so that everybody could hear them and keep up-to-date with civilization as represented by the latest Broadway musicals.

The Father is a round man, full of laughter and generous in his love of men. He found a little rum, some coffee, and a hunk of homemade bread, and made me stay for a yarn. He produced a jug of milk, a present, he said, from Mr. Crellin's cow, and we sat and had an afternoon snack.

Afterwards we looked at the new church, designed by the assistant district officer, who is a Protestant, and built by men of Tari who are heathens, to the glory of God who is, said Father Paul happily, prepared to put up with the lot of us if we will only do our best.

"But we have a little bit of a problem at the moment," said Father Paul, "because the old men say that the garden land is becoming poor and needs refertilizing, so they are organizing sing-

sings and pig killings to invoke these old volcanoes to erupt." He swept his hand around the landscape ringed with old volcanic cones.

"They have a story that their land is replenished every few generations by volcanic debris, and the story may well be true, for they have a great sense of history-through-legend, handed on by word of mouth from generation to generation.

"Why," he said, "some of these old men around here can recite their genealogies back for fifteen or twenty 'fathers,' and if you allow only twenty years for each generation, that gives you three hundred years.

"It doesn't seem to bother them that if the volcanoes erupt half the tribe could get wiped out. However, that's not our main problem at the moment." We moved over into the shade of a lean-to where he had a saw-bench and gasoline engine, a gift from friends of the mission in Pittsburgh.

The big problem at the moment, he said, was to stop the headmen around the place from marrying so many wives. It was not that he felt religiously affronted by the custom, and in any case it was too soon to attempt to introduce drastic changes into the traditional domestic pattern of local life, but with the old men having a monopoly of young women, frustrations set in among the younger men and caused endless trouble.

"It was not," he added, "that there was a shortage of women. On the contrary there was usually a surplus because many men were killed in battle each year, leaving more women than men in the tribe. It was simply that the ancients, being rich and having traditional prestige, were able to outbid the younger men and offer more valuables in exchange for brides."

Meantime, Brother Claude had over a hundred boys in the school, although some of the older ones had recently gone off to take part in one of the stages of initiation. It was, he thought, the fire-walking part of the ceremonies.

The men build a special house for this ritual, a building of about forty feet in length although no more than seven or eight feet wide. One end of the building, which is roughly built of bush sticks and kunai grass, is no more than four feet high, and has a small dog-kennel opening through which the boys enter.

The roof of the building slopes upward in a long, easy incline, reaching a peak some ten feet from the ground at a point about three-quarters of the way along its length. Then it slopes down quickly again to the end wall.

In the end part there is a little room with two openings, one allowing ingress from the main part of the building, and the other leading out into the open air. In the main part of the building a raised platform, about eighteen inches from the ground, runs the length of each side, and supporting posts form a colonnade of columns.

When the fire-walking part of the initiation ceremonies takes place, the aisle between the platforms is spread with logs of wood that are fired, and when the wood is burned the charcoal is leveled and a series of smaller fires spaced along the aisle.

Then two of the old men anoint their own feet with tree oil, and others pour similar oil from bamboo tubes onto the fires, causing them to give off a pungent smoke. The two old men with their feet anointed then walk the length of the long room and enter into the smaller room at the end, where they stop.

Meanwhile a pig is killed outside, behind the house, and is kept cooking while the ceremony takes place.

These preparations, beginning with the building of the fire-walking house, or the repair of an old one, take many weeks. During this time the boys who are to be initiated live in a secret place in the bush, well away from any path likely to be used by a woman, for the fire-walking is said by many to be part of the ritual cleansing of the male from any contamination by contact with the female, either mother, aunt, sister, cousin, or acquaintance.

And in this time the lads, aged twelve or thirteen or thereabouts, eat food that is exclusively produced and prepared by men, from gardens in which women have never set foot.

The whole ceremony is a ritual rather than an ordeal, a purification rather than a hardening of the sensibilities. The older men are more solicitous than sadistic, and on the day appointed two of them lead the lads to the house with feelings of sentimental benevolence and spiritual fusion, which probably parallel the thoughts and feelings of Christian, Hebrew, Moslem, or Hindu men when they bring their boys to the temples for traditional and religious ceremonies marking young manhood.

Inside the long house, as the boys approach, the adult men of the clan stand waiting on the raised platforms that run the length of the building, each man carrying a switch or light birch of twigs and leaves. The small fires, spaced at short intervals, are alight, and the charcoal spread between them is hot. The room is filled with smoke and the men are murmuring invocations to ancestors.

The first lad bends down to enter, and is pushed forward and urged to run the length of the building to the opposite exit, and as he runs and stumbles the men on the platforms begin to yell and shout and beat him with the switches, driving the devil out of him as he plunges forward, trying to dodge the fires around his feet and the blows on his back, and to find his way through the smoke to the escape hatch at the other end.

He bends down to pass through the exit and finds himself in the small room with the two old men, who soothe him, and when he is settled and finds himself unhurt (for the fires are not violent and the soles of his feet are thick) he begins to feel proud and lifted up and superior, and eagerly welcomes the other boys as they come struggling through from the long room into the security of the little room.

Then the old men give each lad a piece of the cooked pig, and when the ceremony is done men and boys sit down together and eat. Much of this was told to me by Hingre, son of Kadi, a headman of Tari, and it is likely that there are variations in this ritual among the clans.

Father Paul took me back to the station on the pillion of his motorcycle, and let me off at the hospital.

My host, Medical Assistant Ted Burchett, stood outside dubiously holding a small parcel wrapped in leaves. An elderly male patient, wearing a dilapidated wig, and with a bandaged leg, stood resting on a single crutch watching him with an expression of senile amiability and anticipation.

The hospital staff, four orderlies and three nurses, gathered around as he carefully untied the bindings of bush twine.

Father Paul and I approached. "What have you got there, Ted?"

Ted Burchett looked up, indicating the old man on the crutch. "I don't know exactly, but it's a present from the old gentleman. He had one of his sons bring it to me for a 'thank you' for removing an arrow from his buttock. The silly old goat seems to like it here and says that he's going to stay."

We gathered around and watched. One of the nurses, carrying a baby at her breast, smoked a foot-long cigarette rolled in newsprint. The senior orderly had his eye bandaged, having been involved in a dispute with the husband of a female patient.

"It's warm, whatever it is," said Mr. Burchett, unwrapping the outside envelope of leaves. Father Paul began to chuckle and ripples ran around his stomach.

We all watched closely. Ted Burchett's nose began to twitch and a look of doubt crossed his face as he folded back the inside leaves. Father Paul made choking noises and turned away, hiding laughter behind his hand.

I went in closer to look. Ted Burchett shook his head and said, "Pig's guts, hot." He walked across to the old man, solemnly shook his hand, and speaking without a smile, said, "Thank you, Omgi, you are a true gentleman."

We went inside for a few minutes and he handed the parcel to the smallest nurse-girl, a child of thirteen with hennaed hair, a policeman's daughter, and said that she should take it home for her father's supper, but not to tell the old man, Omgi.

Then as we walked home he explained that a parcel of pig's intestine, cooked and wrapped in leaves, was the usual price paid to a sorcerer for a successful spell.

As we walked past the subdistrict office the Papuan clerk came out, carrying a kundu drum. He looked a little sheepish and said, in explanation, "It is getting close to Christmas and we must practice for the sing-sing."

He, and the schoolteacher from the Methodist mission, the medical orderly, and a couple of house-boys who had come to Tari with their white masters, and some policemen, all being Christians, would get together at Christmastime and play their drums and sing the Motuan songs of the coast, and Tolai chants, and the Methodist hymns that they had learned as children, and would feel more foreign among the Huri, and out of place and remote from their own people, than the white people would.

Father Paul brought his new discs over to the Burchetts after dinner and played them on an antiquated phonograph affectionately referred to as the hi-fi, a contraption with a variable speed regulator and a hand-crank motor with a spring not quite long enough to maintain speed through a full long-playing disc.

A.D.O. Crellin was there with his wife. And Sinclair, in from the Duna country to pick up more stores before going out again on another long patrol. Father Paul, Brother Claude, and the station carpenter, whose hobby is making violins. A young cadet patrol officer on his first assignment, going out with Sinclair for experience. Ted Burchett and his wife, and my friend the linguist. And up from Sydney on vacation, the district commissioner's brother, businessman and amateur magician.

He held the floor, demonstrating sleight-of-hand and conjuring tricks, producing the nominated card from the pack, and poking lighted cigarettes through a handkerchief without scorching it. Mrs. Burchett's kitchen-boy and two friends peered in at the door, wide-eyed, and one of them was asked to come in and hold a hat into which the conjurer from Sydney threw pennies.

He asked the boy to turn the hat upside down and let the coins fall out, but when he did nothing happened, for the coins had vanished. The boy was still for a moment, then turned a dirty gray color and dropped the hat and ran outside and crouched shaking in a corner of the kitchen until Mrs. Burchett went out to assure him that it was not sorcery, but a white man's game that anyone could play. But he would not come back again and left the house the next day.

We heard *Camelot* played at half-speed so that Ted Burchett could learn the words, then passages played at double-speed to hasten over the entractes, and at variable speed as the spring ran down and was rewound *en passant*. All the time Father Paul laughed heartily, and Brother Claude discussed building problems with the carpenter, while the cadet patrol officer listened in awe-struck silence while Assistant District Officers Crellin and Sinclair spoke of recent forays in which each had taken part.

"So they chased me back to the station," said Crellin, "but it was my own fault. I went out to look for a site for a rest house, not too far from the station, and only took a couple of police and half-a-dozen carriers.

"We wandered into the middle of a local brawl and found ourselves between two factions, and seeing us so small a party they ganged up, figuring that together they might stand a good chance of doing us over. But they were cautious, and we managed to work our way back to the station before they attacked."

Sinclair nodded, understanding the situation perfectly, and the cadet looked from one to the other with reverence on his face.

"If they had jumped us," said Crellin, "I would have had to shoot, and the chances were that somebody would have been hurt, and then it would have taken a year or two to make friends again. So I came back to collect a few more police and a bigger carrier line, then went straight back to where they were fighting, and put a stop to it."

The cadet said, "How?" and Crellin raised his eyebrows at the interruption.

"Why, we marched through the middle of them and they were so surprised that they stopped. Then we borrowed a couple of wooden fighting shields and lined the gentlemen up while the police fired a volley at the shields and shattered them into splinters."

He smiled kindly at the cadet, "It works most times, and I doubt if we will have any more trouble in that area." Then he poured himself a rum, looked sternly at the young man, and said, "But I should have known better than to have gone out into Huri country without a force big enough to deal with any kind of situation."

I knew what was in his mind, for it was only a year ago that Crellin had been sent into country, northwest of Tari and on the Sepik side of the divide, to investigate the murder of two Australians who had been trapped with inadequate forces while patrolling in uncontrolled country. For three months he walked the mountains, gathering in the tribesmen, asking questions, piecing together the story and the evidence. And eventually he rounded up 178 suspects and witnesses and took them out to Wewak, on the coast; and in that time lost thirty pounds body weight.

"It's the same in the Duna country," said Jim Sinclair. "It's too soon yet to move about freely, although on the whole the people are friendly enough."

Sinclair is in direct line of descent through the pioneer explorers of inland New Guinea: Karius and Champion, the Leahy brothers and Jim Taylor, and other men obsessed with looking at what lies on the other side of the mountain. He moves as though articulated with strong springs, and frequently withdraws into some quite private and personal world where he lives a life of phenomenal spiritual activity in absolute solitude.

"I got jumped the other day not far from Yetemari where you and I camped six months ago, no more than a decent day's walk from Koroba station." He looked at me almost indignantly. "You remember the place, just down from the Wagafugwa swamp."

I said yes I did remember, but the remembrance was vague because when one has walked day after day behind Sinclair the topography ceases to be impressive, and a succession of temporary camps, changing night after night, leave only an overlapping and out-of-focus picture in the memory.

"I had Corporal Peroro with me, and Constable Pahun and some of the other police who came with us out to the Strickland River last year, and because there had been fight rumors going on all around the district for weeks, and talk of the Tagari clans doing me in, we were watching for trouble.

"But when we made camp there were only a few old men about, and no one came with food to sell for salt or shell, so we figured that the local warriors were away fighting elsewhere, and we had it in mind to keep after them and stop whatever they were doing."

A faraway look came into his eyes as he went on speaking, and he seemed to forget us, and went back again in his mind to his camp on the edge of the Wagafugwa swamp.

"I had picked a fairly good camp site from the defensive point of view. Good angles of vision most of the way around, and nothing overlooking us at the back. And the swamp on one side with a great thicket of reeds as high as sugar cane. There was a lot of scrub on the western side but we couldn't do much about that.

"It was a cloudy evening, just about half-past six, and very quiet. A bird of paradise was screeching away over in the bush and I could see that Peroro would have liked to go after it with the shotgun to get the feathers, but he knew that I wouldn't let him. In any case he's too sensible to take that kind of risk.

"I was sitting in my tent writing up the diary and waiting for young Pitjarra to get me some dinner. He's a lousy cook as you know, just an untutored little savage, and slow, but a man shouldn't pamper himself on patrol." He was getting at me, I knew, because I like to eat as well as possible at any time, even in primitive New Guinea, and usually take a few tins of luxury along.

Over in the corner Father Paul and Ted were playing *My Fair Lady* at half-speed, and arguing about the words, but Sinclair stayed in the Duna and refused to be put off.

"It came right out of the blue, without warning. A bellow in the scrub and then a rain of arrows dropping down into the camp. One of them right through the roof of my tent, which nearly put me out of the patrolling business for good.

"Then they broke out into the open, about three hundred of them, and an arrow got Pahun in the shoulder and made him sick. Peroro yelled at me, and I ducked and saw him lift his rifle and shoot a bloke who had a bead on me.

"That steadied them for a minute, and there was a little lull which gave me time to look around and see what damage had been done. Five carriers had been hit, and a chap who had joined up with us at Yetemari and come along for the ride was running around like a frightened chicken.

"Peroro called out to him to stay put, but he panicked and made a bolt for it, heading back homeward. I saw one of their men stand up and take deliberate aim at him as he ran, and bingo, he got him with an arrow right through the back and dropped him like a log, and that started it up again. So I told my boys to let them have a volley, and we fired one round, dropping two of them stone dead and winging another.

"The whole bunch of them went off, whooping and shouting and crashing through the scrub until they figured they were safely out of range, and there they stayed yelling at us while our medical orderly looked after the wounded carriers, and I got the rest to work strengthening our defenses and picking up arrows. We collected a hundred and thirteen in the camp clearing alone.

"Then we cut the scrub back another thirty yards or so and burned it to give us a wider field of defense, and built fires around our perimeter and gathered fuel to stack alongside them, for it was dark now and we meant to keep watch all night.

"They came back twice before daybreak and fired a few more arrows at us, but couldn't get close enough to do much damage, though they stayed as near as they dared to the edge of the scrub, yelling threats and insults, which helped to keep us awake.

"They moved off at dawn and although we stayed around for a couple of days they didn't come back to collect their arrows, so we figured they had gone off to bury the two dead men and hold a wake for them."

The young cadet was silent, remembering that by the end of the week he would be on the way to the Duna to go on patrol with Sinclair. He wasn't sure if he was looking forward to it or whether he would rather be back in Sydney, lying on Bondi Beach with a golden-brown sunburned girl.

I lay awake in the guest house on the edge of the gully and once or twice in the night sat up quickly, disturbed by sounds of movement in the house and in the bush just outside.

There was no danger of molestation. I knew that the sounds were made by bush rats scuffling and scampering, and an opossum nesting in the kunai roof, or perhaps a cockroach, or small snake.

Rain dripped from the thick grass eaves into a little puddle, and from somewhere on the station came the dull, sad, monotonous thud of a single kundu drum. As I lay listening I heard Crellin shout from his house on the hill, abusing the drummer, telling him to shut up and go to bed. I turned over, comforted, and tried to sleep.

But there were Dunas dancing with whipped-up rage, and firing arrows, and creeping into a tent and suddenly slashing with an ax at the head of a sleeping white man. Me. But then I remembered that Corporal Peroro or Constable Pahun would be walking about the camp keeping watch, and the sounds that I would hear were their footsteps in the sharp grass.

So I went to sleep.

Seven

I sat on a spare wheel in the shade of the corrugated iron shed that serves Crellin as a workshop, and watched him working on the Land-Rover. In an hour it would be completely assembled and ready for the road.

"After lunch we'll give it a go." He straightened up, looking satisfied, and wiped his greasy hands on a wad of cotton waste, then lit a cigarette and relaxed for a while.

A few elderly Tari men were hanging around the shed watching the operation, among them the ancient Ivahi, his tatty wig decorated with thin spirals of metal foil stripped from the inside of a packing case, which made him look like a senile fairy queen.

And Neni, the sorcerer, was with them, but standing a little apart.

In the beginning Neni had been against the white men, seeing in their coming the end of his authority, for their magic was so much more spectacular than his own. But in time it became clear that their wonders tended to be entertaining rather than relevant to the essentials of everyday life.

They could not, for instance, kill anybody secretly but must make a great show of it, pointing their magic sticks and making great bangs and splashing blood all over the place, whereas Neni could kill a man merely by thinking about it and whispering the appropriate spells in secret.

Nor did the white men seem to know any of the proper magic for making pigs and women fertile, or food gardens abundantly productive. So, whereas he had at first stayed away from them, he now spent much of his time on the station gathering scraps of gossip and knowledge, finding that he could use them to increase his reputation as a soothsayer and prophet.

He was able to foretell, for instance, the arrival of the missionaries, a piece of information obtained from his nephew Punga, the station interpreter, only a few days before they came. He had also maneuvered another nephew onto the staff of the hospital, and had begun to build a small private stock of aspirin and antimalarial tablets, together with a collection of printed leaflets giving instructions for the use of various medical preparations and patent medicines.

They were proving efficacious with many of his own patients who suffered internal or muscular pain, especially if a paper was laid on the affected part at the same time as the incantation of the proper spell. Indeed, it was held by many that Neni's treatment with the leaflets cured more clansmen than did the medicines themselves, administered by the hospital staff.

But he had not been able to develop a satisfying theory about the Land-Rover, and spent much time watching closely while Crellin put it together. Nor could he accept wholeheartedly the story put forward by the station workers who came from outside, that the strange contraption was intended solely to run along the road that Mr. Crellin had so adamantly insisted should be built out into the Duna country to join distant Koroba with Tari.

The road had been a puzzle all along. It had no apparent purpose, and the amount of work entailed seemed gratuitous and useless. If the Government wanted a track to join the two places it should be sufficient, surely, to make it just wide enough for a man to walk along in comfort and in as straight a line as possible. Neni had moments of doubt in which he secretly conceded that the foreigners on the station might have occult information or experience of which he was himself entirely ignorant, but a pathway wide enough for twelve men to walk abreast, and which wandered aimlessly along hillsides in twists and turns, made no sense, not even in relation to this thing taking shape before his eyes. Nor was he alone in this attitude toward the road.

For many weeks Assistant District Officer Crellin had realized that most of the Tari men were tired of working on a project that seemed so pointless, and it was to give fresh fillip to their enthusiasm that he had undertaken "Operation Land-Rover."

It is often difficult for visitors to New Guinea to distinguish between the truly remarkable and the merely unusual. The country is so lacking in civilized norms that undertakings which might most likely seem amazing in other places are commonplace and excite little or no comment here. One needs to be excessively simple and direct in all things in order to exist in New Guinea.

Take the Land-Rover. It could not be driven in from the coast because Tari has no road link with the outside world, and the airstrip at that time could not accommodate aircraft big enough to take the chassis or the tray. So the vehicle was driven from the port of Lae, up the rough Markham Valley road to Goroka and thence to Minj in the Wahgi Valley; and here Crellin stripped it down into portable components. The engine, wheels, and other compact parts were flown in the Norseman straight to Tari, but the chassis and tray, being too big to fit into this aircraft, were lifted by Dakota into Laiagam, a Western Highlands station only sixty air miles from Tari.

From here the two large parts were manhandled across the mountains by a team of fifty carriers, who took thirteen days to make the journey.

Crellin accompanied them.

It would be asking enough of fifty men to carry a motorcar chassis and its body-work sixty miles in a straight and level line. But Laiagam is in a high valley, closed in on one side by an escarpment rising some eleven hundred feet to the top plateau, which is itself closed in by a range of even higher peaks. So the carriers crossed the rough roof of the highlands from New Guinea into Papua struggling through moss forests, or walking in long, narrow passes just below the timber line, hot by day and perishing cold by night.

For the first part they had help, in fact the hardest climb was the most fun, for two thousand Laiagam men, urged on by their patrol officer, cut a laddered track up the sheer side of their valley to the top of the escarpment, and passed the chassis and its tray hand-to-hand above their heads, chanting and laughing and hugely enjoying every moment.

They came on a little way from the top but soon the novelty wore off and instinct and superstition took over, and after one night camped on the heights they went home again, whooping and racing down into their own lands with relief, but happy and filled with a sense of achievement. They had done well, and had given the cavalcade a fine start on its way to Tari.

Crellin and his carriers walked eleven desolate days in one of the earth's most lonely places, through valleys unknown to the outside world, carrying an automobile. And no one in New Guinea was surprised, or gave it more than a minute's thought.

They carried this strange artifact from the white man's world through thick and head-high kunai grass, day after day, where no white man had walked before.

For the first two hours of each day the grass was wet and cold, saturated with overnight rain. Then as the sun climbed the ground gave off vapors, and myriads of little insects attacked the skin. By midday it was blazing, and in the afternoon it rained again. But the landscapes at twilight were majestic and awe-inspiring.

They crossed into Papua at ten thousand feet and waded two great rivers. In one of them, the Andabare, they were nearly washed away. Then they began to descend into the valley of the Tari and followed it down, and were met two days out from the station by a patrol officer and a relieving gang of carriers who had cut a track to this meeting place. In this way they brought these two big parts to the station, and now, a few days later, the Land-Rover was almost assembled and ready to test.

Crellin went off to lunch leaving word with Neni that in the afternoon the vehicle would "run about," and that the people should come and watch. There were a hundred or more men beside the airstrip and some women in the background when he came back, and Neni and a few of the big-men were waiting at the workshop to see the performance begin.

The corporal came with Crellin to keep order, and moved the old men back out of harm's way, clear of the entrance to the shed. They seemed a little resentful and reluctant to move, until the engine suddenly spluttered into life, and then they backed away hastily, holding their hands extended in front of their faces.

When the vehicle began to move slowly forward they turned and ran without shame, scurrying to get out of its way. But when it had passed them and was headed toward the airstrip they ran after it, not wishing to miss anything of the demonstration, their lean, ungainly legs, knotted with old, unsupple muscles, leaping anxiously over ditches and rough ground. Even Neni ran, and old Ivahi, for this was the biggest happening since the day when the first plane came.

The Land-Rover roared along the length of the airstrip, then turned and came back toward the loading bay, and as it swerved in to the edge of the strip, in the direction of the people, they scattered, and women snatched up their babies and ran to hide behind the station buildings.

Crellin called Punga, telling him to bring Neni and Ivahi, and some of the older men, and put them in the back of the vehicle, it being proper and politic to do them this initial courtesy before the fact of riding in the Land-Rover became a matter of no consequence, and something that anybody could boast about.

They came reluctantly, unable to refuse without losing face, and climbed uncomfortably over the backboard and sat along the sides, carefully tucking their buttock coverings under them and modestly smoothing their frontal aprons down between their thighs.

Some of them looked openly terrified and covered their eyes with their hands, and when Crellin accidentally pressed the horn they scrambled out over the side in panic, and fell onto the ground in their haste to be away, while some of the police and station hands who were watching, doubled up, helpless with high-pitched hysterical laughter.

The corporal sent two of his men to fetch the old men back and put them in the tray once more, and when they were installed again, clinging to any hand-hold for support, the vehicle moved slowly along the strip and back again, sedately in case any of them should take fright again and attempt to jump out while in motion, and so risk injury.

When their ride was over they clambered out as quickly as age and dignity would permit, grinning sheepishly as the onlookers congratulated them and praised them for their courage. Afterwards some of the other important men had rides, and soon everyone was clamoring, even one or two of the more forward of the women; but Crellin called to me and said that we might drive down to the Tagari River bridge to see Father Barard, a matter of a dozen miles or so, and the limit of the road.

So with two policemen, and two young men to push if things went wrong, we set out. And as we left the airstrip and turned onto the road leading to the Tagari bridge a great shout went up from all the men who were watching, for now they could see the reason and the meaning of the road, and they ran after us, hooting with excitement.

We stopped briefly at the workshop to load a bundle of shovels and picks, and as the two young men lifted them into the tray the crowd, having caught up, stood wide-eyed, enlightenment and understanding flooding even more fully into their minds as they nudged each other and pointed out that this thing carried a man's load for him, and more than one man's load, but as much as many men could carry.

Some tried to look wise, saying that this was obvious from the beginning, and that they had understood all along the purpose of this new machine, but most of them just shook their heads, wondering what other marvels Mr. Crellin would produce for them.

Half an hour later an astounded workman who had withdrawn briefly, in private, to the top of the hill behind the Tagari bridge came rushing and stumbling down, crying out in wonder and astonishment, "Father, Father, there is a house running along the road and coming this way."

Father Barard, who would have made a saintly model for El Greco, had they been contemporaries, smiled, and lifting his head listened to the familiar sound of a motorcar engine, never before heard in this valley, and said, "It is Mr. Crellin, coming to see how we are getting on." But no one believed him until the Land-Rover appeared over the brow of the hill and drove down toward them.

Most of them ran away. Those who were widening and leveling ground at the approaches jumped down into the river bed and stood behind boulders, or disappeared into the bush on the far side and stayed hidden. And the men who were working on the bridge itself, laying bearers and making ready for the decking, swung themselves like monkeys across to the other side and safety. But seeing the policeman and the two young men get out of the back and begin to unload the picks and shovels, they were reassured, and stood out in the open again to watch with excited curiosity.

We stopped for a while, chatting with Father Barard, who is a Capuchin friar from California and, like most of his missionary brethren in the Southern Highlands vicariate, a professional man; in his case a construction engineer.

He and Crellin discussed the progress being made on the bridge and tried to estimate a possible date for its official opening by the district commissioner, who would come from Mendi for the occasion. Afterwards Father Barard would bless the bridge and there would be a feast and sing-sing for the Huri and Duna men who had done the work, for the Tagari River is the traditional boundary between their tribal lands, and the bridge which they have built is a symbol of future peace, co-operation, and unity. And perhaps the Government would buy them a pig to kill and eat.

It is a small thing, perhaps, a bridge over a river. Not even a big bridge. The span is some seventy feet long with tower posts thirty feet high on each bank, and the whole some twenty feet above the water when the river is running at its normal height.

Yet when the two white men had first stood on the banks of the Tagari and discussed the building of this bridge with local leaders, there was head-shaking. It was impossible. The Government and the missionary had many marvels to show and much powerful magic, but they could not tell Duna and Huri men much about bridging the river, for they had been doing it for generations.

First, one looked for the narrowest part of the river, no matter how steep the approaches, for it was necessary to be able to pass a length of cane across and secure it to trees on either side. This was the governing factor. If the gap was too wide it was not possible to gain sufficient tension to keep the vine bridge even moderately rigid, and it would break in the middle. This, to the Duna and Huri men, was elementary.

These vine bridges are cleverly made, with a footway three or four inches wide, made of thin saplings, suspended from two swinging vines that form the handrails and main supports, strengthened every few feet with short verticals of similar vine. They sway violently and will carry the weight of only two or three men at a time, and then the men must be spaced out. And these bridges need to be renewed every two or three years even if they are not cut down in between times in the course of tribal wars.

But for the Tagari River bridge Father Barard chose a site with long and gently sloping approaches, where the river has a wide bottom so that flood rains can get away and not rise so high as to undermine the pylons; and this confused the people. And when he explained that the decking of the bridge would be twelve feet wide they refused to believe that he was serious.

But they were impressed when he set up the tower posts and slung thick steel cables between them, using a light pontoon as a working bridge to move back and forth across the river, and before very long the few faithful were joined by other groups who came only to watch this curious thing, but stayed to help.

Soon the Father had a gang of some two hundred men working, some from Tari, and others from up to twenty miles away in the Duna country where white men had not yet been seen.

This sort of thing goes on all over New Guinea, with missionaries not only assisting the Government to build, maintain, and staff hospitals and schools and infant welfare clinics, but to construct bridges and roads and airstrips, to run air-charter services, timber mills, farm schools, shipyards, and engineering workshops.

So with the Tagari bridge.

The missionary was the engineer and planner, the Government provided tools and materials, nuts, bolts, turnbuckles, shackles and cables, picks and shovels and explosives. Assistant District Officer Crellin did the blasting to shift rocks and boulders from the roadway. He supplied a young patrol officer and police to act as foremen to the laborers, and found rations and pay where needed.

Now he has the Land-Rover to fetch and carry and make things easier for the Father, who lives alone in a grass house just above the bridge, and who for the purposes of the operation has become, officially, a Government employee because this is uncontrolled territory and it is forbidden to civilians to enter without a special permit.

We went up, briefly, to the house and had coffee, and I said that I would come back when the bridge was opened and would drive from Tari to Koroba luxuriously in the Land-Rover, maybe in two hours, having walked the distance once before in two long, exhausting days. By which time there might be an airstrip, a school, and a hospital, and the Duna men would soon be electing a Local Government Council.

When we got into the vehicle and turned to go back to Tari, we drove too close to the edge of the road and sank in thick clay to the axle, and had to be pushed and almost lifted out by the laborers, shouting and heaving and laying bags under the wheels. But they were still impressed with the Land-Rover and gave a great shout as we got free and roared up the hill, away from the river, back to the station at Tari.

Eight

Early next morning, soon after daylight, a Cessna aircraft flew over Tari and went on to make a circuit around the Methodist mission to announce itself, then came back to land on the station strip. The pilot helped his passenger to alight, unloaded a heap of baggage, then came with her across to the Burchett's house for breakfast. He had brought her from Madang where she had arrived only yesterday, coming by ship from Holland to join Sister Walker's nursing staff.

The pilot, flying for the Missionary Aviation Fellowship, said that he was going back via Mount Hagen where he had a passenger to pick up, and when I asked if he would take me he agreed, saying that it was perhaps wise of me to get out of Tari straightaway as the weather was making up for a change, and it might not otherwise be possible to get to Hagen tomorrow morning in time for the opening of the agricultural show.

We breakfasted together with the hospitable Burchetts, then leaving the new nurse to be collected by the missionaries, I packed my bag and took off in the Cessna, northward again over the border, out of Papua once more and back into New Guinea.

We flew a devious route to avoid high clouds building in the east around Mount Giluwe, and cut across the top of the plateau where Crellin had come with his carriers and the Land-Rover, and so flew over the valley of the Lai River where it runs swift and turbulent in a deep gorge near the patrol post at Wapenamanda.

The road here is cut out of a steep mountainside and drops hundreds of feet in long, winding loops into the gorge. We could see hundreds of men working on it, and great umber scars and scarfs where shale and clay had been tipped in tons over embankments.

Somewhere in this topographical extravagance there might be a mass of gold if anyone can find it, the gold that the Leahy brothers were looking for when they found these valleys in 1933, though the lode, if there is one, eluded them.

They panned a bit of color out of one of the creeks and Daniel Leahy stayed on to work it, finding local men to labor for him, and paying them with shell and mirrors, knives and colored cloth, which in those days were riches beyond belief to primitives. With the money made from his gold he cleared land and planted coffee in the Hagen area, and so became the first immigrant settler in these western highlands.

A few other gold-seekers followed and went farther out to try their hands, and although they found nothing to encourage them to stay, they taught the few highland men who worked with them how to pan and puddle gold from the mountain streams that rise here to feed the big rivers of the southern fall—the tributaries of the Ok, the Om, and the Laigaip[1] which, with many others, fill the Strick-land River, then run into the Fly and so down into the Gulf of Papua, debouching from a delta fifty miles wide.

These highland men, taught by the pioneer prospectors, now wash the rivers for gold themselves, and every few weeks come down from the hills bringing their dust and little nuggets to the patrol post in pill bottles begged from medical orderlies on the station. They have little idea what the Government does with the gold, what it is for or why they get paid for it. It is another of the white man's mysteries.

They are wild men, quite primitive, who wear great wigs which have the shape of crescent moons and have horns extending up and outward, with almost two feet between the points.

They watch, fascinated, while the patrol officer carefully weighs their gold in the balance, then locks it away in the office safe before paying them their money. Most times the patrol officer is also the bank agent and prevails upon them to leave much of the money with him for safe-keeping, and this is put away, too, but first is en-tered into the man's bankbook.

The cash they keep to spend goes straight to the trade store in exchange for white man's goods: picks and shovels for the mining operation, knives, axes, plastic bags, mirrors, and oil lamps; woolen

[1] Pronounced L'*guy*-ip.

jerseys to keep out the cold, and cotton singlets for a status symbol; even umbrellas, made in Hong Kong and imported by the Chinese traders on the coast, to replace the traditional rain capes of pandanus leaf.

We flew on.

A Dakota aircraft, out from Hagen, passed us going westward. Its cargo doors were off and we came close enough to see men piling sacks of stores close to the opening, where they could be quickly kicked out at a given signal.

Somewhere, farther out toward the border that divides the Western Highlands from West Irian, a patrol would be exploring new valleys not yet known, estimating population, and bringing the people their first personal communication with our civilization.

There are ninety-six hundred square miles of this Western Highlands district and a known population of a quarter of a million people. Ten years ago the whole of this area, except around the district station at Mount Hagen, was largely uncontrolled, and movement within its valleys was restricted to armed patrols. Now it is considered safe to move about almost anywhere, although officially some twelve hundred square miles or more remains to be properly explored and the people brought fully within the influence of the Government.

In these past ten years something like six hundred miles of rough roadway have been driven through its mountains, mainly by hand labor, and twenty-five airstrips have been laid down in places that seemed at first inaccessible; and this has been achieved without punitive pressures or force, and mostly with much local enthusiasm.

We flew a little longer and came in sight of Mount Hagen, the thirteen-thousand-foot landmark and name-place of the administrative center of the Western Highlands district.

This mountain, the highest for miles around, was named for Count von Hagen. He was principal director of the New Guinea Company which, until 1899, was the official ruling authority on behalf of the German Government, of what was then German New Guinea.

Neither Von Hagen nor any other official of the company ever saw the mountain, but during his reign a German naturalist came over the ranges from the coast on a journey of exploration and saw, even if he did not enter, this western end of the highland valley system. He sighted the mountain and named it after the most important man in the colony, by whose courtesy he had been enabled to make his scientific travels.

The present Government station, sitting in the valley in sight of Mount Hagen, inherited the name, and the count's Prussian eagle is still the insignia of the district, standing on a low column in a small formal garden overlooking the airstrip, under the Australian flag.

The station, in recent years, has grown from a Government outpost into a modest township, and begins to consciously rival Goroka as the commerical and social center for the whole of the New Guinea highlands. But in the ninety-six hundred square miles that the station officially serves there are less than eight hundred white people.

Of these about a hundred belong to coffee-planting families, and another hundred are traders or tradesmen, airline pilots and mechanics, commerical men or company clerks. The other six hundred whites are fairly evenly divided between the various Government departments and twelve different missionary organizations which between them operate forty-one mission stations with thirteen hospitals, seventy-eight schools recognized by the Government, and 552 village schools; all these in the Western Highlands area.

And there is the hotel staff.

The hotel, built recently to cope with the ever-increasing flow of official visitors and tourists, and already being extended, stands alongside the airstrip, so that conversation in the bar and dining room is punctuated with the clamor of engines as planes race by to take off, almost continuously, or swish down onto the strip and gun along to the loading bay.

This activity continues to increase as the outback highlands are opened up and the center of communications moves farther westward, leaving Minj and the lower Wahgi Valley behind in the upsurge of development. Now Hagen is the biggest and busiest center west of Goroka for the distribution of cargoes coming in from the coast, and for the export of coffee and other goods going out. Its daily tally of traffic, as with some other New Guinea airstrips, exceeds that of many Australian state capitals.

When we arrived the hotel was filled with people visiting for the show, some of them planters from the eastern end of the valley, but mostly officials from other districts, and from Port Moresby. There were a few Australian tourists, excited at the prospect of seeing

primitive New Guinea without the inconvenience of going far to
find it, and already rehearsing stories for retelling to their friends
at home. Many of them, of course, would live out the rest of their
social lives as experts on New Guinea, its people and its problems.

By midnight Mount Hagen would have a thousand visitors, more
than double its own population, sleeping on the floors of friends'
houses, in spare rooms with beds laid side by side and touching, on
verandas and balconies, or "in with the kids."

Some were to sleep in spare beds in the hospital, others in grass
houses especially built for the occasion to accommodate the over-
flow. The missionaries have their guests. Other visitors bring tents
and camp in back gardens. There is nobody in Mount Hagen without
a full house for the show. District Commissioner Ellis has ordered
hospitality all around. There is no more to be said.

Mr. Ellis is a determinedly tough and angular man; a wartime
fighter pilot with a record of the most ruthless pursuit of Japanese
shipping on the New Guinea coast, and with a high-rating decoration to prove it.

His father was also an officer in the New Guinea service, and the
fact that the district commissioner, as a wartime pilot, was flying
and fighting above his own homeland might in part explain the
violent and venomous ferocity with which he sought to eliminate
the enemy, and for which he built an almost legendary reputation.
It seems to be not only a reputation but an attitude that has carried over, for as district commissioner of the Western Highlands he
treats each administrative problem, however small, as a personal
challenge; and anyone who stands between him and its immediate
solution is seen as an enemy, to be eliminated, implacably, or ren-
dered expeditiously ineffectual.

But it must not be thought that he is an ogre of unrelieved efficiency. These seemingly severe characteristics overlay a fine sense
of protocol, social duty, and domestic graciousness, so that a manner apparently sardonic, which seems suited to a man charged with
civilizing a quarter of a million primitives, is softened by an unexpected, easy courtesy that makes being his guest a pleasure.

I had lunch with him, and afterwards he spared time to drive
me for a while on a circuit of the station to see its most recent improvements, for I have been a regular visitor here for several years
and have acquired an interest beyond that of a mere observer.

The commissioner's character has superimposed itself on the district and shows through in what one sees and hears, driving along its tidy avenues of casuarina, past spacy lawns and massed flower beds. It has an atmosphere that, to me, makes it unique among all other New Guinea Government stations; a keyed-up, tight tempo, that seems to sing, not sweetly but with decisive insistency, like an electric drill or a predatory mosquito.

People move quickly, so unlike the languor of the coast or even the easy rhythms of the other highland areas. The airstrip is continuously active with aircraft coming and going, clerks trotting to and from with bills of lading and manifests, cargo boys shuffling in long lines, loading and unloading, and the almost unceasing exchange of information between the chief clerk in the district office beside the airstrip, and the air control officer in Madang.

Graders and rollers and gangs of laborers work all day keeping the strip in order, for it is inadequate for the traffic and needs continuous maintenance until the new strip, a few miles farther down the valley and with more open approaches, can be completed. Five hundred men are almost continuously at work on this second strip which, when finished, will take multiengined aircraft that can come straight from Sydney and Brisbane. This is but one of the district commissioner's many ambitions.

There is no quiet at Mount Hagen between early morning and sundown. All day the powerhouse hammers out its rhythm. Sawmills scream, turning out timber for new buildings. Machines whine and grind in the motor workshops, keeping trucks on the road. Wood-working machines clatter in the joinery shop where school and hospital furniture, household fittings, and office equipment are being made.

A suburb is being built, the coffee factory extended, brick-making machines installed, a hydroelectric scheme constructed. It is all restless and nervous and progressive. If there is a deadline for the civilization of New Guinea the Western Highlands will be the first to keep it, whether the highland tribesmen like it or not. The United Nations is not going to say that District Commissioner Ellis stood in the way of progress.

But the highlanders do like it, or seem to, for they have a satisfied and smiling look about them except when they are temporarily of-

fended by some unusually sharp-shafted rebuke administered by
"Master Ellis."

These Western Highlands people are a bourgeoisie. They lack
the gay and sexually extroverted flamboyance of the Minj and Middle Wahgi people, nor do they demonstrate the simple surface emo-
tionalism of the peasant-like Chimbu. They have an eye to profit
rather than to effect, riches for power rather than for display.

The Hagen tribes are friendly enough but tend to be analytical
in their relationships. They are hospitable but make no great dem-
onstrations of affection or respect. They are the Swiss of New
Guinea. Businessmen. Interested in solidity, respectability, acquisi-
tion, and orderliness.

Their one unique decoration is the *aumak*, a lattice of bamboo
slats, some six inches in width, suspended by a cord around the
neck and hanging down the breast. It is a bankbook, a ledger or
reckoning. The longer a man's aumak the richer and more influential
he is. If an ambitious or frustrated young man, pretending to be
more wealthy than he is, wears a falsified aumak he is laughed out
of countenance.

Each slender bamboo slat represents an amount of wealth, either
shell, pigs, feathers, or ceremonial axes, owned, lent, or invested in
marriage payments and other traditional economic enterprises.

These transactions are the main preoccupation of the older men.
In this respect the Hagen people, among the most recently primitive
of all New Guinea tribes, come closest to our civilized concept of a
solid and successful citizen.

People of this kind need a man like District Commissioner Ellis
to lead them, and in choosing him to administer this district the
Government has shown an unusual felicity of decision.

We drove a few miles out from the station, then stopped to watch
progress on a stretch of roadwork in which some two hundred men
and women were engaged, and two tractors being used to pull car-
loads of river gravel back to the station to surface the airstrip.

Ninji, the patriarch of Hagen was there, keeping an eye on the
operation of the tractors, which he owns.

It is some years since I saw Ninji and at first glance failed to
recognize him, although we had been first introduced seven years
ago, when he was a Paramount Luluai.

In those days he wore the traditional costume of a local big-man and looked impressive. Now he wears a neat white shirt and a necktie, white shorts, and a councilor's badge. But he has aged a great deal and clearly has not long to live.

A few years ago he stood straight for me, to have his picture taken, and stared at the camera, holding a spear in one hand and a fine ceremonial ax in the other. His hair was done at that time in the traditional manner of these Hagen tribes, teased up into little plaits and twists made stiff with pig grease, then pinned up with slithers of bamboo. Over this thick, high pad of hair he wore a cloth of beaten bush rope flattened to a width of eight or nine inches, and laid across the head and tied around the temples so that it fits like a tight beret.

The practical purpose of this hair style, still common among the mass of Hagen men, was to cushion ax blows received in tribal fights, but the covered pad also served a decorative function, acting as a pincushion into which feathers and other ornaments might be stuck.

Ninji, in that picture, looked impressive. He wore the tail feathers of a cassowary on his head, a headband of cowrie shells six inches deep, and the polished base of a cone shell suspended from his nose and covering his lips. His waistband was a foot wide, decorated with clan and family designs dyed or burned in. To put it on he stepped into it and drew it up tightly over his thighs.

His frontal apron hung down heavily, almost to his ankles, and he wore the usual bunch of tanket leaves behind.

His aumak was the longest I had seen, emerging from beneath his full black beard to disappear for several inches underneath two great Kina shells hanging on his chest, then to be lost somewhere below the waistband in the region of his navel. In all it would have been about eighteen inches long, while the average aumak is between six or eight inches.

Now he wears his hair trimmed neatly and ungreased. He has a councilor's badge instead of an emu tail, and a bankbook instead of an aumak. He also owns the two tractors that are working on the road, one of them being his personal property, and the other belonging to the native local council of which he is president. The Government, through the district commissioner, has lent part of the money for the purchase of these machines; the rest has come from coffee.

Mr. Ellis hires the tractors from Ninji and the council on behalf of the Government, to work on the roads and the airstrip. The transaction fits neatly into the traditional economic system.

But although Ninji is still rated the most important of the traditional headmen in the district, he no longer looks impressive, and because he has no English or Pidgin he can only smile defensively when visitors speak to him. He has accepted the new symbols of wealth, authority, and status, but in his Western clothes he no longer seems to feel important to himself. He has a lost look. He has ceased to be a great tribal figure and has become, instead, a figurehead.

And he is dying.

Perhaps Ninji is afraid that his ancestors will not recognize him, and that when he dies he will have to wander through the spirit world looking for a people who will accept a man who is neither one thing nor the other. Civilization has come a little late in his life. It has taken too much and given back too little. It is bad luck for him, but for the majority of Hagen men the future holds much promise.

In the old days men like Ninji were guardians of the tribal wealth, and young men had to borrow from them before they could buy a bride or acquire pigs, or trade or engage in any of the ceremonial exchanges. Now, with the coming of the white men, there has been an economic boom and a free flow of wealth in which almost everybody has shared. This disruption of the old economic system has had other effects on the social order, changing the economic if not the domestic status of a class of highlanders who were virtually serfs or slaves at the beginning of this present generation.

Ninji, when I first knew him, had five such serfs, who worked for him and lived as part of his household. It is possible that he still has them, for the relationship between serf and serf-owning family was for the most part mutually agreeable, and the bond a personal one, by no means intolerable.

Father Ross, a New Yorker and the oldest missionary in these parts, says that when he came to the Western Highlands thirty years ago, a quarter of the people who lived around about Mount Hagen had the status of serfs. Most of them, he said, were refugees from tribal wars, the male remnants of clans which had been decisively beaten in battle, whose women and children had been slaughtered or taken captive, their villages and gardens destroyed, and the tribal lands occupied by the victors.

These refugees roamed the highlands seeking people who would take them in and give them food and shelter, and when they found a man with sufficient wealth to be able to offer them refuge they bound themselves to work for him without wages. They lived as members of their patron's family, were accepted almost as distant kin, and provided with women; but they had no share in the family wealth nor any active part in rituals involving the exchange of riches held in common by the clan.

It was an accepted relationship, as it was in medieval Europe, and in the context of a primitive society it offered security on reasonably dignified terms, no less at least than those available to the penniless refugees of our twentieth-century wars.

It may be then, that the young men who drive Ninji's tractors with such exuberance are serfs or the sons of serfs, but the status is no longer socially important. If they work for him they are covered by the same labor regulations as govern the employment of tribesmen by the white settlers, so that they must be fed and clothed and paid wages, and provided with medical care.

But on our way back to the station we met another man, named Kup Ogut. He was driving a truck piled high with bags of green coffee beans bought from local people in the hamlets round about, a bucketful here, half a sackful there. He will spread the coffee out on trays behind his trade store and regrade it, then take it to the factory and make his middleman's profit, for Kup, like Ninji, is one of the new capitalists of the Western Highlands.

But whereas Ninji is a traditional clan-leader with ancient authority and mystique and many wives, and a great household of relatives and adopted sons and serfs, Kup is an opportunist whose initial capital consists of his wits. He is an operator, an up-and-coming tycoon who will soon have a finger in the political pie.

At present he is vice-president, under Ninji, of the Hagen local government council. He is also a member of the Highland Planters and Settlers' Association, of which the planter Ian Downs is president, and which is becoming a powerful influence inside New Guinea.

Ninji is old, and Kup is middle-aged.

Kup learned to speak Pidgin English as a boy, when he was a

medical orderly, and soon became a teacher to other orderlies and traveled a good deal and learned the white man's ways. Now he has a truck and trade stores. He not only wears shirt and trousers, but shoes also, because he has a son at school in Australia and does not wish to embarrass the boy when he visits him.

When the district commissioner needs five hundred men to work on the new airstrip he tells Ninji. When he wants to place a Hagen man in the councils of the white people he picks on Kup. So Kup was chosen to go to Canberra with a party of potential politicians from Papua and New Guinea, to see the Australian Parliament in action. When he came back a month later he made a public statement saying, "If Australia is wise she will quickly make New Guinea her seventh state, for her own protection as well as ours."

Privately he debated the proposition that he might himself sit in the Parliament in Canberra to represent the people of New Guinea, but concluded with some reluctance that his son might fit more comfortably into this niche while he himself would concentrate upon becoming wealthy. Kup is wise in his generation.

By late afternoon Mount Hagen Station was busy with people coming in from the countryside to camp for the night, so to be ready for the opening of the show the next day.

They came in clan and family groups, in dozens, scores, and hundreds, strung out along all the roads that lead to the station. The men carried spears and ceremonial decorations wrapped in pandanus leaves to keep them from the rain. The women walked behind, bringing food in net bags, rolls of sleeping mats, and the children. Some carried favorite piglets in their arms like babies. Others led bigger pigs on strings. Many families had been walking for several days. Tomorrow, early in the morning, the men would put on their finery and paint their faces, then get together with their friends to practice for the intertribal dancing contests. Some were already at it on the showground.

Planes came, one after the other, swooping low above their bobbing heads, drowning out the booming of the kundu drums. The planes brought visitors from other stations, from Goroka and Mendi and Minj, and from the coastal towns to the north, Madang and Lae, even from as far as Wewak in the Sepik, and Rabaul.

Trucks, cars, and station wagons came to collect visitors at the airstrip; men struggling with baggage and women with babies and paper bags, excited voices calling above the din of idling engines, promises being made to visit, invitations to drink and "to see you later."

Bob Gibbes, a planter in the Wahgi Valley, came flying in on the uttermost edge of dusk, flipping through the darkening sky like a bat and landing his brand-new Cessna aircraft with abandon, as if it were a toy. He is a professional flyer, and like District Commissioner Ellis was a wartime pilot, leader of a famous fighter squadron and afterwards a private airline operator in these highlands. He was, he says, the first to base a commercial aircraft in the Wahgi Valley.

Now he talks gaily about the dangers of those days, when hastily cut landing grounds were so short that pilots had to maneuver their machines within a foot or two of the threshold of the runway, then cut the engines and drop them dead. "Otherwise," he said, "you couldn't bring your aircraft to a stop before running out of airstrip."

He opened little trading stores near these early strips, and made money, bought more aircraft, leased land, and planted coffee; not motivated by avarice but by a compelling and restless spirit of adventure. His wife kept the accounts.

One of his old aircraft crashed in the far western valleys while dropping supplies to a Government patrol, so he sent in a mechanic with 150 carriers from Tari, the Government lending a patrol officer to lead them. They found the aircraft in a swamp sixty-five miles from the nearest patrol post, out in Sinclair's country where the tribes were fighting each other and attacking Government patrols.

The battle stopped when they arrived, and the tribesmen came to watch while the mechanic stripped the wreck and cut it into one hundred and twenty pieces, small enough to be carried. When it was ready the tribesmen helped move the wreckage from their territory, then went back to their fighting. The carriers brought the pieces of aircraft to Tari where the mechanic reassembled them on the airstrip, welding the aircraft together again, putting it back into service.

But the airline operating has become big business, even in New Guinea, and the Government now frowns on the pioneer approach to flying and enforces normal safety regulations, thus making life difficult for people who fly because they like it, and are not businessmen at heart. So Gibbes sold his old planes and turned to full-time planting and trading operations. He was among the first to go into business with the highlanders, and now has New Guinea men as partners in a coffee-buying and -marketing company.

Kondom Agaundo, the Chimbu leader, is one of them. And Somu Sigob of Finschhafen is another. They are both members of the Legislative Council. Among the highland people, black and white, the principle of multiracial partnerships has ceased to be a visionary theory. Many of the white men regard it as an essential prerequisite to their own survival.

"If we are going to stay in this country," said Gibbes, "we must play along with the people who own it. In this I agree with Ian Downs, the Farmers and Settlers' president."

Downs says that the New Guinea people have let white settlers buy land to live on and, in return, the settlers have shown them how to use their own land profitably and in a way that allows them to live better lives.

"We have taught them," says Downs, "to grow commercial crops, and we help them to sell their produce. Partnership on every level is our only hope. If we don't want to live with these people on equal terms we should get out."

We talked about these things later in the evening, over a drink at the doctor's house, where guests stepped over each other on verandas packed with makeshift beds and mattresses spread on the floor.

Danny Leahy was there, the first white man to settle in the Hagen area. Tomorrow, as patron of the show, he would make a speech, but he was not looking forward to this, being a shy and modest man. We listened to him talk of the early days.

"When brother Mick and me came looking for gold we had visions of a big and thriving mining industry here. We never thought of being farmers and living out our lives among these people. I did my share of milking cows when I was a boy in Australia, for fifteen shillings a week and rough keep, and if you'd told me then that I would one day be patron of the biggest agricultural show in New Guinea I would have thought you mad." He shook his head, thinking back, and added, "Why, in those days Hagen wasn't even a place on the map."

He showed us a copy of the show program, with a foreword signed by himself, in which he had written, "I came here with my brothers looking for wealth beneath the ground . . . but like all who have followed after, I came to realise that the true wealth of this country is to be found above the ground in agriculture."

And he set out to prove it, growing coffee, tea, ground nuts, soya beans, corn, and vegetables of all kinds, cattle, sheep, pigs and goats, fowl, ducks, and geese. And he taught the Hagen people to do these things, and gave the tribesmen plants and stock so that they could imitate him.

"Well," said Gibbes, "we've achieved a fair bit in a short time and I don't know that we've got much to be ashamed of, but if I could get a good price for my plantation today, I'm not so sure that I wouldn't get out of New Guinea, for the future is none too bright."

There was an astonished silence. Bob Gibbes is an optimist by instinct and a man of intellect and proven courage. "Why," we said, "would you want to sell out?"

"I've just spent three weeks visiting our neighbors in West Irian where I was flying an aircraft for the United Nations, and believe me, my eyes have been opened." Everybody looked surprised. It is not like Gibbes to cry wolf. He became suddenly embarrassed and went red in the neck, and apologetic.

"Not that I'm any expert, I'm only a poor bloody aviator, but I do have a stake in this country, and a home here, and I think it's time we Australians began to face the facts of life in today's world."

"What facts are you talking about?" said the district commissioner, sternly.

"Well," said Gibbes, "when the Indonesians took over West Irian many native leaders on both sides of the border protested, and talked of betrayal by the United Nations and the Americans. And some said that Australia had let them down and that the Papuans in West Irian were being sold out.

"They're not saying that any more. They say, instead, that the Indonesians are more like themselves. That they are more friendly, and treat them as human beings. The New Guinea men who complained the loudest are now working pretty well with their new rulers, and like them."

He went on. "Sooner or later some of the West Irian Papuans will be coming over the border into our territory and they will repeat these things to our native leaders. They might suggest that the Indonesian rulers would be better rulers than the Australians. That brown men are able to get along more easily together than brown men do with white men."

My mind slipped back to a hotel room in Lae, to Somu Sigob who has a business partnership with Gibbes. And I remembered him saying, "You white people have taken men like me and have made us the key to your own future in this country. If you turn us one way the door will be open for you. If you turn us the other way you will be shut out."

Bob Gibbes was saying much the same thing and felt uncomfortable about it. He slopped some whisky into a glass.

"Sorry, chaps, about the speech-making, but this trip shook me a bit. I think, maybe, that someone in Canberra should consider making our New Guinea folk into real Australians before they decide they'd rather be something else."

A New Guinea man might yet sit in the Parliament in Canberra.

Nine

Some officials thought that there were about forty thousand people on the showground, while others more excitedly imaginative said sixty thousand tribesmen and at least two thousand white people. Aircraft were coming and going every few minutes as though Hagen had suddenly become an international airport, and by lunchtime the station clerk, who is meticulous about such things, said that there were forty-eight aircraft parked on the edge of the landing strip.

The Governor-General of Australia came up from Canberra, accompanied on the last part of his trip by officials from Port Moresby. A special flight brought the constabulary brass band to lead the Grand Parade.

Shy tribesmen from isolated hamlets in the mountains beyond the Lai River, who previously had seen only occasional white men and strangers coming through their country on patrol, walked nervously through the crowd in twos and threes, keeping close together, unsure of themselves and seeing no escape and no allies if fighting should break out. Each wore a wig protected from the weather by a mob cap of bark, and each carried a long, slender fighting spear and a wooden shield, for these men have never before known the luxury of peace, and were suspicious of all the many strangers who surrounded them.

The energetic Wabag people, fully five years introduced to the modern world, built a complete hamlet on the showground to exhibit their traditional way of life. They built a man's house and a woman's house, complete with food garden, the whole hamlet fenced with wooden billets for protection against any enemy.

Inside their hut, divided into sections for living and sleeping, the women gossiped, spun threads, and wove aprons and net bags as they do at home. They sat along three sides of the main room, the fourth side being divided into pens for the pigs. In the middles they had a fire, with sweet potatoes and a cluster of peanuts roasting. To flavor the cooking the women chewed salt and sprayed salinated saliva onto the food through their lips.

The gold-miners came down from Liaigan and the Porgera Valley in a plane chartered for them by their patrol officer, and under his guidance set up the replica of an alluvial gold mine, with race and cradle and puddling gear, and two men washing dirt in pans. They displayed their gold in a showcase made for the occasion, with cards neatly printed by the patrol officer, giving statistics of their industry. They also brought with them a dead friend, smoked, and set him up in the midst of the exhibit because he had expressed a wish to attend the show but had died seven months too soon. He was a headman, and had been buried with due ceremony but uncased for the occasion and brought along out of sentiment and a proper respect for his wishes.

Jimmi River men, from the hills above Minj, came down with assurance and set up their exhibit unaided. They are craftsmen, famous all through the highlands for the ceremonial stone axes which they make, traditionally, for trading. These great axes are prized artifacts and a major item of intertribal trade. Double-bladed, with delicate, halbert-shaped heads bound to the haft with fine cane, and covered with plaited grasses, they are perhaps the most elegant of all New Guinea arts and crafts.

The Jimmi River people have almost a monopoly of this craft because the smooth, deep-green-and-gray volcanic stone from which the ax blades are split and ground, outcrops mainly on their tribal lands. In the old days the axes were traded for salt which, before the coming of the white man, was one of the most highly valued of all commodities. A handful would buy an ax or a ceremonial girdle, or some other major item of wealth and status.

The making of the salt was also, by and large, a monopolistic industry, for the best salt was evaporated from mineral springs found only in a few places in the mountains, or else leached tediously from the ashes of certain sparse grasses and timbers, carefully charred, so that the axes of the Western Highlands, and the salt, were equally valuable. Now, of course, the white man's salt can be bought at any trade store for a few pence, and before long the axes will become valuable only as collectors' items and museum pieces.

These and other exhibits were displayed along one side of the showground in a row of spacious, open-fronted booths, especially erected to house the produce, handicrafts, and natural resources of each part of the highlands. In these booths the tribesmen displayed their arts and crafts and produce, their flora and fauna; wild orchids unknown to the outside world, curious birds and animals, phalangers, tree-climbing kangaroos, hornbills, birds of paradise and parrots, pythons, and strange insects, some edible and others with iridescent carapaces, used for ornament.

District Commissioner Ellis seemed proud and almost on the point of smiling as he walked around with the official party, being host and guide to His Excellency who, with great good sense and dignity, wore a ceremonial cocked hat for the occasion. Later, the distinguished visitor made a speech giving praise to everyone, commending them for the splendor of the exhibits.

Few of the tens of thousands of New Guinea people understood a word of his speech, but they listened attentively, pleased because he had come all the way from Canberra to visit them; and after Mr. Ellis had repeated the speech in Pidgin the interpreters turned it into place-talk for each clan. Then His Excellency shook hands with the big leaders; with Kibunki from Wabag, and Nopnop from Minj, Puk, Komp, Wak, and the rest of them.

The tribal dancing contest went on all through the day and late into the night, and was won eventually, to everybody's astonishment, by the group from Mendi who, for their skill and pains, received a prize of fifty pounds. It was a memorable occasion for the Mendis, for at Hagen they also took delivery of a tractor purchased by their local government council, and carried it back with them to their own valley, over the still uncompleted road that is being pushed across the mountains between Hagen and Mendi.

I met Tau Boga, who was once a leper, and having been cured on Gemo Island is now teaching in the highlands. He took me to see the display of schoolchildren's work and was quietly proud when I showed surprise at the copper-plate precision of the handwriting of his ten-year-old pupils who live in grass huts, and whose parents are utterly illiterate, and did not know what paper was until their children went to school.

I realize that this ability to write neatly means nothing much except, perhaps, that most human beings are born with attributes and potentialities common to all humanity. That the rest depends on genetics, education, and environment, and the mysterious working of the Holy Ghost. Or, if you wish, of chance. More importantly it suggests that those who say that it will be fifty or even a hundred years before the Papuans and New Guineans are ready to govern themselves are not simply wrong, but are much less intelligent than the highlander himself, who only yesterday changed his stone ax for a steel one.

I left Tau Boga talking to other visitors, and went across the showground to the coffee planters' exhibit, and stood there for a while listening to a planter explaining new mechanical equipment to a young man, Western-dressed, who held a young girl's hand, and she wearing her family's best feathers and shells.

At another booth crowds of women and old men watched young girls spin and weave wool grown locally, using old-fashioned spinning wheels worked by foot pedal, and hand looms suitable for village industry, to make blankets and bedspreads. Danny Leahy taught the girls to do these things, importing the simple equipment as well as the sheep, teaching the men to tend the flocks and to shear, and the women to spin and weave.

Dan, having delivered his patronal speech with dignity, now walked around with his brother Jim, from Goroka. Both are big men, with wide Irish faces. Now in their fifties, they came here thirty years ago, slim and adventurous youths, to be greeted by the highlanders as tribal spirits back from the dead.

Many of the highland men walking about the showground came to speak to them, or passing, gave them greeting as friends, for the Leahy brothers belong with these people and have no other home. They have taught the tribesmen much since they have lived here, and have set many of them up as farmers, providing them with stock and seedlings. Government agricultural officers now do most of this work, but the brothers and other settlers who live on the land are key figures in the evolving pattern of change that is taking place in the lives of the highland people.

Dan's pigs were on display in the animal pavilions on the showground, enormous beasts bred from Australian stock; so big that the highlanders clustered around their pens drawing in their breath and clicking their tongues with admiration and envy. Around one great sow, a black and yellow brute standing three feet high and measuring seven feet from snout to tail, a row of young girls stood, stretching out their hands tentatively to stroke its skin, as city women might stroke a mink coat, covetously.

To these Hagen girls, not yet married but at courting age, with minds on bride-price and a husband's wealth, the ownership of such a pig would be heavenly. And this is possible if their fathers care to buy the progeny from Dan, who offers them for a few pounds to help the highland people improve their native stock. The Government does the same, and keeps stud boars to serve the village sows.

The girls moved along the pens, from pig to pig, huddling close together and clutching at each other, uttering little squeals, their bare breasts and stomachs shining with fat, hair in ringlets stiff with grease, and wearing great displays of family wealth.

Their fathers and elder brothers were busy in their own way, many of them taking part in contests in the arena, spear-throwing, or shooting arrows at a target. And full-bearded, stately clan leaders raced around the oval on shiny bicycles, purchased with money earned from coffee and other crops, their bare buttocks set firmly on the saddles, with tail leaves draped behind, pedaling with grave dignity for a prize of two pounds.

At the stockyards Ian Downs was selling cattle by auction, two hundred head raised on the Government experiment farm at Baiyer River, twenty miles away. Settlers, traders, and missionaries were bidding for them, some intending to start or increase their own herds, others buying the beasts to provide meat for their plantation laborers.

Scores of tribesmen stood or sat on the high rails around the stockyard, among them a great many who had never before seen any animal bigger than a village pig; and to give them a chance to bid for the cattle Downs kept a pen in reserve. Agricultural officers gave advice and bargained with the auctioneer on behalf of clan leaders, and later there was much excitement and confusion as men with bones through their noses coaxed stubborn cattle out of pens and led them westward along the new roads. One, at least, of the beasts was killed before nightfall to make a clan feast.

When the sale was over I walked back to the main arena with

Ian Downs, and as we walked, making our way among the tribesmen, he spoke earnestly. "We have shown that we people in the
highlands can work with each other to develop this country as a
common home. We believe that a nonracial way of life and a nonracial society is not only possible but practicable. Certainly, we have
a long way to go before this is completely achieved, but all around
there are sure signs of progress."

Yet he seemed reluctant to talk much about these things, and
almost shy, as though trying to avoid the implication that he was
setting himself up as a leader and a politician. And there was an
edge of impatience in his voice, as though it should not be necessary to say the things that he was saying.

"We white settlers know and have always known that some day
we would have to adapt ourselves to the transfer of political authority to the New Guinea people themselves, and we will support
this transfer. But we believe that if the New Guinea people are to
succeed in self-government they will need Australia's help for a
long time to come."

We could hear the constabulary band playing a marching tune,
and coming to the main arena stood on a bank to watch the Grand
Parade. Tens of hundreds of men in full ceremonial finery, with
high plumes and ritual wigs, great trident spears and shields, war
bows and arrows, axes and bone daggers, faces painted, shells shining in the fierce sunlight. Some of them had fought with the white
men, many had only known white men for a few years. Some still
live primitive lives only a step removed from the stone age and
prehistoric anonymity. Some clans are still feuding with others taking part in this procession on the showground, others are meeting
each other for the first time. Before the show was ended they ran
wild all over the ground, chasing a greasy pig, which they caught
and killed with much shouting and laughing.

Ninjikama, chief of the Hagen clans, sat in the grandstand with
Mr. Ellis, watching. Too ill to take part, he leaned his chin on a
stick and stared out through dim eyes across the crowded arena,
beyond the big shelters that housed the district exhibits. It was, he
thought, a very good show. So many people on his land, so much
dancing, so much shell and rich displays of fine feathers. But not as
exciting as in the old days when the tribes were all fighting and

life had some meaning, and on such an occasion as this they would have killed, maybe, five hundred pigs or even more.

On the other side of the showground Kup Ogut was looking at a new coffee grader, wondering if he should buy it.

EPILOGUE

Ninji, last of the great Highland fight-leaders, died soon after the Hagen show. Masses were offered and many hundreds of pigs were slaughtered for the repose of his soul.

Soon afterwards elections were held all over Papua and New Guinea, and a House of Assembly met in June 1964 to replace the old Legislative Council.

Many of the old leaders were rejected. Kondom Agaundo lost his seat and returned to the Chimbu Valley and his eight wives. Somu Sigob, the puzzled politician of Finschhafen, was also defeated and has gone back to his coffee and cocoa trees, leaving the problem of New Guinea's future to men more confident, who by and large are less likely to be inhibited by a simple sense of loyalty to old ideas and emblems of authority.

A new wind blows across the great Stone Age Island of New Guinea—the wind of change—stirring a cool, damp draft that may soon be felt in the corridors of Canberra.

The following authors and authorities were consulted during the writing of this book:

Anthropos. Vol. 31, 1936. Ethnological notes on Mount Hagen tribes. Father William Ross.

Australian Institute of Political Science. Papers published under the title "New Guinea and Australia." Sydney: Angus & Robertson, 1958.

Australian National Library. Correspondence.

Belshaw, Cyril. *The Great Village*. London: Routledge & Kegan Paul, 1957.

Bevan, Thomas. *Toil, Travel and Discovery in British New Guinea*. London: Routledge & Kegan Paul, 1890.

Brongersma, L. D., and Venema, G. F. *To the Mountains of the Stars*. London: Hodder & Stoughton, 1962.

Brown, Rev. George. *An Autobiography*. London: Hodder & Stoughton, 1908.

Chalmers, Rev. James. *Work and Adventure in New Guinea*. London: Religious Tract Society, 1885.

Champion, Ivan F. *Across New Guinea from the Fly to the Sepik*. London: Constable & Company, 1932.

Clune, Frank. *Prowling through Papua*. Sydney: Angus & Robertson, 1943.

Dampier, William. *A Voyage to New Holland in the Year 1669*. London: 1703.

Dupeyrat, André. *Mitsinari*. London: Staples Press, 1954.
———. *Festive Papua*. London: Staples Press, 1955.

Essai, Brian. *Papua and New Guinea—A Contemporary Survey*. Melbourne: Oxford University Press, 1961.

Fairhall, Constance. *Where Two Tides Meet*. London: Edinburgh House Press, 1945.

——. *Island of Happiness.* London: Edinburgh House Press, 1951.
Fortune, Dr. Reo. *Sorcerers of the Dobu.* New York: E. P. Dutton & Company, 1932.

Gitlow, A. L. *Economics of the Mount Hagen Tribes, New Guinea.* American Ethnological Society Monographs, No. 12. New York: J. J. Augustin, 1947.

Groves, Dr. Murray. Various manuscripts, published and unpublished (contemporary).

Hides, Jack. *Papuan Wonderland.* London: Blackie & Son, 1936.
——. *Savages in Serge.* Sydney: Angus & Robertson, 1938.

Hogbin, Dr. Ian. *Transformation Scene—The Changing Culture of a New Guinea Village.* London: Routledge & Kegan Paul, 1951.

Leahy, Michael, and Crain, Maurice. *The Land that Time Forgot.* New York: Funk & Wagnalls Company, 1937.

Lett, Lewis. *Papuan Achievement.* Melbourne University Press, 1942.
——. *Sir Hubert Murray of Papua.* New York: William Collins Sons & Company, 1951.
——. *Papua—Its People and Its Promises.* Melbourne University Press, 1944.

Malinowski, B. *Argonauts of the Western Pacific.* New York: E. P. Dutton & Company, 1922.
——. *The Natives of Mailu.* Adelaide: Royal Society of South Australia, 1915.

Markham, Sir Clements. *The Voyages of de Quiros 1595–1606.* London: 1904.
——. *Famous Sailors of Former Times.* London: 1876.

Mead, Margaret. *Growing Up in New Guinea.* New York: William Morrow & Company, 1930.
——. *Male and Female.* London: Penguin Books, 1962.

Moresby, John. *Discoveries and Surveys in New Guinea & the D'Entrecasteaux Islands.* London: John Murray, 1876.

Oceana. Articles on Native Custom by G. Bateson, M. Megget, and W. Read.

Pineau, Rev. André. *Marie-Therese Noblet*. Issoudun: 1938.

Reay, Marie. *The Kumu—Freedom and Conformity*. Melbourne University Press, 1959.

Romilly, H. H. *The Western Pacific and New Guinea*. London: David Nutt, 1886.
———. *From My Verandah in New Guinea*. London: David Nutt, 1889.

Royal Geographical Society. Various papers.

Salisbury, Dr. Richard. *From Stone to Steel*. Melbourne University Press, 1962.

Seligman, Dr. C. G. *Melanesians of British New Guinea*. London: Cambridge University Press, 1910.

Sharp, Andrew. *The Discovery of the Pacific Islands*. New York: Oxford University Press, 1960.

Simpson, Colin. *Adam with Arrows*. New York: Frederick A. Praeger, 1956.
———. *Adam in Plumes*. Sydney: Angus & Robertson, 1954.

Sinclair, Dr. Alex. Field & Clinical Survey Report on Mental Health of the Indigenes of Papua & New Guinea. Port Moresby: 1959.

Spencer, Margaret. *A Doctor's Wife in New Guinea*. Sydney: Angus & Robertson, 1960.

Stevens, Henry N. (ed.) *New Light on the Discovery of Australia* (as revealed by Diego de Prado y Tobar's journal). London: Henry Stevens, Son & Stiles, 1930.

Vaudin, Rev. Jean. *Monseigneur Henri Verjus*. Lille: 1924.

Williams, F. E. "The Vailala Madness," "The Blending of Cultures," and other anthropological papers issued by the Government Printer, Port Moresby.

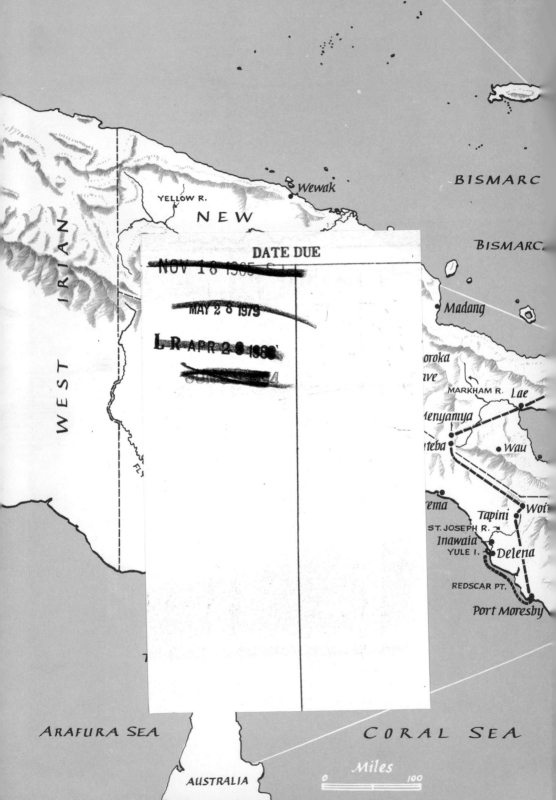

PACIFIC OCEAN

BISMARC

BISMARC

WEST IRIAN

NEW

YELLOW R.

Wewak

Madang

oroka

ve

MARKHAM R. Lae

Menyamya

teba

Wau

ema

Tapini

Wot

ST. JOSEPH R.

Inawaia

YULE I.

Delena

REDSCAR PT.

Port Moresby

ARAFURA SEA

CORAL SEA

AUSTRALIA

Miles

0   100